Hugh Johnson's Pocket Encyclopedia of Wine

Simon and Schuster/New York

KEY TO SYMBOLS

r.	red	
p.	rosé	(in brackets) means relatively unimportant
w.	white	
br.	brown	
sw.	sweet	
s/sw.	semi-sweet	
dr.	dry	
sp.	sparkling	

*	plain, everyday quality
**	above average
***	well known, highly reputed
****	grand, prestigious, expensive
☐	usually particularly good value in its class

70 71 etc.

    recommended years which may be currently available.

70 etc.   years in **bold** should be ready for drinking (the others should be kept). Where both reds and whites are indicated the red is intended unless otherwise stated.

    N.B. German vintages are codified by a different system. See note on p. 64.

D.Y.A.	drink the youngest available
NV	vintage not normally shown on label

Cross-references are in SMALL CAPS

See p. 5 for extra explanation

A quick-reference vintage chart for France and Germany appears on p. 156.

Hugh Johnson's Pocket Encyclopedia of Wine
© 1977 Mitchell Beazley Publishers Limited
Text © Hugh Johnson 1977, 1978, 1979
Revised edition published 1978
Revised and enlarged edition published 1979
© 1979 Mitchell Beazley Publishers Limited
All rights reserved
including the right of reproduction
in whole or in part in any form
A Fireside book
Published by Simon and Schuster
A Division of Gulf & Western Corporation
Simon and Schuster Building
Rockefeller Center
1230 Avenue of the Americas
New York, New York 10020

ISBN 0-671-25333-6
Library of Congress Catalog Card Number 77-79242
Printed in Great Britain
Designed by Florianne Henfield
Assistant Editor Kathie Gill

Contents

Introduction 4
How to read an entry 5
Grape Varieties 6
Wine & Food 10
France 18–61
    Châteaux of Bordeaux 26–40
Germany 62
Switzerland 79
Italy 82
Spain & Portugal 99
North Africa & Asia 109
Central & South-east Europe 110–123
    Austria 112
    Hungary 115
    Romania 117
    Jugoslavia 118
    Bulgaria 121
    Greece 122
    Cyprus 123
California 124
New York 135
South America 137
England 138
Australia 140
South Africa 145
Sherry, Port & Madeira 150
Wine newspeak 155
Quick-reference vintage charts
for France and Germany 156

Introduction

This book is an exercise in crowding angels on a pinhead, or students into a telephone box. It is deliberately the shortest book in which I could possibly squeeze a book's-worth of information. Conversely it holds as much information as I could possibly squeeze into a little diary-format book. Hence no prose: the whole work is played staccato.

Its arrangement is intended to be as helpful as possible when you are buying a bottle, whether you are on the nursery slopes or an old hand with a bad memory. You are faced with a list of wines or an array of bottles in a restaurant, wine merchant or bottle store. Your mind goes blank. You fumble for your little book. All you need to establish is what country a wine comes from. Look up the principal words on the label in the appropriate country's section. You will find enough potted information to let you judge whether this is the wine you want.

Specifically, you will find information on the colour and type of wine, its status or prestige, whether it is usually particularly good value, which vintages are good and which are ready to drink—and often considerably more ... about the quantity made, the grapes used, ownership and the rest. Hundreds of cross-references help you go further into the matter if you want to.

The introduction to each national section will help you to establish which label-terms are the ones that count. In many cases you will find you can look up almost all the words on the label: estate, grape, shipper, quality-rating, bottling-information....

For your browsing moments the introduction contains important background information about grape types; the first of all determining factors for the quality and essential flavour of any wine.

Notes on the 1979/80 Edition

Tumultuous fermentation in the wine industry combined with break-neck expansion over the last 12 months has made it necessary to add more pages to this edition, incorporating much completely new material, particularly on Bordeaux (where many "petits châteaux" are finding international acceptance for the first time), on Italy, Spain, California, Australia and England, which makes its debut in this edition.

The whole book has been revised and reset, with vintage information brought up to date in detail both as regards the latest vintages (where interesting information is already available) and the state of maturity of older ones.

How to read an entry

The top line of most entries consists of the following information in an abbreviated form.

1. Which part of the country in question the wine comes from. (References to the maps in this book.)

2. Whether it is red, rosé or white (or brown/amber), dry, sweet or sparkling, or several of these.

3. Its general standing as to quality: a necessarily rough and ready guide based principally on the following ascending scale:

    ⋆ plain, everyday quality

    ⋆⋆ above average

    ⋆⋆⋆ well known, highly reputed

    ⋆⋆⋆⋆ grand, prestigious, expensive

So much is more or less objective. Additionally there is a subjective rating: a box round the stars of any wine which in my experience is usually particularly good (which means good value) within its price range. There are good everyday wines as well as good luxury wine. The box system helps you find them.

4. Vintage information: which were the more successful of the recent vintages which *may* still be available. And of these which are ready to drink this year, and which will probably improve with keeping. Your first choice for current drinking should be one of the vintage years printed in **bold** type. Buy light-type years for further maturing.

The German vintage information works on a different principle: see the Introduction to Germany, page 62.

Acknowledgements

This store of detailed recommendations comes partly from my own notes and partly from those of a great number of kind friends. Without the generous help and co-operation of every single member of the wine trade I have approached, I could not have attempted it. I particularly want to thank the following for giving me material help with research or in the areas of their special knowledge.

Martin Bamford	Patrick Matthews
Anthony Barton	Christian Moueix
Jean-Claude Berrouet	Reginald Nicholson
Michael Broadbent M.W.	David Peppercorn M.W.
Sheila Cavanagh-Bradbury	Alain Querre
Jan Critchley-Salmonson	Jan Read
Len Evans	Rosamond Richardson
Georges Fouquier	Dr. Bruno Roncarati
Francis Fouquet	Steven Spurrier
Jean-Paul Gardère	Keith Stevens
Robert Hart M.W.	Serena Sutcliffe M.W.
Tony Laithwaite	Hugh Suter M.W.
Michael Longhurst	Bob Thompson
Tim Marshall	Peter Vinding-Diers

Grape varieties

The most basic of all differences between wines stems from the grapes they are made of. Centuries of selection have resulted in each of the long-established wine-areas having its favourite single variety, or a group of varieties whose juice or wine is blended together. Red burgundy is made of one grape, the Pinot Noir; red Bordeaux of three or four: two kinds of Cabernet, Merlot, Malbec and sometimes others. The laws say which grapes must be used, so the labels assume it.

So in newer vineyards the choice of a grape is the planter's single most crucial decision. Where he is proud of it, and intends his wine to have the character of a particular grape, the variety is the first thing he puts on the label—hence the useful, originally Californian, term "varietal wine".

A knowledge of grape varieties, therefore, is the single most helpful piece of knowledge in finding wines you will like wherever they are grown. Learn to recognize the characters of the most important. At least seven—Cabernet, Pinot Noir, Riesling, Sauvignon Blanc, Chardonnay, Gewürztraminer and Muscat—have memorable tastes and smells distinct enough to form international categories of wine.

Further notes on grapes will be found on page 126 (for California) and in the sections on central and south-east Europe, South Africa, etc.

The following are the best and commonest wine grapes.

Grapes for white wine

Aligoté

Burgundy's second-rank white grape. Crisp (often sharp) wine, needs drinking young. Perfect for mixing with cassis (blackcurrant liqueur) to make a "Kir". Also grown in the USSR.

Blanc Fumé

Another name for SAUVIGNON BLANC, referring to the "smoky" smell of the wine, particularly on the upper Loire. Makes some of California's best whites.

Bual

Makes sweet Madeira wines.

Chardonnay

The white burgundy grape, one of the grapes of Champagne, and the best white grape of California. Gives dry wine of rich complexity. Trials in Australia and eastern Europe are also successful.

Chasselas

A prolific and widely grown early-ripening grape with little flavour, also grown for eating. Best known as Fendant in Switzerland, Gutedel in Germany. Perhaps the same as Hungary's Leányka and Romania's Fetească.

Chenin Blanc

>The leading white grape of the middle Loire (Vouvray, Layon, etc.). Wine can be dry or sweet (or very sweet), but always retains plenty of acidity—hence its popularity in California, where it rarely distinguishes itself.

Clairette

>A dull neutral grape widely used in the s. of France.

Fendant

>See Chasselas

Folle Blanche

>The third most widely grown grape of France, though nowhere making fine wine. High acid and little flavour makes it ideal for brandy. Known as Gros Plant in Brittany, Picpoul in the Midi. At its best in California.

Furmint

>A grape of great character: the trade mark of Hungary both in Tokay and as vivid vigorous table wine with an appley flavour. Called Sipon in Jugoslavia.

Gewürztraminer (or Traminer)

>The most pungent wine grape, distinctively spicy to smell and taste. Wines are often rich and soft, even when fully dry. Best in Alsace; also good in Germany, eastern Europe, Australia, California.

Gros Plant

>See Folle Blanche

Grüner Veltliner

>An Austrian speciality. Round Vienna and in the Wachau and Weinviertel can be delicious: light but lively. For drinking young.

Italian Riesling

>Grown in n. Italy and all over central eastern Europe. Inferior to German or Rhine Riesling with lower acidity, but a good all-round grape. Alias Wälschriesling, Olaszriesling (or often just "Riesling").

Malvasia

>Known as Malmsey in Madeira, Malvasia in Italy: also grown in Greece, Spain, eastern Europe. Makes rich brown wines or soft whites of no great character.

Müller-Thurgau

>Dominant variety in Germany's Rheinhessen and Rheinpfalz; said to be a cross between Riesling and Sylvaner. Ripens early to make soft flowery wines to drink young. Makes good sweet wines. Grows well in Austria, England.

Muscadet

>Makes light, very dry wines round Nantes in Brittany. Recently some have been sharper than they should.

Muscat (many varieties)

>Universally grown easily recognized pungent grape, mostly made into perfumed sweet wines, often fortified (as in France's VIN DOUX NATURELS). Muscat d'Alsace is alone in being dry.

Palomino

>Alias Listan. Makes all the best sherry.

Pedro Ximénez

>Said to have come to s. Spain from Germany. Makes very strong wine in Montilla and Malaga. Used in blending sherry. Also grown in Australia, California, South Africa.

Pinot Blanc

>A close relation of CHARDONNAY without its ultimate nobility. Grown in Champagne, Alsace, n. Italy (good sparkling wine), s. Germany, eastern Europe, California.

Pinot Gris

Makes rather heavy full-bodied whites with a certain spicy style. Known as Tokay in Alsace, Tocai in n.e. Italy and Jugoslavia, Ruländer in Germany.

Pinot Noir

Superlative black grape (see under Grapes for red wine) used in Champagne and occasionally elsewhere for making white wine.

Riesling

Germany's finest grape, now planted round the world. Wine of brilliant sweet/acid balance, flowery in youth but maturing to subtle oily scents and flavours. Successful in Alsace (for dry wine), Austria, parts of eastern Europe, Australia, California, South Africa. Often called White, Johannisberg or Rhine Riesling.

Sauvignon Blanc

Very distinctive aromatic, herby and sometimes smoky scented wine, can be austere (on the upper Loire) or buxom (in Bordeaux, where it is combined with SEMILLON, and parts of California). Also called Fumé Blanc.

Semillon

The grape contributing the lusciousness to great Sauternes; subject to "noble rot" in the right conditions. Makes soft dry wine. Called "Riesling" in Australia.

Sercial

Makes the driest wine of Madeira—where they claim it is really Riesling.

Seyval Blanc

French-made hybrid between French and American vines. Very hardy and attractively fruity. Popular and successful in the eastern States and England.

Steen

South Africa's best white grape: lively fruity wine. Said to be the Chenin Blanc of the Loire.

Sylvaner

Germany's workhorse grape: wine rarely better than pleasant except in Franconia. Good in the Italian Tyrol and useful in Alsace. Wrongly called Riesling in California.

Tokay

See Pinot Gris. Also a table grape in California and a supposedly Hungarian grape in Australia.

Traminer

See Gewürztraminer

Trebbiano

Important grape of central Italy, used in Orvieto, Chianti, Soave, etc. Also grown in s. France as Ugni Blanc, and Cognac as "St-Emilion".

Ugni Blanc

See Trebbiano

Verdelho

Madeira grape making excellent medium-sweet wine.

Verdicchio

Gives its name to good dry wine in central Italy.

Vernaccia

Grape grown in central and s. Italy and Sardinia for strong wine inclining towards sherry.

Viognier

Rare but remarkable grape of the Rhône valley, grown at Condrieu to make very fine soft and fragrant wine.

Welschriesling (or Wälschriesling)

See Italian Riesling

Grapes for red wine

Barbera

One of several good standard grapes of Piemonte, giving dark, robust, fruity and often rather sharp wine. High acidity makes it a good grape for California.

Cabernet Franc

The lesser of two sorts of Cabernet grown in Bordeaux; the Cabernet of the Loire making Chinon and rosé.

Cabernet Sauvignon

Grape of great character; spicy, herby and tannic. The first grape of the Médoc, also makes the best Californian, Australian, South American and eastern European reds. Its wine always needs ageing and usually blending.

Carignan

By far the commonest grape of France, covering hundreds of thousands of acres. Prolific with dull but harmless wine. Also common in North Africa, Spain and California.

Gamay

The Beaujolais grape: light fragrant wines at their best quite young. Makes even lighter wine on the Loire and in Switzerland and Savoie. Known as Napa Gamay in California.

Gamay Beaujolais

Not Gamay but a variety of PINOT NOIR grown in California.

Grenache

Useful grape giving strong and fruity but pale wine: good rosé. Grown in s. France, Spain, California and usually blended.

Grignolino

Makes one of the good cheap table wines of Piemonte. Also used in California.

Merlot

Adaptable grape making the great fragrant and rich wines of Pomerol and St-Emilion, an important element in Médoc reds, and making lighter but good wines in n. Italy, Italian Switzerland, Jugoslavia, Argentina, etc.

Nebbiolo (also called Spanna)

Italy's best red grape, the grape of Barolo, Barbaresco, Gattinara and Valtellina. Intense, nobly fruity and perfumed wine taking years to mature.

Pinot Noir

The glory of Burgundy's Côte d'Or, with scent, flavour, texture and body unmatched anywhere. Less happy elsewhere; makes light wines of no great distinction in Germany, Switzerland, Austria; good ones in Hungary; generally dull ones in California.

Sangiovese

The main red grape of Chianti and much of central Italy.

Syrah

The best Rhône red grape, with heavy purple wine, which can mature superbly. Said by some to come from Shiraz in Persia; others say Syracuse in Sicily. Very important as "Shiraz" in Australia.

Zinfandel

Fruity adaptable grape peculiar to California.

Wine & Food

There are no rules and regulations about what wine goes with what food, but there is a vast body of accumulated experience which it is absurd to ignore.

This list of dishes and appropriate wines records most of the conventional combinations and suggests others that I personally have found good. But it is only a list of ideas intended to help you make quick decisions. Any of the groups of recommended wines could have been extended almost indefinitely, drawing on the whole world's wine list. In general I have stuck to the wines that are widely available, at the same time trying to ring the changes so that the same wines don't come up time and time again—as they tend to do in real life.

The stars refer to the rating system used throughout the book: see opposite Contents.

First courses

Aïoli
> A thirst-quencher is needed with so much garlic. ★→★★ white Rhône, or Verdicchio, and mineral water.

Antipasto (see also Hors d'oeuvre)
> ★★ dry or medium white, preferably Italian (e.g. Soave) or light red, e.g. Valpolicella, Bardolino or young ★ Bordeaux.

Artichoke
> ★ red or rosé.
> **vinaigrette** ★ young red, e.g. Bordeaux.
> **hollandaise** ★ or ★★ full-bodied dry or medium white, e.g. Mâcon Blanc, Rheinpfalz or California "Chablis".

Asparagus
> ★★→★★★ white burgundy or Chardonnay, or Tavel rosé.

Assiette anglaise (assorted cold meats)
> ★★ dry white, e.g. Chablis, Graves, Muscadet, Dão.

Avocado
> **with prawns, crab, etc.** ★★→★★★ dry to medium white, e.g. Rheingau or Rheinpfalz Kabinett, Graves, California Chardonnay or Sauvignon, Cape Stein, or dry rosé.
> **vinaigrette** ★ light red, or fino sherry.

Bisques
> ★★ dry white with plenty of body: Verdicchio, Pinot Gris, Graves.

Bouillabaisse
> ★→★★ very dry white: Muscadet, Alsace Sylvaner, Entre-Deux-Mers, Pouilly Fumé, Cassis.

Caviare
> ★★★ champagne or iced vodka.

Cheese fondue
> ★★ dry white: Fendant du Valais, Grüner Veltliner.

Chicken Liver Pâté
> Appetizing dry white, e.g. ★★ white Bordeaux, or light fruity red; Beaujolais, Gamay de Touraine or Valpolicella.

Clams and Chowders
> ★★ big-scale white, not necessarily bone dry: e.g. Rhône, Pinot Gris, Dry Sauternes.

Consommé
> ★★→★★★ medium-dry sherry, dry Madeira, Marsala, Montilla.

Crudités
> ★→★★ light red or rosé, e.g. Côtes-du-Rhône, Beaujolais, Chianti, Zinfandel.

Eggs (see also Soufflés)

These present difficulties: they clash with most wine and spoil good ones. So ★→★★ of whatever is going.

Empanadas

★→★★ Chilean Cabernet, Zinfandel.

Escargots

★★ red or white of some substance: e.g. Burgundy; Côtes-du-Rhône, Chardonnay, Shiraz, etc.

Foie gras

★★★→★★★★ white. In Bordeaux they drink Sauternes. Others prefer vintage champagne or a rich Gewürztraminer Vendange tardive.

Gazpacho

Sangria (see Spain) is refreshing, but to avoid too much liquid intake dry Manzanilla or Montilla is better.

Grapefruit

If you must start a meal with grapefruit try port, Madeira or sweet sherry with it.

Ham, raw

See Prosciutto

Herrings, raw or pickled

Dutch gin or Scandinavian akvavit, or ★★ full-bodied white Mâcon-Villages, Graves or Dão.

Hors d'oeuvre (see also Antipasto)

★→★★ clean fruity sharp white: Sancerre or any Sauvignon, Alsace Sylvaner, Muscadet, Cape Stein—or young light red Bordeaux, Rhône or equivalent.

Mackerel, smoked

★★→★★★ full-bodied tasty white: e.g. Gewürztraminer, Tokay d'Alsace or Chablis Premier Cru.

Melon

Needs a strong sweet wine: ★★ Port, Bual Madeira, Muscat, Oloroso sherry or Vin doux naturel.

Minestrone

★ red: Grignolino, Chianti, etc.

Omelettes

See observations under Eggs

Onion/Leek tart

★→★★★ fruity dry white, e.g. Alsace Sylvaner or Riesling. Mâcon-Villages of a good vintage, California or Australian Riesling.

Pasta

★→★★ red or white according to the sauce or accompaniments, e.g.

with fish sauce (vongole, etc.) Verdicchio or Soave.
meat sauce Chianti, Beaujolais or Côtes-du-Rhône.
tomato sauce Barbera or Sicilian red.
cream sauce Orvieto or Frascati.

Pâté

★★ dry white: e.g. Chablis, Mâcon Blanc, Graves.

Peppers or aubergines (egg-plant), stuffed

★★ vigorous red: e.g. Bull's Blood, Chianti, Zinfandel.

Pizza

Any ★★ dry Italian red or a ★★ Rioja, Australian Shiraz or California Zinfandel.

Prawns or Shrimps

★★→★★★ dry white: burgundy or Bordeaux, Chardonnay or Riesling. ("Cocktail sauce" kills wine.)

Prosciutto with melon

★★→★★★ full-bodied dry or medium white: e.g. Orvieto or Frascati, Fendant, Grüner Veltliner, Alsace Sylvaner, California Gewürztraminer, Australian Riesling.

Quiches

    ★→★★ dry white with body (Alsace, Graves, Sauvignon) or young red according to the ingredients.

Ratatouille

    ★★ vigorous young red, e.g. Chianti, Zinfandel, Bull's Blood, young red Bordeaux.

Salade niçoise

    ★★ very dry not too light or flowery white, e.g. white (or rosé) Rhône, white Spanish, Dão, California Sauvignon Blanc.

Salads

As a first course: any dry and appetizing white wine. After a main course: no wine.

N.B. Vinegar in salad dressings destroys the flavour of wine. If you want salad at a meal with fine wine, dress the salad with wine instead of vinegar.

Salami

    ★→★★ powerfully tasty red or rosé: e.g. Barbera, young Zinfandel, Tavel rosé, young Bordeaux.

Salmon, smoked

A dry but pungent white, e.g. fino sherry, Alsace Gewürztraminer, Chablis Grand Cru.

Soufflés

As show dishes these deserve ★★→★★★ wines.

Fish soufflés Dry white, e.g. burgundy, Bordeaux, Alsace, Chardonnay, etc.

Cheese soufflé Red burgundy or Bordeaux, Cabernet Sauvignon, etc.

Taramasalata

Calls for a rustic southern white of strong personality; not necessarily the Greek Retsina.

Terrine

As for pâté, or the equivalent red: e.g. Beaune, Mercurey, Beaujolais-Villages, fairly young ★★ St-Emilion, California Cabernet or Zinfandel, Bulgarian or Chilean Cabernet, etc.

Fish

Abalone

    ★★→★★★ dry or medium white: e.g. Sauvignon Blanc, Chardonnay, Verdicchio.

Cod

A good neutral background for fine dry or medium whites, e.g. ★★→★★★ Chablis, cru classé Graves, German Kabinetts and their equivalents.

Coquilles St. Jacques

An inherently slightly sweet dish, best with medium-dry white wine.

in cream sauces ★★★ German wines.

grilled or fried Hermitage Blanc, Gewürztraminer, California Chenin Blanc or Riesling.

Eel, smoked

Either strong or sharp wine, e.g. fino sherry or Bourgogne Aligoté.

Haddock

    ★★→★★★ dry white with a certain richness: e.g. Meursault, California Chardonnay.

Herrings

Need a white with some acidity to cut their richness. Burgundy Aligoté or Gros Plant from Brittany or dry Sauvignon Blanc. **Kippers:** a good cup of tea, preferably Ceylon.

Lamproie à la Bordelaise

    ★★ young red Bordeaux, especially St-Emilion or Pomerol.

Lobster or Crab

    salad **→**** white. Non-vintage champagne, Alsace Riesling, Chablis Premier Cru.

    richly sauced Vintage champagne, fine white burgundy, cru classé Graves, California Chardonnay, Rheinpfalz Spätlese, Hermitage Blanc.

Mackerel

    ** hard or sharp white: Sauvignon Blanc from Bergerac or Touraine, Gros Plant, vinho verde, white Rioja.

Mullet, Red

    ** Mediterranean white, even Retzina, for the atmosphere.

Mussels

    *→** Gros Plant, Muscadet, California "Chablis".

Oysters

    →* white. Champagne (non-vintage), Chablis or (better) Chablis Premier Cru, Muscadet or Entre-Deux-Mers.

Salmon, fresh

    *** fine white burgundy: Puligny- or Chassagne-Montrachet, Meursault, Corton-Charlemagne, Chablis Grand Cru, California Chardonnay, or Rheingau Kabinett or Spätlese, California Riesling or equivalent.

Sardines, fresh grilled

    *→** very dry white: e.g. vinho verde, Dão, Muscadet.

Scallops

    See Coquilles St. Jacques

Shad

    →* white Graves or Meursault.

Shellfish (general)

    Dry white with plain boiled shellfish, richer wines with richer sauces.

Shrimps, potted

    Fino sherry or Chablis.

Skate with black butter

    ** white with some pungency (e.g. Alsace Pinot Gris) or a clean one like Muscadet.

Sole, Plaice, etc.

    plain, grilled or fried An ideal accompaniment for fine wines: * up to **** white burgundy, or its equivalent.

    with sauce Depending on the ingredients: sharp dry wine for tomato sauce, fairly sweet for Sole véronique, etc.

Trout

    Delicate white wine, e.g. *** Mosel.

    Smoked, a full-flavoured **→*** white: Gewürztraminer, Pinot Gris, Rhine Spätlese or Australian Hunter white.

Turbot

    Fine rich dry white, e.g. *** Meursault or its Californian equivalent.

Meat

Beef, boiled

    ** red: e.g. Cru Bourgeois Bordeaux (Bourg or Fronsac), Côtes-du-Rhône-Villages, Australian Shiraz or Claret.

Beef, roast

    An ideal partner for fine red wine. *→**** red of any kind.

Beef stew

    →* sturdy red, e.g. Pomerol or St-Emilion, Hermitage, Shiraz.

Beef Strogonoff

    →* suitably dramatic red: e.g. Barolo, Valpolicella, Amarone, Hermitage, late-harvest Zinfandel.

Cassoulet

** red from s.w. France, e.g. Cahors or Corbières, or Barbera or Zinfandel.

Chicken or Turkey, roast

Virtually any wine, including your very best bottles of dry or medium white and fine old reds.

Chili con carne

*→** young red: e.g. Bull's Blood, Chianti, Mountain Red.

Chinese food

** dry to medium-dry white: e.g. Jugoslav Riesling, Mâcon-Villages, California "Chablis".

Choucroute

Lager.

Confit d'Oie

→** rather young and tannic red Bordeaux helps to cut the richness. Alsace Tokay or Gewürztraminer matches it.

Corned beef hash

** Zinfandel, Chianti, Côtes-du-Rhône red.

Coq au Vin

→** red burgundy. In an ideal world one bottle of Chambertin in the dish, one on the table.

Curry

*→** medium-sweet white, very cold: e.g. Orvieto abboccato, certain California Chenin Blancs, Jugoslav Traminer.

Duck or Goose

*** rather rich white, e.g. Rheinpfalz Spätlese or Alsace Réserve Exceptionelle, or *** Bordeaux or burgundy.

Wild Duck *** big-scale red: e.g. Hermitage, Châteauneuf-du-Pape, Calif. or S. African Cabernet, Australian Shiraz.

Frankfurters

*→** German or Austrian white.

Game birds

Young birds plain roasted deserve the best red wine you can afford. With older birds in casseroles **→*** red, e.g. Gevrey-Chambertin, St-Emilion, Napa Cabernet.

Game Pie

*** red wine.

Goulash

** strong young red: e.g. Zinfandel, Bulgarian Cabernet.

Grouse

See under Game birds

Ham

→* fairly young red burgundy, e.g. Volnay, Savigny, Beaune, Corton, or a slightly sweet German white, e.g. a Rhine Spätlese, or Chianti or Valpolicella.

Hamburger

*→** young red: e.g. Beaujolais, Corbières or Minervois, Chianti, Zinfandel.

Hare

Jugged hare calls for **→*** red with plenty of flavour: not-too-old burgundy or Bordeaux. The same for saddle.

Kebabs

** vigorous red: e.g. Greek Demestica, Turkish Doluca, Hungarian Pinot Noir, Chilean Cabernet, Zinfandel.

Kidneys

→* red: Pomerol or St-Emilion, Rhône, Barbaresco, Rioja, California or Australian Cabernet.

Lamb cutlets or chops

As for roast lamb, but less grand.

Lamb, roast

One of the traditional and best partners for very good red Bordeaux—or its equivalents.

Liver

    ** young red: Beaujolais-Villages, Rhône, Médoc, Italian Merlot, Zinfandel.

Meatballs

    →* red: e.g. Mercurey, Madiran, Rubesco, Dão, Zinfandel.

Mixed Grill

    A fairly light easily swallowable red; ** red Bordeaux from Bourg, Fronsac or Premières Cotes; Chianti; Bourgogne Passetoutgrains.

Moussaka

    *→** red or rosé: e.g. Chianti, Corbières, Côtes de Provence, California Burgundy.

Oxtail

    →* rather rich red: e.g. St-Emilion or Pomerol, Burgundy, Barolo or Chianti Classico, Rioja Reserva, California Cabernet.

Paella

    ** Spanish red, dry white or rosé, e.g. Panades or Rioja or vinho verde.

Partridge, pheasant

    See under Game birds

Pigeons or squabs

    →** red Bordeaux, Chianti Classico, Cabernet Sauvignon, etc.

Pork, roast

    The sauce or stuffing has more flavour than the meat. Sharp apple sauce or pungent sage and onion need only a plain young wine. Pork without them, on the other hand, is a good neutral background to very good white or red wine.

Rabbit

    *→*** young red: Italian for preference.

Sauerkraut

    Beer.

Shepherd's Pie

    *→** rough and ready red seems most appropriate, but no harm would come to a good one.

Steak and Kidney Pie or Pudding

    Red Rioja Reserva or mature **→*** Bordeaux.

Steaks

    Au poivre a fairly young *** Rhône red or Cabernet.

    Tartare ** light young red: Bergerac, Valpolicella.

    Filet or Tournedos *** red of any kind (but not old wines with Béarnaise sauce).

    T-bone **→*** reds of similar bone-structure: e.g. Barolo, Hermitage, Australian Cabernet.

    Fiorentina (bistecca) Chianti Classico.

Stews and Casseroles

    A lusty full-flavoured red, e.g. young Côtes-du-Rhône, Corbières, Barbera, Shiraz, Zinfandel, etc.

Sweetbreads

    These tend to be a grand dish, suggesting a grand wine, e.g. *** Rhine Kabinett or Spätlese, or well-matured Bordeaux or Burgundy, depending on the sauce.

Tongue

    Ideal for favourite bottles of any red or white.

Tripe

    *→** red: Corbières, Mâcon Rouge, etc., or rather sweet white, e.g. Liebfraumilch.

Veal, roast

    A good neutral background dish for any old red which may have faded, or a *** German white.

Venison

    *** big-scale red (Rhône, Bordeaux of a grand vintage) or rather rich white (Rheinpfalz Spätlese or Tokay d'Alsace).

Wiener Schnitzel

    →* light red from the Italian Tyrol (Alto Adige) or the Médoc: or Austrian Riesling, Grüner Veltliner or Gumpoldskirchener.

Cheese

    Very ripe cheese completely masks the flavour of wine. Only serve fine wine with mild cheeses.

Bleu de Bresse, Dolcelatte, Gorgonzola

    Need fairly emphatic accompaniment: young ** red wine (Barbera, Dolcetto, Moulin-à-Vent, etc.) or sweet white.

Cream cheeses: Brie, Camembert, Bel Paese, Edam, etc.

    In their mild state go perfectly with any good wine, red or white.

English cheeses

    On the whole are strong and acidic. Sweet or strong wine is needed.

    Cheddar, Cheshire, Wensleydale, Stilton, Gloucester, etc. Ruby, tawny or vintage-character (not vintage) port, or a very big red: Hermitage, Châteauneuf-du-Pape, Barolo, etc.

Goat cheeses

    →* white wine of marked character, either dry (e.g. Sancerre) or sweet (e.g. Monbazillac, Sauternes).

Hard Cheese, Parmesan, Gruyère, Emmenthal

    Full-bodied dry whites, e.g. Tokay d'Alsace or Vernaccia.

Roquefort, Danish Blue

    Are so strong-flavoured that only the youngest, biggest or sweetest wines stand a chance.

Desserts

Apple pie, apple strudel

    →* sweet German, Austrian or Hungarian white.

Baked Alaska

    Sweet champagne or Asti Spumante.

Cakes

    Bual or Malmsey Madeira, Oloroso or cream sherry.

Cheesecake

    →* sweet white from Vouvray or Coteaux du Layon.

Chocolate cake, mousse, soufflés

    No wine.

Christmas pudding

    Sweet champagne or Asti Spumante.

Creams and Custards

    →* Sauternes, Monbazillac or similar golden white.

Crème brûlée

    The most luxurious dish, demanding ***→**** Sauternes or Rhine Beerenauslese, or the best Madeira or Tokay.

Crêpes Suzette

    Sweet champagne or Asti Spumante.

Fruit flans (i.e. peach, raspberry)

    *** Sauternes, Monbazillac or sweet Vouvray.

Fruit salads, orange salad

    No wine.

Nuts

    Oloroso sherry, Bual, Madeira, vintage or tawny port.

Sorbets, ice-creams

    No wine.

Stewed fruits, i.e. apricots, pears, etc.
> Sweet Muscatel: e.g. Muscat de Beaumes de Venise, Moscato di Pantelleria.

Strawberries and cream
> *** Sauternes or Vouvray.
> **Wild strawberries** Serve with *** red Bordeaux poured over them and in your glass (no cream).

Summer Pudding
> Fairly young Sauternes of a good vintage (e.g. 70, 71, 75).

Treacle Tart
> Too sweet for any wine but a treacly Malmsey Madeira.

Trifle
> No wine: should be sufficiently vibrant with sherry.

Sweet Soufflés
> Sweet Vouvray or Coteaux du Layon.

Zabaglione
> Light gold Marsala.

Savoury

Cheese straws
> Admirable meal-ending with a final glass (or bottle) of a particularly good red wine.

Temperature

No single aspect of serving wine makes or mars it so easily as getting the temperature right. White wines almost invariably taste dull and insipid served warm and red wines have disappointly little scent or flavour served cold. The chart below gives an indication of what is generally found to be the best and most satisfactory temperature for serving each class of wine.

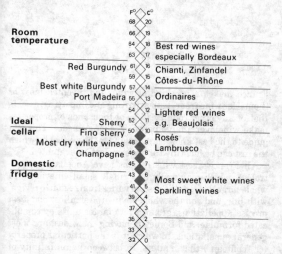

	F°	C°	
Room temperature	68	20	
	66	19	
	64	18	Best red wines especially Bordeaux
	63	17	
Red Burgundy	61	16	Chianti, Zinfandel Côtes-du-Rhône
	59	15	
Best white Burgundy	57	14	
Port Madeira	55	13	Ordinaires
	54	12	Lighter red wines e.g. Beaujolais
Ideal cellar	52	11	Sherry
	50	10	Fino sherry · Rosés
Most dry white wines	48	9	
Champagne	46	8	Lambrusco
Domestic fridge	45	7	
	43	6	
	41	5	Most sweet white wines Sparkling wines
	39	4	
	37	3	
	35	2	
	33	1	
	32	0	

France

Brittany

Loire **Lo**

R. Loire

Cognac

Bordeaux

• Borde

R. Garor

SW F

France makes every kind of wine, and invented most of them. Her wine trade, both exporting and importing, dwarfs that of any other country. Tens of thousands of properties make wine over a large part of France's surface. This is a guide to the best known of them and to the system by which the rest can be identified and to some extent evaluated.

All France's best wine regions have Appellations Controlées, which may apply to a single small vineyard or a whole large district: the system varies from region to region, with Burgundy on the whole having the smallest and most precise appellations, grouped into larger units by complicated formulae, and Bordeaux having the widest and most general appellations, in which it is the particular property (or "château") that matters. In between lie an infinity of variations.

Abbreviations of regional names shown in bold type are used in the text.

An Appellation Controlée is a guarantee of origin and of production method, of grape varieties and quantities produced: not of quality. France does not have a quality-testing system as Germany does. The scale of the problem is too vast and the French are too French.

Appellations therefore help to identify a wine and indicate that it comes from a major area. They are the first thing to look for on a label.

Wine regions without the overall quality and traditions required for an appellation can be ranked as Vins Délimités de Qualité Supérieure (VDQS), or (a new third rank created largely to encourage the improvement of mediocre wines in the south of France) Vins de Pays. VDQS wines are often good value, on the Avis principle. Vins de Pays are worth trying for curiosity's sake.

Recent vintages

Red Burgundy

Côte d'Or Côte de Beaune reds generally mature sooner than the bigger wines of the Côte de Nuits. Earliest drinking dates are for lighter commune wines: Volnay, Beaune, etc. Latest for the biggest wines of Chambertin, Romanée, etc. Different growers make wines of different styles, for longer or shorter maturing, but even the best burgundies are much more attractive young than the equivalent red Bordeaux.

1978	Poor summer saved by miraculous autumn. A small vintage of outstanding quality.
1977	Very wet summer. Better wine than expected, especially in northern côtes.
1976	Hot summer, excellent vintage. Some wines may be too big and tannic.
1975	Rot was rife, particularly in the Côte de Beaune. Mostly very poor. A few good wines from the northern Côte de Nuits with careful vinification.
1974	Another big wet vintage; mostly poor, even the best light and lean. Drink up.
1973	Again, vintage rain stretched the crop. Light wines, but many fruity and delicate. Many are already too old.
1972	High acidity posed problems, but the wines are firm and full of character, ageing well and beginning to be delicious.
1971	Very powerful and impressive wines, not as long-lasting as they first appeared. Most now ready.
1970	Attractive soft fruity wines, but should be drunk up now. Big crop.
1969	A magnificent vintage with very few exceptions. Small crop. The best will mature as long as any modern burgundy. The rest are ready.

Older fine vintages: '66, '64, '62, '61, '59.

Beaujolais

1978	A very good vintage in profusion. The best Crus will keep well.
1977	Generally poor, some pleasant light wines and good Crus.
1976	Was the best vintage since 1971. Most wines are now delicious. Its best will keep for 3–4 years.

White Burgundy

Côte de Beaune Well-made wines of good vintages with plenty of acidity as well as fruit will improve and gain depth and richness for some years—anything up to ten. Lesser wines from lighter years are ready for drinking after two or three years.

1978	Good wines, perhaps too soft to keep for long.
1977	Rather light; some well-balanced and good.
1976	Hot summer, rather heavy wines; good but not for laying-down.
1975	Hot summer, then vintage rain. Whites did much better than reds. Rot reduced quantity, but the grapes were ripe and the wine can be excellent. No hurry to drink.
1974	Spring frosts reduced the crop, but the hot summer made fine wines, some great.
1973	Very attractive, fruity, typical and plentiful, but not wines to keep they lack acidity.
1972	Awkward wines to make with high acidity, even greenness, but plenty of character. The best are developing into classical wines.
1971	Great power and style, some almost too rich, but the best have good balance. Small crop.
1970	Large and very good. Attractive soft gentle style has matured quickly. Drink soon.
1969	An excellent all-round vintage, strong, tasty and well balanced. Small crop. Mostly mature.

The white wines of the Mâconnais (Pouilly-Fuissé, St Véran, Mâcon-Villages) follow a similar pattern, but do not last as long. They are more appreciated for their freshness than their richness.

Chablis Grand Cru Chablis of vintages with both strength and acidity can age superbly for up to ten years. Premier Crus proportionately less. Only buy Petit Chablis of ripe years, and drink it young.

1978	Excellent wines for fairly early drinking.
1977	Reduced quantity, but typical and fresh like 1974.
1976	A great vintage. Should be kept.
1975	Very good wines maturing rather quickly.
1974	A trifle sharp at first, but lively, attractive and typical.
1973	Very good ripe and plentiful vintage for drinking young.
1972	Poor and sharp. Some have improved in bottle.
1971	Excellent, if not classic; some as rich as Côte d'Or. Drink soon.

Red Bordeaux

Médoc/red Graves For some wines bottle-age is optional: for these it is indispensable. Minor châteaux from light vintages need only two or three years, but even modest wines of great years can improve for fifteen years or so, and the great châteaux of these years need double that time.

1978	A miracle vintage: magnificent long warm autumn saved the day. Some very good wines.
1977	Very wet summer. Pleasant light wine, many better than 1974.
1976	Excessively hot, dry summer; rain just before vintage. Difficult year, but its best wine will be very good, maturing rather quickly.
1975	A splendid summer and very fine vintage, with deep colour, high sugar content and some tannin. For long keeping.
1974	Diluting vintage rain ruined hopes of a really good vintage. Oceans of disappointing light wines, though the best have good colour and have developed some character.
1973	Again, last-minute rain turned quality into quantity. A huge vintage, attractive to drink young but lacking acidity and tannin.
1972	High acidity from unripe grapes. Unripe wines, though the best will soften with age. Do not pay much for '72s.
1971	Small crop. Less fruity than '70 and less consistent. Some châteaux made outstanding wine. Most are ready to drink.
1970	Abundance *and* uniform quality. Big fruity wines with elegance and attractive suppleness. Although not tannic they are wines of great distinction for long keeping.
1969	Heavy September rain after a good summer. Mean wines lacking fruit and colour. Should all be drunk soon.
1968	This time a wet August was the culprit. Very few drinkable wines.
1967	Large; first judged to be light and for early drinking, has developed well and gained body and interest, though not always charm.
1966	A very fine vintage with depth, fruit and tannin. Still needs time to open out. Classic claret.

Older fine vintages: '62, '61, '59, '55, '53, '52, '50, '49, '48, '47, '45, '29, '28.

St-Emilion/Pomerol

1978	Lovely wine, to everyone's surprise.
1977	Very wet summer. Mediocre with few exceptions.
1976	Very hot, dry summer and early vintage, but vintage rain made complications. Some excellent wines: the best great.
1975	Most St-Emilions good, the best superb. Frost in Pomerol reduced crops and made splendid concentrated wine.
1974	Vintage rain again. Mainly disappointing light wines.
1973	Good summer, big wet vintage. Pleasant: wines to drink young.
1972	Poor summer but fine for the late vintage. Many unripe wines, but some are pleasant enough. Choose carefully.
1971	Small crop: fine wines with length and depth, on the whole better than Médocs but generally now ready.
1970	Glorious weather and beautiful wines with great fruit and strength throughout the district. Very big crop.
1969	Fine summer, small wet vintage. At best agreeable.
1968	A disaster. Endless rain.
1967	Large and generally very good; on the whole better than Médoc and Graves. Some good buys here.
1966	Ripe, powerful, round. Maturing well.

Older fine vintages: '64, '61, '59, '53, '52, '49, '47, '45.
For other areas see under A–Z entries.

Ajaccio   Corsica r. p. or w. dr. ★ NV
>The capital of Corsica and its strong plain wines.

Aligoté
>Second-rank burgundy white grape and its often sharp wine, often agreeable and with considerable local character when young.

Aloxe-Corton   B'y. r. or w. ★★★ 69 70 71 72 73 76 77 78
>Northernmost village of CÔTE DE BEAUNE: best v'yds.: CORTON (red) and CORTON-CHARLEMAGNE (white). Village wines lighter but often good value.

Alsace   Al. w. or (r.) ★★ 71 73 74 75 76 77 78
>Aromatic, fruity dry white of Germanic character from French Rhineland. Normally sold by grape variety (RIESLING, GEWÜRZTRAMINER, etc.). Matures well.

Alsace Grand Cru   ★★★
>Appellation restricted to the best named v'yds

Alsace Grand Vin or Réserve
>Wine with minimum 11° natural alcohol.

Anjou   Lo. (r.) p. or w. (sw. dr. or sp.) ★→★★★ 69 70 71 73 75 76 78
>Very various Loire wines, incl. good CABERNET rosé, luscious COTEAUX DU LAYON. Maturity depends on style.

Appellation Controlée
>Government control of origin and production of all the best French wines (see France Introduction).

Apremont   Savoie w. dr. ★★ D.Y.A.
>One of the best villages of SAVOIE for pale delicate whites.

Arbois   Jura r. p. or w. (dr. sp.) ★★ D.Y.A.
>Various pleasant light wines; speciality VIN JAUNE.

Armagnac
>Region of s.w. France famous for its excellent brandy, a fiery spirit of rustic character. The chief town is Condom.

Auxey-Duresses   B'y. r. or w.   ★★   69 71 72 73 74 75w 76 77 78
>Second-rank CÔTE DE BEAUNE village: has affinities with VOLNAY and MEURSAULT. Best estates: Duc de Magenta, Prunier, Roy, HOSPICES DE BEAUNE Cuvée Boillot.

Avize   Champ. ★★★★
>One of the best white-grape villages of CHAMPAGNE.

Ay   Champ. ★★★★
>One of the best black-grape villages of CHAMPAGNE.

Bandol   Prov. r. p. or (w.) ★★ 70 71 72 73 74 76
>Little coastal region near Marseille with tasty reds.

Banyuls   Pyr. br. sw. ★★ NV
>One of the best VIN DOUX NATURELS (fortified sweet red wines) of the s. of France. Not unlike port.

Barsac   B'x. w. sw. ★★→   ★★★
>Neighbour of SAUTERNES with similar superb luscious golden wines. Top ch'x.: CLIMENS and COUTET.

Barton & Guestier
>Important Bordeaux shipper dating from the 18th century, now owned by Seagram's.

Bâtard-Montrachet   B'y. w. dr.   ★★★★   67 69 71 72 73 74 76 77 78
>Neighbour and almost equal of MONTRACHET, the top white burgundy. As rich in flavour as dry white wine can be.

Béarn   S.W. France r. p. or w. dr. ★
>VDQS of local interest.

Beaujolais   B'y. r. (p. w.) ★ 76 78 D.Y.A.
>The simple appellation of the big Beaujolais region: light short-lived fruity red.

Beaujolais Primeur (or Nouveau)
>The same made in a hurry (only 4–5 days fermenting) for drinking from 15 November. The best come from light sandy soil and are as strong as 12.5% alcohol.

Beaujolais de l'année

In effect, the same as Primeur or Nouveau.

Beaujolais Supérieur B'y. r. (w.) ★ 76 78

Beaujolais 1° of natural alcohol stronger than the 9° minimum. Since sugar is almost always added this makes little difference to the final product.

Beaujolais Villages B'y. r. ★★ 76 78

Wine from the better (northern) half of Beaujolais, stronger and tastier than plain Beaujolais. The 9 (easily) best "villages" are the "crus": FLEURIE, BROUILLY, etc. Of the 30 others the best lie around Beaujeu. Cannot be released 'en primeur' before December 15th.

Beaumes de Venise Rh. (r. p.) br. sw. ★★★ NV

France's best dessert muscat, from the s. Côtes-du-Rhône; high-flavoured, subtle, lingering. The red and rosé from the co-operative are also good.

Beaune B'y. r. or (w. dr.) ★★★ 69 71 72 73 76 78

Middle-rank classic burgundy. Négociants' "CLOS" wines (usually "Premier Cru") are often best.

Bellet Prov. p. (r. w. dr.) ★★

Highly fashionable, much above average, local wine from near Nice. Tiny production.

Bergerac Dordogne r. or w. sw. or dr. ★★ 75 76 78

Light-weight, often tasty, Bordeaux-style. Drink young, the white very young.

Beyer, Leon

Ancient and excellent Alsace family wine business at Eguisheim.

Blagny B'y. r. or w. dr. ★★ 69 71 72 73 76 78

Hamlet between MEURSAULT and PULIGNY-MONT-RACHET; affinities with both and VOLNAY for reds. Ages well.

Blanc de Blancs

Any white wine made from (only) white grapes, esp. champagne, which is usually made of black and white.

Blanc de Noirs

White wine made from black grapes.

Blanquette de Limoux Midi w. dr. sp. ★ NV

Good cheap sparkler from near Carcassonne made by a version of the MÉTHODE CHAMPENOISE. Very dry and clean.

Blaye B'x. r. or w. dr. ★→★★ 70 71 73 75 76 78

Your average Bordeaux from e. of the Gironde. PREMIÈRES CÔTES DE BLAYE are better.

Bollinger NV "Special Cuvée" and 62 64 66 69 70 73

Top champagne house, at AY. Dry full-flavoured style. Luxury wines "Tradition R. D."; and "Vieilles Vignes Françaises" from ungrafted vines.

Bommes

Village of SAUTERNES. Best ch'x.: LA TOUR-BLANCHE, LAFAURIE-PEYRAGUEY, etc.

Bonnes Mares B'y. r. ★★★★ 66 69 70 71 72 73 76 77 78

37-acre Grand Cru between CHAMBOLLE-MUSIGNY and MOREY-SAINT-DENIS. Reliably noble, often better than CHAMBERTIN.

Bonnezeaux Lo. w. sw. ★★★ 67 69 70 71 73 75 76 78

Unusual fruity/acidic wine from CHENIN BLANC grapes.

Bordeaux B'x. r. or (p.) or w. ★ 73 75 76 78 (for ch'x. see p. 26)

Basic catch-all appellation for low-strength Bordeaux wine.

Bordeaux Supérieur

Ditto, with slightly more alcohol.

Bordeaux Côtes-de-Castillon B'x. r. ★ 70 71 73 75 76 78

Fringe Bordeaux from east of ST-EMILION, and not far from some St-Emilions in quality.

Bordeaux Côtes-de-Francs B'x. r. or wh. dr. * 71 73 75 **76** 78
Fringe Bordeaux from east of ST-EMILION. Light wines.

Borie-Manoux
Bordeaux shippers and château-owners, incl. Ch'x.
BATAILLEY, HAUT BAGES-MONPELOU, DOMAINE DE L'EGLISE,
TROTTEVIEILLE.

Bouchard Ainé
Famous and long-established burgundy shipper and grower
with 60 acres in Beaune, Mercurey, etc.

Bouchard Père et Fils
Important burgundy shipper (est. 1731) with 200 acres of
excellent v'yds., mainly in the CÔTE DE BEAUNE, and cellars at
the Château de Beaune.

Bourg B'x. r. or (w. dr.) ** **70** 71 73 75 78
Meaty, un-fancy claret from e. of the Gironde. CÔTES DE BOURG
are better.

Bourgogne B'y. r. (p.) or w. dr. ** **76** 78
Catch-all appellation for burgundy, but with higher stan-
dards than basic BORDEAUX. Light but often good flavour.
BEAUJOLAIS crus can be sold as Bourgogne.

Bourgogne Grand Ordinaire B'y. r. or (w.) * D.Y.A.
The lowest burgundy appellation. Seldom seen.

Bourgogne Passetoutgrains B'y. r. or (p.) ⊡ D.Y.A.
Often enjoyable junior burgundy. ⅓ PINOT NOIR and ⅔ GAMAY
grapes mixed. Not as "heady" as BEAUJOLAIS.

Bourgueil Lo. r. *** 71 73 75 **76** 78
Delicate fruity CABERNET red from Touraine. Drink cool.

Bouzy Rouge Champ. r. *** **66** 67 69 70 71 73 75 76
Still red wine from famous black-grape CHAMPAGNE village.

Brédif, Marc
One of the most important growers and traders of VOUVRAY.

Brouilly B'y. r. *** **76** 78
One of the 9 best CRUS of BEAUJOLAIS: fruity, round, refreshing. One year in bottle is enough.

Brut
Term for the driest wines of CHAMPAGNE until recently, when
some completely unsugared wines have become available as
"Brut Intégrale", "Brut non-dosé", "Brut zéro" etc.

Bugey Savoie w. dr. or sp. * D.Y.A.
District with a variety of light sparkling, still or half-
sparkling wines.

Cabernet
See Grapes for red wine

Cabernet d'Anjou Lo. p. ** D.Y.A.
Delicate, often slightly sweet, grapy rosé.

Cahors S.W. France r. *→ ** 70 71 72 75 76 78
Very dark, traditionally hard "black" wine, now made more
like Bordeaux but can be full-bodied and distinct.

Cairanne Rh. r. p. or w. dr. ** 72 73 74 76 78
Village of CÔTE-DU-RHÔNE-VILLAGES. Good solid wines.

Calvet
Great family wine business, originally on the Rhône, now
important in Bordeaux and Burgundy.

Canon-Fronsac
See Côtes-Canon-Fronsac

Cantenac B'x. r. ***
Village of the HAUT-MÉDOC entitled to the Appellation
MARGAUX. Top ch'x. include PALMER, BRANE-CANTENAC, etc.

Cassis Prov. (r. p.) w. dr. ** D.Y.A.
Seaside village e. of Marseille known for its very dry white,
above the usual standard of Provence. Not to be confused with
cassis, a blackcurrant liqueur made in Dijon.

Cave
>   Cellar, or any wine establishment.

Cave co-opérative
>   Wine-growers' co-operative winery. Formerly viticultural dustbins, most are now well run, well equipped and making some of the best wine of their areas.

Cépage
>   Variety of vine, e.g. CHARDONNAY, MERLOT.

Cérons   B'x. w. dr. or sw. ** 70 71 75 76
>   Neighbour of SAUTERNES with some good sweet-wine ch'x.

Chablis   B'y. w. dr. ** 73 74 75 76 77 78
>   Distinctive full-flavoured greeny gold wine. APPELLATION CONTROLÉE essential. Petit Chablis is less fine, but often good.

Chablis Grand Cru   B'y. w. dr.   ****   67 69 71 73 74 75 76 77 78
>   Strong, subtle and altogether splendid. One of the great white burgundies.

Chablis Premier Cru   B'y. w. dr.   ***   69 71 73 74 75 76 77 78
>   Second-rank but often excellent and more typical of Chablis than Grands Crus.

Chai
>   Building for storing and maturing wine, esp. in Bordeaux.

Chambertin   B'y. r. **** 66 69 70 71 72 73 76 77 78
>   32-acre Grand Cru giving the meatiest, most enduring and often the best red burgundy. Many growers.

Chambertin-Clos-de-Bèze   B'y. r. **** 66 69 70 71 72 73 76 77 78
>   37-acre neighbour of CHAMBERTIN. Similarly splendid wine.

Chambolle-Musigny   B'y. r. (w. dr.) *** 66 69 70 71 72 73 76 77 78
>   420-acre CÔTE DE NUITS village with fabulously fragrant, complex wine. Best v'yds.: MUSIGNY, Les Armoureuses, Les Charmes. Best grower: de Vogüé.

Chambré
>   At (old-fashioned) room temperature; normal for drinking red wines. Modern room temperature is often too high.

Champagne
>   Sparkling wine from 55,000 acres 90 miles e. of Paris, made by the MÉTHODE CHAMPENOISE: the world's best (see also name of brand).

Champagne, Grande
>   The appellation of the best area of COGNAC.

Champigny
>   See Saumur

Chanson Père et Fils
>   Growers and traders in fine wine at BEAUNE.

Chante-Alouette
>   A famous brand of white HERMITAGE.

Chapelle-Chambertin   B'y. r. *** 66 69 70 71 72 73 76 77 78
>   13-acre neighbour of CHAMBERTIN. Similar wine, not quite so full and meaty.

Chapoutier
>   Long-established family firm of growers and traders of Rhône wines, particularly HERMITAGE.

Chardonnay
>   See Grapes for white wine

Charmes-Chambertin   B'y. r. *** 66 69 70 71 72 73 76 77 78
>   76-acre neighbour of CHAMBERTIN. Similar but lighter wine.

Chassagne-Montrachet   B'y. r. or w. dr. *** 69 70 71 72 73 74w. 75w. 76 77w. 78.
>   750-acre CÔTE DE BEAUNE village with superlative rich dry whites and sterling hefty reds. Best v'yds.: MONTRACHET, BÂTARD-MONTRACHET, CRIOTS-BÂTARD-MONTRACHET, Ruchottes, Caillerets, Boudriottes, Morgeot (r. w.), CLOS-ST-JEAN (r.).

Châteaux of Bordeaux

Some 200 of the best-known châteaux of Bordeaux are listed below in alphabetical order.

References to their classifications into "growths" (crus) can be confusing. The following may help.

Only the Médoc châteaux have been classified as first- to fifth-growths, followed by Crus Exceptionnels and Crus Bourgeois. The 1855 order is still official. But today it helps understand the prestige of the châteaux more than the quality of their wine.

In St-Emilion, "Premier Grand Cru Classé" (the top rank, roughly equating to the top three ranks of the Médoc) has been translated as "first-growth" and all the rest as simply "classed-growth". Pomerol has no classification. The Graves châteaux are either "classed" or not (for red or white or both); there is no pecking order. Sauternes is effectively classified into two ranks below Château d'Yquem, which is given a class of its own.

General information about the quality and style of vintages will be found in the vintage charts on page 21. The particular information about the relative success and maturity of each vintage at each château is incomplete, for obvious reasons. It has been supplied by many friends in the wine trade whose impartiality I trust, supplementing my own notes, but since no one person has ever tasted all these wines it should be treated with a modicum of reserve. Further information about each village or appellation will be found under the general entries.

d'Agassac Ludon, Haut-Médoc r. ★★
>14th-century moated fort with 85 acres. Same owners as Ch'x CALON-SÉGUR and DU TERTRE and a growing reputation.

L'Angélus St-Em. r. ★★ 66 70 75 76
>Well-situated classed-growth of 65 acres on the St-Emilion Côtes w. of the town. Recent vintages have not been exciting.

d'Angludet Cant-Mar. r. ★★ 66 67 70 71 73 75 76 77
>70-acre British-owned Cru Exceptionnel of classed-growth quality.

D'Arche Sauternes w. sw. ★★ 70 71 73 76
>Substantial second-rank classed-growth of 120 acres. Ch. d'Arche-Lafaurie is its lesser wine.

Ausone St-Em. r. ★★★★ 66 67 69 70 71 75 76
>Celebrated first-growth with 20 acres in a commanding position on the Côtes and famous rock-hewn cellars under the v'yd. Off form in the last decade but made a great 1975.

Balestard-la-Tonnelle St-Em. r. ★★ 64 66 67 70 71 75 76
>Historic little classed-growth on the plateau near the town. Mentioned by the 15c poet Villon and still in the same family.

de Barbe Côtes de Bourg r. (w.) ★★ 70 71 73 75 76
>The biggest and best-known ch. of the right bank of the Gironde. Good full-bodied red.

Baret Graves r. and w. dr. ★★ 75
>Little estate of good quality, better known for its white wine.

Batailley Pauillac r. ★★★ 61 62 64 66 70 71 72 73 75 76 77
>The bigger of the famous pair of fifth-growths (with HAUT-BATAILLEY) on the borders of Pauillac and St-Julien. 125 acres. Firm strong-flavoured wine for long maturing.

Beaumont Cussac, Haut-Médoc r. ★★
>Considerable Cru Bourgeois, well-known in France for full-bodied, consistent, not brilliant wines.

Beauregard Pomerol r. ★★ 66 67 70 71 73 74 75 76
>30+ acre v'yd. with pretty 17th-century ch. near LA CONSEILLANTE. Well-made typical "round" wines.

Beauséjour St-Em. r. ★★★ 69 70 71 73 75 76
>Half of the famous old Beauséjour estate on the w. slope of the Côtes. 20 acres. Restored from serious decline since 1969.

Beauséjour-Duffau-Lagarosse St-Em. r. ★★★ 66 70 71 75 76
>The other half of the above, in old family hands and making good traditional wine for long maturing.

Beau-Site-Haut-Vignoble St-Est. r. ★★ 70 75 76
>Well-regarded 35-acre Cru Bourgeois near Ch. CALON-SÉGUR.

Belair St-Em. r. ★★★ 70 75 76
>Sister-ch. and neighbour of AUSONE with 30+ acres on the Côtes. Steady improvement in recent vintages.

de Bel-Air Lalande de Pomerol r. ★★ 73 74 75 76
>The best-known estate of this village just n. of Pomerol, with very similar wine. 30 acres.

Bel-Air-Marquis d'Aligre Sou-Mar. r. ★★★ 69 70 71 73 75 76
>Reliable Cru Exceptionnel with about 35 acres.

Belgrave St-Lau. r. ★★
>Obscure fifth-growth in St-Julien's back-country. 100+ acres.

Bellevue St-Em. r. ★★
>Well-known little classed-growth on the w. Côtes.

Bel-Orme-Tronquoy-de-Lalande St-Seurin-de-Cadourne (Haut-Médoc) r. ★★ 66 69 70 71 75 76
>Reputable 70-acre Cru Bourgeois n. of St-Estèphe.

Beychevelle St-Jul. r. ★★★ 61 64 66 67 69 70 71 73 74 75 76 77
>115-acre fourth-growth with the Médoc's finest mansion. Wine of great distinction and more elegance than power.

Le Bourdieu   Vertheuil (Haut-Médoc) r. **
> Cru Bourgeois with sister ch. Victoria known for steady typical middle-Médocs.

Bourgneuf-Vayron   Pomerol r. **
> 20-acre vineyard on clay soil making good rather heavy wines.

Bouscaut   Graves r. w. dr. *** 70 71 73 75
> Neglected classed-growth at Cadaujac brought back to life by American enthusiasts since 1969. Recent wines have not quite lived up to promise.

du Bousquet   Côte de Bourg r. ** 75
> Reliable estate with 100 acres making attractive solid wine.

Boyd-Cantenac   Margaux r. *** 66 70 71 74 75 76
> 60-acre third-growth united with Ch. POUGET to produce attractive soft wines. The best are sold as Boyd-Cantenac.

Branaire-Ducru   St-Jul. r. ***   61 66 70 71 73 74 75 76 77 78
> Fourth-growth of 110 acres producing notably flowery and flavoury wine: attractive and reliable. Also, most unusually for Bordeaux, a non-vintage wine rather than poor vintages.

Brane-Cantenac   Cant-Mar. r. ***   61 64 66 67 70 71 73 74 75 76 77
> Big (180 acres) well-run and reliable second-growth. Round, smooth and delightful wines. Same owners as Chx. DURFORT-VIVENS, VILLEGEORGE, CLIMENS.

Brillette   Moulis, Haut-Médoc r. **
> 75-acre v'yd. whose pebbly soil is said to "shine" – hence the name. Reliable rather country-style wine, improving.

A Bordeaux label

CHATEAU GISCOURS
GRAND CRU CLASSE
APPELLATION MARGAUX CONTROLEE
MIS EN BOUTEILLES AU CHATEAU

A château is an estate, not necessarily with a mansion or a big expanse of v'yd. Over 200 are listed on pages 26–40. Reference to the local classification. It varies from one part of Bordeaux to another—see p. 26. The Appellation Controlée: look up Margaux in the France A–Z. "Bottled at the château"— becoming the normal practice with classed-growth wines.

La Cabanne   Pomerol r. ***   71 73 75 76
> Highly-regarded 20-acre property near the great Ch. TROTANOY.

Cadet Piola   St-Em. r. 70 71 73 74 75 76
> Reliable little property (17 acres) on the plateau just n. of the town of St-Emilion.

Calon-Ségur   St-Est. r. ***   61 62 66 67 70 71 73 74 75 76 77
> Big (145-acre) third-growth of great reputation. Often the best St-Estèphe but rather casually run. Bottles can be disappointing.

Camensac   St-Lau. r. **   66 70 72 73 74 75 76 77
> Re-emerging fifth-growth neighbour of Ch. BELGRAVE, re-planted in the '60s with new equipment and expert direction. Fine vigorous full-bodied wines.

Canon   St-Em. r. *** 66 70 71 75 76
> Famous first-classed-growth with 45+ acres on the plateau w. of the town. Conservative methods; impressive wine.

Canon-la-Gaffelière   St-Em. r. ** 66 70 71 75 76
> 50-acre classed-growth on the lower slopes of the Côtes.

Cantemerle Macau r. ★★★ 61 **62** 64 66 **67** 70 71 **73** 74 75 76 77 78
> Superb estate at the extreme s. of the Médoc, with a romantic ch. in a wood and 50 acres of vines. Officially fifth-growth: in practice nearer second-growth. Traditional methods make deep, longlasting, richly subtle wine.

Cantenac-Brown Cant-Mar. r. ★★★ 61 **62** 66 70 71 **73** 75 76
> Formerly old-fashioned 72-acre third-growth, now well run and making classical wine for long development.

Cap de Mourlin St-Em. r. ★★★
> Well-known 40-acre chateau n. of St-Emilion making reliable, if sometimes rather light, wine.

Capbern St-Est. r. ★★
> 80-acre Cru Bourgeois; same owner as Ch. CALON-SÉGUR.

Carbonnieux Graves r. and w. dr. ★★★ 64 66 70 71 74 75 76 77
> Historic estate at Léognan making good fairly light wines with modern methods. The white is much the better.

La Cardonne Blaignan (Médoc) r. ★★
> Large Cru Bourgeois in the n. Médoc recently bought by the Rothschilds of Ch. LAFITE.

Les Carmes-Haut-Brion Graves r. ★★
> Small but not unworthy neighbour of HAUT-BRION.

Caronne-Ste-Gemme St-Lau. (Haut-Médoc) r. ★★
> Substantial Cru Bourgeois of 80 acres.

du Castéra Médoc r. ★★ 70 73 75
> Beautiful property at St-Germain in the n. Médoc managed by LICHINE. Fine, longlasting wine.

Certan de May Pomerol r. ★★ 70 71 73 75 76
> Neighbour of VIEUX-CHÂTEAU-CERTAN. Tiny property with fine rather hard wine, needing time to mature.

Certan-Giraud Pomerol r. ★★★ 71 73 75 76
> Minute (8½-acre) property next to the great Ch. PETRUS.

Chasse-Spleen Moulis r. ★★ 64 66 67 69 70 71 73 74 75 76
> 12-acre Cru Exceptionnel of classed-growth quality. Consistently good long-maturing wine.

Cheret-Pitre Graves r. (w. dr.) ★★ 75 76
> 35-acre property at Portets making full and meaty wines.

Cheval Blanc St-Em. r. ★★★★ 61 **62** 64 66 **67** 69 70 71 **73** 74 75 76 77
> The best wine of St-Emilion, rich and full-blooded, from an old family estate of 80 acres on the border of Pomerol. 70, 71 and 75 are outstanding vintages.

Cissac Cissac r. ★★ 66 70 71 73 75 76
> Small Cru Bourgeois well known in Britain.

Citran Avensan, Haut-Médoc r. ★★★
> One of the best Crus Bourgeois at present. Full-bodied tough wine. Same owners as Ch. COUFRAN and Verdignan.

Clerc-Milon Pauillac r. ★★★ 70 71 73 75 76 77
> Unimpressive little fifth-growth until 1970, when it was bought by Baron Philippe de Rothschild. Now 75 acres and new equipment are making first-rate wine.

Climens Sauternes w. sw. ★★★ **62** 67 69 70 71 75 76
> Famous 80-acre classed-growth at Barsac making some of the best and richest sweet wine in the world. Same owners as Ch. BRANE-CANTENAC.

Clinet Pomerol r. ★★ 70 71 73 75 76
> 17-acre property in central Pomerol making elegant wine with more finesse than force.

Clos l'Eglise Pomerol r. ★★★ 71 73 75 76
> 13-acre vineyard in one of the best sites in Pomerol. Excellent wine.

Clos Fourtet St-Em. r. ★★★ 67 70 73 75 76
> Well-known 33-acre first-growth on the plateau with cellars in the town. Not up to its reputation recently.

Clos des Jacobins　St-Em. r.　******
>　Well-known and well-run little classed-growth owned by the
>　shipper CORDIER.

Clos René　Pomerol r.　*******　**61 66 67** 70 71 73 75 78
>　Leading ch. on the w. of Pomerol. 30 acres making powerful
>　wine, which matures to great delicacy.

La Clotte　St-Em. r.　******　**66 70 71** 75 76 77
>　Small Côtes classed-growth with attractive "supple" wine.

La Conseillante　Pomerol r. ******* 64 66 67 70 71 73 75 76
>　30-acre classed-growth on the plateau between PETRUS and
>　CHEVAL BLANC. At its best gloriously rich but not always as
>　fine as its position would suggest.

Corbin　St-Em. r. ******
>　50-acre classed-growth in n. St-Emilion where a cluster of
>　Corbins occupy the edge of the plateau.

Corbin-Michotte　St-Em. r.　******　66 70 71 73 75 76
>　Well-run small property making attractive and reliable wine.

Cos-d'Estournel　St-Est. r.　*******　**61 62 64** 66 67 70 71 **72 73** 75 76
>　77
>　140-acre second-growth with eccentric chinoiserie building
>　overlooking Ch. LAFITE. Usually full-flavoured, often mag-
>　nificent, wine.

Cos Labory　St-Est. r. ****** 66 70 71 73 75 76
>　Little-known fifth-growth neighbour of COS D'ESTOURNEL
>　with 40 acres. Typical robust St-Estèphe, said to be improving
>　in quality.

Coufran　St-Seurin-de-Cadourne (Haut-Médoc) r. ******
>　Coufran and Ch. Verdignan, on the northern-most hillock of
>　the Haut-Médoc, are under the same ownership.

Couhins　Graves (r.) w. dr.　******
>　25-acre v'yd. at Villenave-d'Ornon producing one of the
>　best dry white Graves.

La Couronne　Pauillac r.　******　**67 70 73** 75 76
>　Small but excellent Cru Exceptionnel under the same direc-
>　tion as Ch. HAUT-BATAILLEY.

Coutet　Sauternes w. sw.　*******　**62 67 69 70** 71 73 75 76
>　Rival to Ch. CLIMENS; also 80 acres in Barsac. Said to be
>　slightly less fine but certainly equally fine.

Couvent des Jacobins　St-Em. r. *******
>　Well-known vineyard of 20 acres adjacent to the town of
>　St-Emilion on the east.

Le Crock　St-Est. r. ******
>　Well-situated Cru Bourgeois of 80 acres in the same family as
>　Ch. LÉOVILLE-POYFERRÉ.

La Croix　Pomerol r. ****** 70 71 74 75 76
>　Well-reputed little property of 25+ acres. La-Croix-de-Gay
>　has the same owner. Old-fashioned tough wine; matures well.

La Croix de Gay　Pomerol r. ******* 71 73 75 76
>　One of the larger Pomerol v'yds. 27 acres in the best part of
>　the commune.

Croizet-Bages　Pauillac r. ****** 61 64 66 70 71 73 75 76
>　50-acre fifth-growth (lacking a ch.) owned by the same family
>　as Ch. RAUZAN-GASSIES. Sound sturdy wines without flair.

Croque-Michotte　St-Em. r.　******　**66 70 72** 75 76
>　Small but well-known classed-growth on the Pomerol border.

Curé-Bon-la-Madeleine　St-Em. r. ******* 66 70 72 75 76
>　Small property among the best of the Côtes; between AUSONE
>　and CANON.

Dauzac　Lab-Mar. r. ****** 66 70 73 75
>　Substantial but somewhat neglected fifth-growth near the
>　river s. of Margaux. 100 acres.

Dillon Haut-Médoc r. **★★**
Often very well-made wine. Run by local wine college of Blanquefort.

Doisy-Daene Barsac w. sw. and dr. **★★★**
Forward-looking estate making crisp dry white (incl. Riesling grapes) as well as traditional sweet Barsac.

Doisy-Védrines Sauternes w. sw. **★★★** 67 70 71 75 76
50-acre classed-growth at Barsac, near CLIMENS and COUTET and only slightly less fine.

Domaine de Chevalier Graves r. and w. dr. **★★★** 61 64 66 67 70 71 72 73 74 75 76 77
Superb small estate of 36 acres at Léognan. The red is stern at first, richly subtle with age. The white is delicate but matures to rich flavours.

Domaine de l'Eglise Pomerol r. **★★** 66 67 70 71 75 76
Small property: good wine distributed by BORIE-MANOUX.

La Dominique St-Em. r. **★★★** 70 71 73 75 76
44-acre classed-growth next door to Ch. CHEVAL BLANC.

Dubreuil Cissac, Haut-Médoc r. **★★**
V'yd. with a 10th-century castle producing full-bodied stylish wine, generally ageing well.

Ducru-Beaucaillou St-Jul. r. **★★★** 61 62 64 66 67 70 71 72 73 74 75 76 77
Outstanding second-growth; about 100 acres overlooking the river. The owner, M. Borie, makes classical long-lived but not harsh wines with noticeable oak flavour.

Duhart-Milon-Rothschild Pauillac r. **★★★** 66 70 71 75 76
Fourth-growth neighbour of LAFITE under the same management. Wines tend to typical Pauillac toughness rather than Lafite's elegance.

Durfort-Vivens Margaux r. **★★** 66 70 75
Relatively small and obscure second-growth known for tough wine, owned by M. Lurton of BRANE-CANTENAC.

Dutruch-Grand-Poujeaux Moulis r. **★★**
Rising star of Moulis, making typically hard tannic wines.

L'Eglise-Clinet Pomerol r. **★★★** 66 70 71 74 75 76
Highly ranked little property; typical, full, fleshy wine.

L'Enclos Pomerol r. **★★★** 64 67 70 71 73 74 75 76
Respected little property on the w. side of Pomerol, near CLOS-RENÉ. Big, well-made, long-flavoured wine.

L'Evangile Pomerol r. **★★★** 66 67 70 71 73 74 75 76
30+ acres between PETRUS and CHEVAL BLANC. Impressive wines. In the same area and class as LA CONSEILLANTE.

Fargues Sauternes w. sw. **★★** 75 76
50-acre v'yd. in same ownership as Ch. YQUEM. Fruity and good but much lighter wines.

Ferrière Margaux r. **★★** 66 70 75
Little-known third-growth of only 12 acres. The wine is made at Ch. LASCOMBES and sold to a chain of French hotels.

Feytit-Clinet Pomerol r. **★★** 64 70 71 74 75 76
Little property next to LATOUR-POMEROL. Has made some fine big strong wines. Managed by J-P MOUEIX.

Fieuzal Graves r. and (w. dr.) **★★** 64 66 67 69 70 71 72 73 75 76
40-acre classed-growth at Léognan. Changed hands in peak condition in 1973; now making some of the best GRAVES.

Figeac St-Em. r. **★★★** 61 62 64 66 67 70 71 73 74 75 76 78
Famous first-growth neighbour of CHEVAL BLANC. Superb 70+ acre v'yd. gives one of Bordeaux's most attractive full-bodied wines.

Filhot Sauternes w. sw. and dr. **★★★** 67 69 70 71 72 75 76
Second-rank classed-growth with splendid ch., 120-acre v'yd. Very good sweet wines.

La Fleur-Petrus Pomerol r. ★★★ 66 67 70 71 73 74 75 76
>20-acre v'yd. flanking PETRUS and under the same MOUEIX management. Very fine rich plummy wines.

Fombrauge St-Em. r. ★★
>Major property of St-Christophe-des-Bardes, e. of St-Emilion. Reliable, if never great.

Fonbadet Pauillac r. ★★
>Well-known Cru Bourgeois with 70 acres next door to Ch. PONTET-CANET. Same owner as Ch. GLANA.

Fonplégade St-Em. r. ★★ 71 73 75 76
>35-acre v'yd. on the Côtes w. of St.-Emilion in another branch of the MOUEIX family.

Fonréaud Listrac r. ★★
>One of the better Crus Bourgeois of its area, selling mainly in France and at the cellar door.

Fonroque St-Em. r. ★★★ 66 67 70 71 73 74 75 76
>50 acres on the plateau n. of St-Emilion, the property of another branch of the ubiquitous family MOUEIX.

Les Forts de Latour Pauillac r. ★★★ 66 67 70 75 76
>The second wine of Ch. Latour; well worthy of its big brother. Fetches the price of a second-growth Château.

Fourcas-Dupré Listrac r. ★★
>A top-class Cru Bourgeois making consistent and elegant wine. To follow.

Fourcas-Hosten Listrac r. ★★ 66 70 71 73 75 76
>Reliable Cru Bourgeois of the central Médoc. Same owners as Ch. GRESSIER-GRAND-POUJEAUX; similar rather hard wine.

Franc-Mayne St-Em. r. ★★ 70 71 73 75 76
>Small but reliable v'yd. on the Côtes w. of St-Emilion.

La Gaffelière St-Em. r. ★★★ 61 66 67 70 71 75 76
>Excellent and reliable 50-acre first-growth at the foot of the Côtes below Ch. BEL-AIR.

La Garde Graves r. ★★
>Substantial ESCHENANER property making reliably sound red.

Le Gay Pomerol r. ★★★ 70 71 74 75 76
>Well-known 14-acre v'yd. on the northern edge of Pomerol.

Gazin Pomerol r. ★★★ 66 67 70 71 75 76
>Large property (for Pomerol) with nearly 60 acres. Well known but below the top rank.

Giscours Lab-Mar. r. ★★★ 66 67 69 70 71 72 73 74 75 76 77
>Splendid 200-acre third-growth s. of CANTENAC. Dynamically run and making excellent wine for long maturing.

Glana St-Jul. r. ★★ 66 70 75
>Big Cru Bourgeois in centre of St-Julien. Variable quality.

Gloria St-Jul. r. ★★★ 66 67 70 71 73 75 76 77 78
>Outstanding Cru Bourgeois making wine of vigour and finesse, among good classed-growths in quality. 100+ acres. Ch. Haut-Beychevelle-Gloria is the same property.

Grand-Barrail-Lamarzelle-Figeac St-Em. r. ★★ 66 67 70 71 72 73 75 76
>Substantial property near FIGEAC. Well-reputed and popular.

Grand-Corbin-Despagne St-Em. r. ★★
>One of the larger classed-growths on the CORBIN plateau.

Grand-Puy-Ducasse Pauillac r. ★★ 66 70 75 76 77
>Well-known little fifth-growth recently bought, renovated and enlarged to 70 acres under expert management.

Grand-Puy-Lacoste Pauillac r. ★★★ 66 67 70 71 72 73 75 76 77
>Leading fifth-growth famous for fine full-bodied typical Pauillac. 70 acres among the "Bages" ch'x. s. of the town, recently bought by M. Borie of DUCRU-BEAUCAILLOU.

La Grave Trigant de Boisset Pomerol r. ⋆⋆ 66 70 71 73 75 76 77
Verdant ch. with small but first-class v'yd. owned by a MOUEIX. One of the lighter Pomerols.

Gressier Grand Poujeaux Moulis r. ⋆⋆ 66 67 70 71 72 73 75 76
See Ch. Fourcas-Hosten. Gressier often has more charm.

Greysac Médoc r. ⋆⋆
Small elegant property whose wine is well-known in the U.S.A., though scarcely exceptional.

Gruaud-Larose St-Jul. r. ⋆⋆⋆ 61 62 66 67 69 70 71 73 75
One of the biggest and best-known second-growths. 190 acres making smooth rich stylish claret. Owned by CORDIER.

Guiraud Sauternes (r.) w. sw. (dr.) ⋆⋆⋆ 61 67 70 71 75 76
Large classed-growth of top quality. 150-acre v'yd. Excellent sweet wine and a small amount of red and dry white.

La Gurgue Margaux r. ⋆⋆⋆
Small well-placed property with fine typical Margaux sold mainly to private customers in France.

Hanteillan Cissac r. ⋆⋆
Large v'yd. recently renovated. To watch.

Haut-Bages-Libéral Pauillac r. ⋆⋆ 75 76
Lesser-known fifth-growth of 50 acres recently bought by the Cruse family. Should improve.

Haut-Bages-Monpelou Pauillac r. ⋆⋆ 70 73 75 76
Cru Bourgeois stable-mate of CH. BATAILLEY.

Haut-Bailly Graves r. ⋆⋆⋆ 64 66 70 71 73 75 77
50-acre estate at Léognan making one of the best red Graves: attractive smooth and perfumed wine.

Haut-Batailley Pauillac r. ⋆⋆⋆ 61 64 66 67 70 71 73 74 75 76 77
The smaller but currently better section of the fifth-growth Batailley estate: 45 acres owned by M. Borie of Ch. DUCRU-BEAUCAILLOU. One of the most reliable Pauillacs.

Haut-Brion Pessac, Graves r. (w.) ⋆⋆⋆⋆ 59 60 61 62 64 66 67 70 71 73 74 75 76 77
The oldest great ch. of Bordeaux and the only non-Médoc first-growth of 1855. 100 acres. Splendid firm reds, though rarely sublime in recent years. A little full dry white.

Haut-Marbuzet St-Estèphe r. ⋆⋆ 70 71 75
One of the best of the many Cru Bourgeois of St-Estèphe.

Haut-Pontet St-Em. r. ⋆⋆ 70 71 73 75
Well-regarded 12-acre v'yd. of the Côtes.

Houissan St-Estèphe r. ⋆⋆
Typical robust well-balanced St-Estèphe Cru Bourgeois, well known in Denmark.

d'Issan Cant-Mar. r. ⋆⋆⋆ 66 67 69 70 71 72 73 75 76
Beautifully restored moated ch. with 74-acre third-growth v'yd. well known for delicate gentle wine.

Kirwan Cant-Mar. r. ⋆⋆ 75 76 77
Well-run 100-acre third-growth owned by SCHRÖDER & SCHYLER. Recently much replanted: worth watching.

Labégorce Margaux r. ⋆⋆ 75 76
Substantial property with rather old-fashioned long-lived wines.

Labégorce-Zédé Margaux r. ⋆⋆ 70 71 72 73 75
Reputable little Cru Bourgeois on the road n. from Margaux. 35 acres. Typical delicate wines.

Lafaurie-Peyraguey Sauternes w. sw. ⋆⋆⋆ 67 69 70 71 75 76
Fine classed-growth of only 40 acres at Bommes, belonging to CORDIER. Excellent wines, though not the richest.

Lafite-Rothschild Pauillac r. ⋆⋆⋆⋆ 59 60 61 62 66 70 71 73 75 76
First-growth of fabulous style and perfume in its great vintages, though too often disappointing recently. 200+ acres. Usually known simply as "Lafite".

Lafleur Pomerol r. *** 66 67 70 71 73 75 76
    Tiny property of 10 acres just n. of PETRUS. Excellent wine of
    the finer, less "fleshy" kind.

Lafleur St-Em. r. ** 70 73 74 75 76
    Very small but well reputed Côtes estate.

Lafleur-Gazin Pomerol r.** 71 73 74 75 76
    Sound small estate on the n.e. border of Pomerol.

Lafon-Rochet St-Est. r. *** 61 64 66 67 70 71 75 76 77
    Fourth-growth neighbour of Ch. COS D'ESTOURNEL, restored
    to prominence in the '60s. 50+ acres. Typical dark full-
    bodied St-Estèphe.

Lagrange Pomerol r. ** 66 67 70 71 75
    Small v'yd. in the centre of Pomerol run by the ubiquitous
    house of MOUEIX.

Lagrange St-Jul. r. *** 62 66 70 71 75 76
    Rather run-down third-growth remote from most of St-
    Julien. 120 acres of the big estate are vines.

La Lagune Ludon r. |***| 62 66 70 71 72 73 74 75 76 77 78
    Well-run ultra-modern 130-acre third-growth in the extreme
    s. of the Médoc. Attractively rich and fleshy wines.

Lamarque Lamarque (Haut-Médoc) r. ** 66 70 75 76
    Splendid medieval fortress of the central Médoc with 100
    acres giving admirable light wine.

Lanessan Cussac (Haut-Médoc) r. |**| 66 67 69 70 71 73 75 76 77
    Well-known 60-acre Cru Bourgeois just s. of St-Julien. Same
    owner as PICHON-LONGUEVILLE-BARON.

Langoa-Barton St-Jul. r. *** 66 67 70 71 72 73 75 76
    Fine 18th-century ch. housing the wine of third-growth
    Langoa (about 40 acres) as well as second-growth
    LÉOVILLE-BARTON. The wines are similar: Langoa slightly
    less fine.

Larcis-Ducasse St-Em. r. *** 66 70 75 76
    The top property of St-Laurent, eastern neighbour of St-
    Emilion, on the Côtes next to Ch. PAVIE. Rather heavy wine.

Laroque St-Em. r. ** 73 74 75 76
    Important 100-acre v'yd. with an impressive mansion on the
    St-Emilion côtes.

Larose-Trintaudon St-Lau. (Haut-Médoc) r. |**| 70 71 73 75 76
    The biggest v'yd. in the Médoc: nearly 400 acres. Modern
    methods and reliable full-flavoured Cru Bourgeois wine.

Laroze St-Em. r. *** 67 70 71 75
    Big v'yd. (70 acres) on the w. Côtes. Substantial solid wines,
    sometimes excellent.

Larrivaux Cissac (Haut-Médoc) r. **
    Small Cru Bourgeois respected for high standards.

Larrivet-Haut-Brion Graves r. (w.) **
    Reputable little property at Léognan.

Lascombes Margaux r. (p.) *** 61 62 64 66 67 70 71 72 73 75 76 77
    240-acre second-growth owned by the British brewers
    Bass-Charrington and recently lavishly restored. Good
    vintages are rich for a Margaux. Also a pleasant rosé from
    young vines.

Latour Pauillac r. |****| 61 62 64 66 67 69 70 71 73 74 75 76 77
    First-growth. The most consistent great wine in Bordeaux, in
    France and probably the world: rich, intense and almost
    immortal in great years, almost always classical and pleasing
    even in bad ones. British-owned. 140 acres. Second wine LES
    FORTS DE LATOUR.

Latour du Haut-Moulin Cussac (Haut-Médoc) r. |**| 73 75 76
    Little-known Cru Bourgeois making classic old-style claret.

Latour-Pomerol Pomerol r. `***` 66 67 70 71 73 74 75 76 77
  Top growth of 20+ acres under MOUEIX management. Rich,
  fruity but firm wine for long maturing.

Laujac Médoc r. `**`
  Cru Bourgeois in the n. Médoc owned by the CRUSE family.
  Well known but scarcely outstanding.

Des Laurets St-Em. r. `**` 75 76
  Major property of Puisseguin-St-Emilion (to the e.) with 66
  acres on the Côtes.

Laville-Haut-Brion Graves w. dr. `***` 70 71 73 75 77
  A small production of very good white Graves made at Ch. LA
  MISSION-HAUT-BRION.

Léoville-Barton St-Jul. r. `***` 61 62 64 66 67 70 71 73 75 76
  80-acre portion of the great second-growth Léoville v'yd. in
  the Anglo-Irish hands of the Barton family for over 150 years.
  Glorious classical claret, made by traditional methods at the
  Bartons' third-growth Ch. LANGOA.

Léoville-Las Cases St-Jul. r. `***` 61 64 66 67 70 71 73 74 75 76
  77
  The largest portion of the old Léoville estate, 140 acres, with
  one of the highest reputations in Bordeaux.

---

*The highest price ever paid for a bottle of wine — so far as anyone
knows — was $28,000. It was paid for a single bottle of Château Lafite
1806 at a Heublein wine auction in Chicago in May 1979.*

Léoville-Poyferré St-Jul. r. `***` 66 67 70 72 75 76
  At present the least outstanding of the Léovilles, though with
  famous old vintages to its credit and some recent ones promising well. 100+ acres. Second label Ch. Moulin-Riche.

Lestage Listrac r. `**`
  100-acre Cru Bourgeois often making fine wine in the best
  vintages.

Liot Barsac w. sw. `**` 71 72 73 75 76
  Consistently fine fairly light golden wines.

Liversan St-Sau. (Haut-Médoc) r. `**` 73 75 76
  Small Cru Bourgeois inland from Pauillac. Recently much
  improved by its new German proprietor.

Livran Médoc r. `**`
  Big Cru Bourgeois at St-Germain in the n. Médoc. More
  consistent than extraordinary.

Loudenne St-Yzans (Médoc) r. `***` 70 71 73 75 76
  Beautiful riverside ch. owned by Gilbeys since 1875. Well-
  made Cru Bourgeois red and a little dry white from 90 acres.

La Louvière Graves r. and w. dr. `**`
  Big estate at Léognan with the same director as Ch. COUHINS.
  Good dry white and agreeable red.

de Lussac St-Em. r. `**` 73 74 75 76
  One of the best estates in Lussac-St-Emilion (to the n.e.).

Lynch-Bages Pauillac r. `***` 61 66 70 71 73 75 76
  One of the biggest and most popular fifth-growths. 140 acres
  making old-style rich robust wine: attractive if never great.

Lynch-Moussas Pauillac r. `**` 66 75
  Neglected little fifth-growth bought by the director of Ch.
  BATAILLEY in 1969. The 12 acres are being expanded and
  better wine is expected.

Magdelaine St-Em. r. `***` 66 67 70 72 73 75 76
  Leading first-growth of the Côtes, 25 acres next to BEL-AIR
  owned by J-P MOUEIX. Particularly good recently.

Magence   Graves r. w. dr.   ** 73 75 77w. 78
> Go-ahead property at St Pierre de Mons, in the s. of the Graves, well known for distinctly SAUVIGNON-flavoured very dry white and fruity red.

Malartic-Lagravière   Graves r. and (w. dr.)   *** 64 66 70 71 73 75 76 77
> Well-known Léognan classed-growth of 50 acres making excellent solid red for long maturing and fruity SAUVIGNON white for early drinking.

Malescasse   Lamarque (Haut-Médoc) r. ** 73 75
> Renovated Cru Bourgeois with 70 acres in a good situation recently bought by M. Tesseron of Ch. LAFON-ROCHET.

Malescot St-Exupéry   Margaux r.   *** 61 64 66 70 71 72 73 75 76
> Third-growth of 55 acres with the same owners as Ch. MARQUIS-D'ALESME-BECKER. Rather hard, long maturing, eventually classically fragrant and stylish Margaux.

de Malle   Sauternes r. w. sw./dr. ** 67 70 71 75 76
> Famous and beautiful ch. at Preignac with 90 acres making good sweet and dry whites and red (Graves) Ch. de Cardaillan.

de Marbuzet   St-Est. r. ** 73 75 76
> The second label of Ch. COS D'ESTOURNEL. (The actual ch. overlooks the river from the hill n. of Cos.)

Margaux   Margaux r. **** 61 66 67 70 71 75
> First-growth, the most delicate and finely perfumed of all in its best vintages. Changed hands in 1977. Noble ch. and estate with 160+ acres of vines.

Marquis-d'Alesme-Becker   Margaux r. **
> The smaller (20 acres), less famous and less fine of twin third-growths. The other is Ch. MALESCOT.

Marquis-de-Terme   Margaux r. *** 66 70 71 75 76 77
> Old-style fourth-growth making fine typical Margaux, tannic and harsh when young. 125 acres. Sells principally in France.

Martinens   Margaux r. ** 75 76
> 50-acre Cru Bourgeois recently much improved.

Maucaillou   Moulis r. ** 70 71 72 73 75
> 60-acre Cru Bourgeois with high standards, property of the shippers DOURTHE FRÈRES. Full fruity wine.

Meyney   St-Est. r. ** 66 70 71 74 75 76
> Big (120-acre) riverside property next door to Ch. MONTROSE, one of the best of many good Crus Bourgeois in St-Estèphe. Owned by CORDIER.

La Mission-Haut-Brion   Graves r. **** 59 61 64 66 70 71 74 75 76 77
> Neighbour and rival to Ch. HAUT-BRION. Serious and grand old-style claret for long maturing.

Monbousquet   St-Em. r. ** 70 71 74 75 76
> Fine 70-acre estate in the Dordogne valley below St-Emilion. Attractive early-maturing wine from deep gravel soil.

Montrose   St-Est. r. *** 59 61 62 64 66 67 70 71 72 73 75 76 77
> 150-acre family-run second-growth well known for deeply coloured, forceful, old-style claret.

Moulin-à-Vent   Moulis r. **
> Small property making efforts to improve its rather hard, typically Moulis wine.

Moulin des Carruades
> The second-quality wine of Ch. LAFITE.

Moulin du Cadet   St-Em. r. *** 70 71 73 74 75 76
> First-class little v'yd. on the Côtes managed by J. P. MOUEIX.

Moulinet   Pomerol r. *** 70 71 73 75 76
> One of Pomerol's bigger estates; 37 acres on light soil.

Mouton-Baron-Philippe Pauillac r. *** **61 66** 70 73 75 76
> Substantial fifth-growth with the enormous advantage of belonging to Baron Philippe de Rothschild, 125 acres making gentler, less rich and tannic wine than Mouton.

Mouton-Rothschild Pauillac r. **** **60 61 62 66 67** 70 71 73 75
> Officially a first-growth since 1973, though for 20 years worthy of the title. 145 acres (90% CABERNET SAUVIGNON) making wine of majestic richness. Also the world's greatest museum of works of art relating to wine.

Nairac Sauternes w. sw. ** **73** 75 76
> Newly restored Barsac classed-growth.

Nenin Pomerol r. *** **66 67 70** 71 75 76
> Well-known 50-acre estate: good but not outstanding quality.

Olivier Graves r. and w. dr. ***
> 60-acre classed-growth, run by the shipper ESCHENAUER, surrounding a moated castle. Well-known, if not exciting, white; less-known but serious red.

Les Ormes-de-Pez St-Est. r. ** **66 70 71** 75 76 77
> Popular 65-acre Cru Bourgeois managed by Ch. LYNCH-BAGES. Reliable full-flavoured St-Estèphe.

Padouen Barsac w. sw. ** 76
> Sandy soil. Good light wines. Australian-owned.

Palmer Cant-Mar. r. **** **59 60 61 66 67 69** 70 71 **73** 74 75 76 77
> The star ch. of CANTENAC; a third-growth often on a level just below the first-growths. Wine of power and delicacy. 100 acres with Dutch, British and French owners.

Pape-Clément Graves r. *** **62 64 66 67** 70 71 **73** 74 75 76 77
> Ancient v'yd. at Pessac named after a medieval Pope from Bordeaux, now 65 acres in fine condition making one of the most attractive red Graves.

Patache d'Aux Bégadan (Médoc) r. ** **70 71** 75 76
> 70-acre Cru Bourgeois of the n. Médoc. Well-made wine.

Pauillac, La Rose Pauillac r. **
> The wine of Pauillac's growers' co-operative, with nearly 200 members. Generally good value.

Paveil-de Luze Margaux r. ** **69** 70 75
> Old family estate at Soussans. Small but highly regarded.

Pavie St-Em. r. *** **64 66 67** 70 71 75 76
> Splendidly sited first-growth of 80 acres on the slope of the Côtes. Typically rich and tasty St-Emilion.

Pavie-Maquin St-Em. r. ** **73 74** 75 76
> Reliable small Côtes v'yd. e. of St-Emilion.

Pedesclaux Pauillac r. ** 70 75
> 50-acre fifth-growth making wine below its full potential.

Petit-Village Pomerol r. *** **66 67** 70 71 75
> One of the best-known little properties: 26 acres next to VIEUX-CH.-CERTAN, same owner as Ch. COS D'ESTOURNEL. Powerful long-lasting wine.

Petrus Pomerol r. **** **61 62 64 66 67** 70 71 **73** 75 76 77
> The great name of Pomerol. 28 acres of gravelly clay giving the world's most massively rich and concentrated wine.

de Pez St-Est. r. *** **66 67** 70 71 **72 73** 75 76 77
> Outstanding Cru Bourgeois of 60 acres. As reliable as any of the classed growths of the village.

Phélan-Ségur St-Est. r. *** **66** 70 71 75 76
> Big and important Cru Bourgeois (140 acres) with the same director as Ch. LÉOVILLE-POYFERRÉ.

Pibran Pauillac r. **
> Reliable, if scarcely stylish, little Cru Bourgeois, mainly drunk in the Low Countries.

Pichon-Longueville-Baron Pauillac r. *** **66 67** 70 71 **73** 75 76
> 70-acre second-growth usually making fine elegant Pauillac.

Pichon-Longueville, Comtesse de Lalande   Pauillac r. ★★★ 61 64
66 70 71 **74** 75 76 78
Important second-growth neighbour to Ch. LATOUR. 110 acres.
Magnificent on form but shaky in recent vintages. '78 v. good.

Pindefleurs   St-Em. r. ★★ 75 76
Up and coming 20-acre v'yd. on the St-Emilion plateau.

de Pitray   Castillon r. ★★ 75 76
Substantial (62 acre) v'yd. on the Côtes de Castillon e. of
St-Emilion. Good lightish wines.

Plince   Pomerol r. ★★
Reputable 20-acre property on the outskirts of Libourne.
Relatively hard and short wines. Excellent '75.

La Pointe   Pomerol r. ★★★ 66 70 71 73 74 75 76
Prominent 60-acre estate for typically fat fruity Pomerol.

Pontet-Canet   Pauillac r. ★★★ 03 61 66 67 70 73 75 76
One of the biggest classed-growths with about 200 acres,
neighbour to MOUTON and potentially far better than its
official rank of fifth-growth. Belonged to the CRUSE family for
many years, now to M. Tesseron of Ch. LAFON-ROCHET.

Potensac   Potensac (Médoc) r. ★★   66 67 70 71 73 75 76 77
The best-known Cru Bourgeois of Ordonnac-et-Potensac in
the n. Médoc. The neighbouring Ch'x. Lassalle and Gallais-
Bellevue belong to the same family, the Delons, owners of Ch.
LÉOVILLE–BARTON.

Pouget   Margaux ★★
Old ch. name now used for the second wine of Ch. BOYD-
CANTENAC. Sold mainly in France.

Poujeaux-Theil   Moulis r. ★★
Family-run Cru Exceptionnel of 100 acres selling its rather
hard wine direct to an appreciative French public.

Prieuré-Lichine   Cant-Mar. r. ★★★   64 66 67 70 71 73 74 75 76
Formerly obscure fourth-growth brought to the fore by Alexis
Lichine since 1952. Excellent finely fragrant Margaux.

Puy Blanquet   St-Em. r ★★ 73 74 75
The major property of St-Etienne-de-Lisse, e. of St-Emilion,
with over 50 acres. Wine below the top class.

Puy-Razac   St-Em. r. ★★
Small property at the foot of the Côtes near Ch. PAVIE,
connected with the well-known Ch. MONBOUSQUET.

Rabaud-Promis   Sauternes w. sw. ★★★ 67 70 71 75 76
Classed-growth of 70 acres at Bommes. Good, not brilliant.

Rahoul   Graves r. and w. dr. ★★   75 76
Australian-owned 34-acre v'yd. at Portets making particularly good wine, 80% red.

Ramage-la-Batisse   Haut-Médoc r. ★★
Oustanding Cru Bourgeois of 75 acres at St-Sauveur, west of
Pauillac. To watch.

Rausan-Ségla   Margaux r. ★★★ 61 66 70 71 73 75 76
100-acre second-growth; famous for its fragrance; one of the
great names of the Médoc, but recently below par. Owned by
the British firm of Holts.

Rauzan-Gassies   Margaux r. ★★★ 61 66 70 73 75 76
50-acre second-growth neighbour of the last with a poor
record in the '60s. Said to be looking up.

Raymond-Lafon   Sauternes w. sw. ★★   75 76
Lesser-known but serious Sauternes estate run by the manager of Ch. YQUEM.

de Rayne-Vigneau   Sauternes w. sw. ★★★ 67 70 71 75 76
100-acre classed-growth at Bommes with rich golden wine.

Respide   Graves (r.) w. dr. ★★
One of the better white-wine ch'x. of s. Graves, at St Pierr
Mons. Full-flavoured wines.

Reysson Vertheuil Haut-Médoc r. ★★
>Recently replanted, up-and-coming Cru Bourgeois.

Rieussec Sauternes w. sw. ★★★ **62 66 67 69** 70 71 75 76
>Worthy neighbour of Ch. D'YQUEM with 120 acres in Fargues.
>Not the sweetest, but can be exquisitely fine.

Ripeau St-Em. r. ★★
>Modest classed-growth in the centre of the plateau.

Rouget Pomerol r. ★★ **67 70 71 74** 75 76
>Attractive old estate on the n. edge of Pomerol. Full round
>wines, maturing well. Popular in smart Paris restaurants.

Royal St-Emilion
>Brand name of the important growers' co-operative.

St-André Corbin St-Emilion r. ★★ **64 66** 75 76
>Considerable property of Montagne-St-Emilion with a long
>record of above-average wines.

St-Estèphe, Marquis de St-Est. r. ⌑ **70 71 73** 75 76
>The growers' co-operative; over 200 members. Good value.

St-Georges St-Geo., St-Em. r. ★★ **70 75 76**
>18th-century ch. overlooking the St-Emilion plateau from the
>hill to the n. Considerable quantities of good wine.

St-Pierre (Bontemps-et-Sevaistre) St-Jul. r. ★★★ 70 **72 73** 75
76
>Well-run small (40-acre) fourth-growth in Belgian owner-
>ship. Attractively ripe and fruity wines.

St-Pierre Graves (r.) w. dr. ★★
>Estate at St Pierre de Mons making old-style Graves of
>notable character and flavour.

de Sales Pomerol r. ★★★ **66 67 70** 71 75 76
>The biggest v'yd. of Pomerol, attached to the grandest ch. But
>relatively dull wine.

Sigalas-Rabaud Sauternes w. sw. ★★ **67 70** 71 75 76
>The lesser part of the former Rabaud estate: 35 acres in
>Bommes, making first-class sweet wine.

Siran Lab-Mar. r. ★★ **61 66** 70 71 75
>Cru Bourgeois sister-ch. to the fifth-growth DAUZAC. Same
>owners but perhaps better wine.

Smith-Haut-Lafitte Graves r. and (w. dr.) ★★★ **66 70** 71 74 75 76
>Run-down old classed-growth at Martillac restored by
>ESCHENAUER in the '60s. Now 120 acres (14 of white). The
>white wine is light and fruity; the red dry and interesting.

Soutard St-Em. r. ★★ **66 67** 70 71 **72 73 74** 75 76
>Reliable 50-acre classed-growth n. of the town. Wine "gener-
>ous" rather than "fine".

Suduiraut Sauternes w. sw. ★★★ **67 70** 71
>One of the best Sauternes: of glorious creamy richness. Over
>200 acres of the top class, under promising new management.

Taillefer Pomerol r. ★★ **70 73** 75 76
>24-acre property on the edge of Pomerol owned by another
>branch of the MOUEIX family.

Talbot St-Jul. r. (w.) ★★★ **61 66** 70 71 **73** 75 76 77
>Important 200-acre fourth-growth, sister ch. to GRUAUD-
>LAROSE, with similarly attractive rich and satisfying wine.

du Tertre Ar-Mar. r. ★★ **66 70** 71 **72 73** 75 76
>Underestimated fifth-growth isolated s. of Margaux.
>Thoroughly well-made claret matures admirably.

Tertre-Daugay St-Em. r. ★★
>Small classed-growth in a spectacular situation on the brow
>of the Côtes. Under new ownership.

La Tour-Blanche Sauternes w. sw. (dr.) ★★★ **62 67 70** 71 75
>Top-rank 60-acre estate at Bommes with a state wine-
>growing school, making sweet wines of only moderate quality
>recently.

La Tour-Carnet St-Lau. r. ★★ **66** 70 75
> Fourth-growth reborn from total neglect in the '60s. Medieval tower with 100+ acres just w. of St-Julien.

La Tour de By Bégadan (Médoc) r. ★★ **70 71** 75 76 77
> Very well-run 100-acre Cru Bourgeois in the n. Médoc.

La Tour-de-Mons Sou-Mar. r. ★★ **66** 70 71 73 75
> Distinguished Cru Bourgeois of 60 acres, three centuries in the same family (which also owns Ch. CANTEMERLE). Sometimes excellent claret with a long life.

La Tour-du-Pin-Figeac St-Em. r. ★★
> 20-acre classed-growth, once part of LA TOUR-FIGEAC. Off form recently.

La Tour-du-Pin-Figeac-Moueix St-Em. r. ★★ **67** 70 75 76
> Another 20-acre section of the same old property, owned by one of the famous MOUEIX family.

La Tour-Figeac St-Em. r. ★★ 70 75
> 40-acre classed-growth between Ch. FIGEAC and Pomerol. Well run by a German proprietor.

La Tour-Haut-Brion Graves r. ★★ **66** 70 75 76
> Small (10-acre) neighbour and sister ch. to Ch. LA MISSION-HAUT-BRION, but a plainer, smaller-scale wine.

La Tour-Martillac Graves r. and w. dr. ★★ 70 71 75
> Small but serious property at Martillac. 10 acres of white grapes; 20 of black. Quantity is sacrificed for quality.

La Tour St-Bonnet Médoc r. ★★
> Consistently well-made and typical n. Médoc from St-Christoly.

La Tour St-Joseph Cissac r. ★★
> Reliable middle-range Haut-Médoc; well-distributed.

Tournefeuille Lalande de Pomerol r. ★★ **67** 70 71 **73** 75 76
> The star of Néac, overlooking Pomerol from the n. A small property, but excellent long-lived wine.

Tronquoy-Lalande St-Est. r. ★★ 70 71 73 75 76
> 50-acre Cru Bourgeois making typical St-Estèphe. Distributed by DOURTHE.

Troplong-Mondot St-Em. r. ★★ **66 70 71** 75 76
> One of the bigger classed-growths of St-Emilion. 70+ acres well sited on the Côtes above Ch. PAVIE.

Trotanoy Pomerol r. ★★★ **67** 70 71 73 74 75 76
> One of the top Pomerols. Only 20 acres but a splendid fleshy perfumed wine. Managed by J-P MOUEIX.

Trottevieille St-Em. r. ★★★ **66 67** 70 71 75 76
> Small but highly reputed first-growth of 25 acres on the Côtes e. of the town. Attractive full wines.

Le Tuquet Graves r. and w. dr. ★★ 76
> Substantial estate at Beautiran making light fruity wines; the white better.

Vieux-Château-Certan Pomerol r. ★★★ **61 66 67 71** 75 76
> By many accounts the second ch. of Pomerol, just s. of PETRUS, the first 30+ acres, Belgian owned.

Vieux-Chateau-St-André St-Emilion r. ★★ 78
> Small v'yd. in Montagne-St-Emilion newly acquired by a leading wine-maker of Libourne. To watch.

Villegeorge Avensan r. ★★ 73 74 75 76
> Small Cru Exceptionnel to the n. of Margaux with the same owner as Ch. BRANE-CANTENAC. Excellent lightish wine.

Vraye-Croix-de-Gay Pomerol ★★★ 71 73 74 75 76
> Very small ideally situated v'yd. in the best part of Pomerol.

d'Yquem Sauternes w. sw. (dr.) ★★★★ **59 62 66 67 68 69** 70 71 75 76
> The world's most famous sweet-wine estate. 240 acres making only 500 bottles per acre of very strong, intense, luscious wine. Good vintages need a decade of maturity.

Château-Chalon Jura w. dr. ★★★

Unique strong dry yellow wine, almost like sherry. Ready to drink when bottled.

Château Corton-Grancey B'y. r. ★★★ 66 69 70 71 72 73 76 78

Famous estate at ALOXE-CORTON, the property of Louis LATOUR. Impressive wine with a long life.

Château de la Chaize B'y. r. ★★★ 76 78

The best-known estate of BROUILLY and possibly all BEAU-JOLAIS.

Château de Panisseau Dordogne w. dr. ★★ D.Y.A.

Leading property of BERGERAC with good dry SAUVIGNON BLANC.

Château de Selle r. p. or w. dr. ★ D.Y.A.

Well-known and typical Provence wines.

Château des Fines Roches Rh. r. ★★★ 69 71 72 73 74 76 78

Large (114 acres) and distinguished estate in CHÂTEAUNEUF-DU-PAPE. Strong old-style wine.

Château du Nozet Lo. w. dr. ★★★ 74 75 76 78

Biggest and best-known estate of Pouilly (Fumé) sur Loire.

Château Fortia Rh. r. ★★★ 69 71 72 73 74 76 78

First-class property in CHÂTEAUNEUF-DU-PAPE. Traditional methods. The late owner, Baron Le Roy, was the father of the APPELLATION CONTRÔLÉE system.

Château-Grillet Rh. w. dr. ★★★★ 66 67 69 70 71 72 76 78

3½-acre v'yd. with one of France's smallest appellations. Intense, fragrant, expensive. Drink fairly young.

Burgundy boasts one of the world's most famous and certainly its most beautiful hospital, the Hospices de Beaune, founded in 1443 by Nicolas Rolin, Chancellor to the Duke of Burgundy, and his wife Guigone de Salins. The hospital he built and endowed with vineyards for its income still operates in the same building and still thrives, tending the sick of Beaune without charge, on the sale of its wine. Many growers since have bequeathed their land to the Hospices. Today it owns 125 acres of prime land in Beaune, Pommard, Volnay, Meursault, Corton and Mazis-Chambertin. The wine is sold by auction every year on the third Sunday in November.

Château-Gris B'y. r. ★★★ 66 69 71 72 73 76 78

Famous estate at NUITS-ST-GEORGES.

Châteaumeillant Lo. r. p. or w. dr. ★ D.Y.A.

Small VDQS area near SANCERRE.

Châteauneuf-du-Pape Rh. r. (w. dr.) ★★★ 69 70 71 72 73 74 75 76 78

7,500 acres near Avignon. Best estate ("domaine") wines are dark, strong, long-lived. Others may be light and/or disappointing. The white is heavy: at best rich, almost sweet.

Château Simone Prov. r. p. or w. dr. ★★

Well-known property in Palette; the only one in this appellation near Aix-en-Provence.

Château Vignelaure Prov. r. ★★ 70 71 72 73 74 75 76 77

Very good Provençal estate near Aix making Bordeaux-style wine with CABERNET grapes.

Chatillon-en-Diois Rh. r. p. or w. dr. ★ D.Y.A.

Small VDQS e. of the Rhône near Die. Good GAMAY reds; white mostly made into CLAIRETTE DE DIE.

Chavignol

Village of SANCERRE with famous v'yd., Les Monts Damnés. Also renowned for goat's cheese.

Chénas B'y. r. ★★★ 71 76 78

Good Beaujolais cru, neighbour to MOULIN-À-VENT and JULIÉNAS. One of the weightier Beaujolais.

Chenin Blanc
See Grapes for white wine

Chevalier-Montrachet B'y. w. dr. ★★★★ 66 67 69 70 71 72 73 74 75 76 77 78
17-acre neighbour of MONTRACHET with similar luxurious wine, perhaps a little less powerful.

Cheverny Lo. w. dr. ★ D.Y.A.
Light sharp Loire country wine from near Chambord.

Chinon Lo. r. ★★★ 70 71 73 75 76 78
Delicate fruity CABERNET red from Touraine. Drink cool.

Chiroubles B'y. r. ★★★ 76 78
Good but tiny Beaujolais cru next to FLEURIE; freshly fruity silky wine for early drinking.

Chusclan Rh. r. p. or w. dr. ⭐ 76 78
Village of CÔTE-DU-RHÔNE-VILLAGES. Good middle-weight wines from the co-operative.

Cissac
HAUT-MÉDOC village just w. of PAUILLAC.

Clair-Daü
First-class burgundy estate of the northern CÔTE DE NUITS, with cellars at GEVREY-CHAMBERTIN.

Clairet
Very light red wine, almost rosé.

Clairette
Mediocre white grape of the s. of France.

Clairette de Bellegarde Midi w. dr. ★ D.Y.A.
Plain neutral white from near Nîmes.

Clairette de Die Rh. w. dr. or s./sw. sp. ★★ NV
Popular dry or semi-sweet rather MUSCAT-flavoured sparkling wine from the e. Rhône, or straight dry CLAIRETTE white.

Clairette du Languedoc Midi w. dr. ★ D.Y.A.
Plain neutral white from near Montpellier.

La Clape Midi r. or w. dr. ★.
Full-bodied VDQS wines from near Narbonne. Gains character after 2–3 years.

Claret
Traditional English term for red Bordeaux.

Climat
Burgundian word for individual named v'yd., e.g. Beaune Grèves, Chambolle-Musigny les Amoureuses.

Clos
A term carrying some prestige, reserved for distinct, usually walled, v'yds., often in one ownership. Frequent in Burgundy and Alsace.

Clos-de-Bèze
See Chambertin-Clos-de-Bèze

Clos de la Roche B'y. r. ★★★ 66 69 70 71 72 73 76 77 78
38-acre Grand Cru at MOREY-ST-DENIS. Powerful complex wine like CHAMBERTIN.

Clos des Lambrays B'y. r. ★★★ 66 69 70 71 72 73 76 78
15-acre Premier Cru v'yd. at MOREY-ST-DENIS. Unreliable.

Clos des Mouches B'y. r. or w. dr. ★★★
Well-known Premier Cru v'yd. of BEAUNE.

Clos de Tart B'y. r. ★★★ 71 72 73 76 77 78
18-acre Grand Cru at MOREY-ST-DENIS owned by MOMMESSIN. Recently much improved.

Clos de Vougeot B'y. r. ★★★ 66 69 70 71 72 73 76 78
124-acre CÔTE-DE-NUITS Grand Cru with many owners. Variable, sometimes sublime. Maturity depends on the grower's technique.

Clos du Chêne Marchand

Well-known v'yd. at Bué, SANCERRE.

Clos du Roi B'y. r. ***

Part of the Grand Cru CORTON; also a Premier Cru of BEAUNE.

Clos St Denis B'y. r. *** 66 69 70 71 72 73 76 77 78

16-acre Grand Cru at MOREY-ST-DENIS. Splendid sturdy wine.

Clos St Jacques B'y. r. |***| 66 67 69 70 71 72 73 76 77 78

17-acre Premier Cru of GEVREY-CHAMBERTIN. Excellent powerful wine, often better (and dearer) than some of the CHAMBERTIN Grands Crus.

Clos St Jean B'y. r. |***| 66 69 70 71 72 73 76 78

36-acre Premier Cru of CHASSAGNE-MONTRACHET. Very good red, more solid than subtle.

Cognac

Town and region of w. France and its brandy.

Collioure Midi r. * 75 76 78

Strong dry red from BANYULS area.

Condrieu Rh. w. dr. *** D.Y.A.

Unusual soft fragrant white of great character from the Viognier grape. CH.-GRILLET is similar.

Corbières Midi r. or (p.) or (w.) |*| 76 78

Good vigorous cheap VDQS reds, steadily improving.

Corbières de Roussillon Midi r. (p.) or (w.) * 75 76 78

The same from slightly farther s.

Cordier, Ets D.

Important Bordeaux shipper and château-owner, including Ch'x. GRUAUD-LAROSE, TALBOT.

Cornas Rh. r. |**| 69 71 72 73 76 78

Small area near HERMITAGE. Typical sturdy Rhône wine of good quality from the SYRAH grape.

The Confrérie des Chevaliers du Tastevin is Burgundy's wine fraternity and the most famous of its kind in the world. It was founded in 1933 by a group of Burgundian patriots, headed by Camille Rodier and Georges Faiveley, to rescue their beloved Burgundy from a period of slump and despair by promoting its inimitable products. Today it regularly holds banquets with elaborate and sprightly ceremonial for 600 guests at its headquarters, the old château in the Clos de Vougeot. The Confrérie has branches in many countries and members among lovers of wine all over the world.

Corse

The island of Corsica. Strong ordinary wines of all colours. Better appellations include PATRIMONIO, SARTÈNE, AJACCIO.

Corton B'y. r. |****| 66 69 70 71 72 73 76 77 78

The only Grand Cru red of the CÔTE DE BEAUNE. 200 acres in ALOXE-CORTON incl. les Bressandes and le CLOS DU ROI. Rich powerful wines.

Corton-Charlemagne B'y. w. dr. **** 69 70 71 72 73 74 75 76 77 78

The white section (one-third) of CORTON. Rich spicy lingering wine. Behaves like a red wine and ages magnificently.

Costières du Gard Midi r. p. or w. dr. * D.Y.A.

VDQS of moderate quality from the Rhône delta.

Coteaux Champenois Champ. r. (p.) or w. dr. *** D.Y.A.

The appellation for non-sparkling champagne.

Coteaux d'Aix-en-Provence Prov r. p. or w. dr. |*| NV

Agreeable country wines tending to improve. CH. VIGNELAURE is far above average.

Coteaux de la Loire Lo. w. dr. sw. ★★★ **69 71 73** 75 76 78
Forceful and fragrant CHENIN BLANC whites from Anjou. The best are in SAVENNIÈRES.

Coteaux de l'Aubance Lo. p. or w. dr./sw. ★★ D.Y.A.
Light and typical minor Anjou wines.

Coteaux de Pierrevert Rh. r. p. or w. dr. ⋆ D.Y.A.
Minor southern VDQS.

Coteaux de Saumur Lo. w. dr./sw. ★★ D.Y.A.
Pleasant dry or sweetish fruity CHENIN BLANC.

Coteaux des Baux-en-Provence Prov. r. p. or w. dr. ⋆ NV
A twin to COTEAUX D'AIX, sharing the same VDQS.

Coteaux du Languedoc Midi r. p. or w. dr. ⋆ D.Y.A.
Scattered better-than-ordinary Midi areas with VDQS status. The best (e.g. Faugères, St Saturnin) age for a year or two.

Coteaux du Layon Lo. w. s./sw. or sw. ★★ **69 70 71 73 75** 76 78
District centred on Rochefort, s. of Angers, making sweet CHENIN BLANC wines above the general Anjou standard.

Coteaux du Loir Lo. r. p. or w. dr./sw. ★★ **64 69 71** 73 76 78
Small region n. of Tours. Occasionally excellent wines. Best v'yd.: JASNIÈRES. The Loir is a tributary of the Loire.

Coteaux du Tricastin Rh. r. p. or w. dr. ★★ D.Y.A.
Fringe CÔTES-DU-RHÔNE from s. of Valence.

Coteaux du Vendomois Lo. r. p. or w. dr. ⋆ D.Y.A.
Fringe Loire from n. of Blois.

Côte(s)
Means hillside; generally a superior v'yd. In ST-EMILION it distinguishes the valley slopes from the higher plateau.

Côte Chalonnaise B'y. r. w. dr. sp. ★★→★★★
Lesser-known v'yd. area between BEAUNE and MÂCON. See Mercurey, Givry, Rully, Montagny.

Côte de Beaune B'y. r. or w. dr. ★★→★★★★
Used geographically: the s. half of the CÔTE D'OR. Applies as an appellation only to parts of BEAUNE.

Côte de Beaune-Villages B'y. r. or w. dr. ★★
Regional appellation for secondary wines of the classic area. They cannot be labelled "Côte de Beaune" without either "Villages" or the village name.

Côte de Brouilly B'y. r. ★★★ **76** 78
Fruity, rich, vigorous Beaujolais cru. One of the best. Leading estate: Ch. Thivin.

Côte de Nuits B'y. r. or (w. dr.) ★★→★★★★
The northern half of the CÔTE D'OR.

Côte de Nuits-Villages B'y. r. (w.) ★★ **71 72 73** 76 78
A junior appellation, rarely seen but worth investigating.

Côte d'Or
Département name applied to the central and principal Burgundy v'yd. slopes, consisting of the CÔTE DE BEAUNE and CÔTE DE NUITS. The name is not used on labels.

Côte Rôtie Rh. r. ★★★ **69 70 71 72 74 76** 78
The finest Rhône red, from just s. of Vienne; achieves complex delicacy with age. Very small production.

Côtes Canon-Fronsac B'x. r. ★★ **70 71 73 75** 76 78
Attractive solid reds from small area w. of ST-EMILION. Ch'x. include Bodet, Canon, Junayme, Moulin-Pey-Labrie, Pichelèvre, Toumalin. The appellation can be simply "Canon-Fronsac". See also FRONSAC.

Côtes d'Agly Midi br. sw. ⋆ NV
Sweet-wine area n. of Perpignan.

Côtes d'Auvergne Central France r. p. or (w. dr.) ⋆ D.Y.A.
Flourishing small VDQS area near Clermont-Ferrand.

Côtes de Blaye B'x. w. dr. ⋆ D.Y.A.
Run-of-the-mill Bordeaux white from BLAYE.

Côtes de Bordeaux Saint-Macaire B'x. w. dr./sw. ★ D.Y.A.
Run-of-the-mill Bordeaux white from e. of Sauternes.

Côtes de Bourg
Appellation used for many of the better reds of **Bourg**. Château incl. de Barbe, La Barde, du Bousquet, de la Croix-Millorit, Eyquem, Font-Guilhem, Lamothe, Mendoce, Mille-Secousses, Domaine de Christoly, Domaine de Taste.

Côtes de Buzet S.W. France r. or w. dr. ★ 76w. 78 D.Y.A.
Pleasant light wines from just s.e. of Bordeaux. An area of promise.

Côtes de Duras Dordogne r. or w. dr. ☆ 75 76 78
Neighbour to BERGERAC. Similar light wines.

Côtes de Fronsac B'x. r. ★→★★ 70 71 73 75 76 78
Some of the best slopes of FRONSAC, making considerable reds. Ch'x incl. la Dauphine, Mayne-Vieil, la Rivière, Rouet, Tasta.

Côtes de Jura Jura r. p. or w. dr. (sp.) ★ NV
Various light tints and tastes. ARBOIS is better.

Côtes de Montravel Dordogne w. dr./sw. ☆ NV
Part of BERGERAC; traditionally medium-sweet wine, now often made dry.

Côtes de Provence Prov. r. p. or w. dr. NV ★→★★
The wine of Provence; often more alcohol than character. Standards have recently been improving.

Côtes de Toul E. France r. p. or w. dr. ★ D.Y.A.
Very light wines from Lorraine; mainly VIN GRIS (rosé).

Côtes de Ventoux Rh. r. p. or w. dr. ☆ 76 78 (D.Y.A.)
Fringe s. Rhône wines, fruity and light.

Côtes du Forez Central France r. or p. ☆ D.Y.A.
Light Beaujolais-style red, can be good in warm years.

Côtes du Fronton S.W. France r. or p. ☆ D.Y.A.
The local VDQS of Toulouse.

Côtes du Haut-Roussillon S.W. France br. sw. ★ NV
Sweet-wine area n. of Perpignan.

Côtes du Luberon Rh. r. p. or w. dr. (sp.) ★ D.Y.A.
Pleasant country wines from n. Provence, e. of the Rhône.

Côtes du Marmandais Dordogne r. or w. dr. ★ D.Y.A.
Undistinguished light wines from s.e. of Bordeaux.

Côtes-du-Rhône Rh. r. p. or w. dr. ★ 76 78
The basic appellation of the Rhône valley. Best drunk young. CÔTES-DU-RHÔNE-VILLAGES is better.

Côtes-du-Rhône-Villages Rh. r. p. or w. dr. ★★ 74 76 78
The wine of the 14 best villages of the southern Rhône. Substantial and on the whole reliable.

Côtes du Roussillon S.W. France r. p. or w. dr. ☆ 75 76 78
Country wine of e. Pyrenees. The hefty dark reds are best. Some whites are sharp VINS VERTS.

Côtes du Vivarais Prov. r. p. or w. dr. ★ NV
Pleasant country wines from s. Massif Centrale.

Côtes Frontonnais
See Côtes du Fronton

Coulée de Serrant Lo. w. dr./sw. ★★★ 64 69 71 73 75 76 78
10-acre v'yd. on n. bank of Loire at Savennières, Anjou. Intense strong fruity/sharp wine, ages well.

Crémant
In champagne means "Creaming"—i.e. half-sparkling. Also a term for high-quality sparkling wines from certain other parts of France.

Crémant de Loire w. dr./sp. ★★ NV
High-quality semi-sparkling wine from ANJOU and TOURAINE. The leading brand is Sablant.

Crépy Savoie w. dr. ★★ D.Y.A.
Light, Swiss-style white from s. of La. Geneva.

Criots-Bâtard-Montrachet B'y. w. ★★★ 69 70 71 72 73 74 76 77 78
7-acre neighbour to BÂTARD-MONTRACHET. Similar wine.

Crozes-Hermitage Rh. r. or (w. dr.) ★★ 69 71 72 73 76 78
Larger and less distinguished neighbour to HERMITAGE.
Robust and often excellent reds but choose carefully.

Cru
"Growth", as in "first-growth"—meaning vineyard.

Cru Bourgeois
Rank of Bordeaux château below CRU CLASSÉ.

Cru Bourgeois Supérieur
Official rank one better than the last.

Cru Classé
Classed growth. One of the first 5 official quality classes of
the Médoc. Also any classed growth of another district (see p.
26).

Cru Exceptionnel
Official rank above CRU BOURGEOIS SUPÉRIEUR, immediately
below CRU CLASSÉ and others.

Cruse et Fils Frères
Long-established Bordeaux shipper famous for fine wine.
Owner of CH. D'ISSAN.

Cubzac, St.-André-de B'x. r. or w. dr. ★ 75 76 78
Town 15 miles n.e. of Bordeaux, centre of the minor Cub-
zaguais region. Sound reds have the appellation Bordeaux.
Estates include: Ch. du Bouilh, Ch. de Terrefort-Quancard,
Ch. Timberley, Domaine de Beychevelle.

---

*The curiously inefficient shape of the traditional shallow champagne-
glass known as a "coupe" is accounted for (at least in legend) by the
fact that it was modelled on Queen Marie Antoinette's breast.
Admirable though that organ undoubtedly was, it was not designed
for dispensing sparkling wine. Champagne goes flat and gets warm
almost as fast in a coupe as it would in your cupped hand. The ideal
champagne glass is a tall, thin "tulip".*

Cussac
Village just s. of ST JULIEN. Appellation Haut-Médoc.

Cuve Close
Short-cut way of making sparkling wine in a tank. The
sparkle dies away in the glass much quicker than with
MÉTHODE CHAMPENOISE wine.

Cuvée
The quantity of wine produced in a "cuve" or vat. Also a word
of many uses, incl. "blend". In Burgundy interchangeable
with "Cru". Often just refers to a "lot" of wine.

d'Angerville, Marquis
Famous burgundy grower with immaculate estate in VOLNAY.

Danglade, L. et Fils
Shipper of St-Emilion and Pomerol, now owned by J-P MOUEIX
of Libourne.

Degré alcoolique
Degrees of alcohol, i.e. per cent by volume.

Delagrange-Bachelet
One of the leading proprietors in CHASSAGNE-MONTRACHET.

Delas Frères
Long-established firm of Rhône-wine specialists at Tournon,
v'yds. at CÔTE RÔTIE, HERMITAGE, CORNAS etc.

Delor, A. et Cie
Bordeaux shippers owned by the English Allied Breweries.

Delorme, André
Leading merchants and growers of the CÔTE CHALONNAISE.

De Luze, A. et Fils
Bordeaux shipper and owners of Ch'x. CANTENAC-BROWN and PAVEIL-DE LUZE.

Demi-Sec
"Half-dry": in practice more than half-sweet.

Depagneux, Jacques et Cie
Well-regarded merchants of BEAUJOLAIS.

Deutz & Geldermann NV and **64 66 70 71**
One of the best of the smaller champagne houses. Luxury brand: Cuvée William Deutz.

Domaine
Property, particularly in Burgundy.

Domaine de Belair
A light-weight branded red Bordeaux of reliable quality made by SICHEL.

Dom Pérignon **62 64 66 69** 70
Luxury brand of MOËT ET CHANDON named after the legendary blind inventor of champagne. Also occasionally a rosé.

Dopff "au Moulin"
Ancient family wine-house at Riquewihr, Alsace. Best wines: Riesling Schoenenbourg, Gewürztraminer Eichberg.

Dopff & Irion
Another excellent Riquewihr (ALSACE) business. Best wines include Muscat les Amandiers, Riesling de Riquewihr.

Doudet-Naudin
Burgundy merchant and grower at Savigny-lès-Beaune. V'yds. incl. BEAUNE CLOS DE ROI.

Dourthe Frères
Well-reputed Bordeaux merchant representing a wide range of ch'x., mainly good Crus Bourgeois, incl. Ch'x. MAUCAILLOU, TRONQUOY-LALANDE.

Doux
Sweet.

Drouhin, J. et Cie
Prestigious Burgundy grower and merchant. Offices in BEAUNE, v'yds. in MUSIGNY, CLOS DE VOUGEOT, etc.

Duboeuf, Georges
Top-class BEAUJOLAIS merchant at Romanèche-Thorin.

Dujac, Domaine
Perfectionist burgundian grower at MOREY-ST-DENIS with v'yds in that village. ECHÉZEAUX, BONNES-MARES, GEVREY-CHAMBERTIN, etc.

Echézeaux B'y. r. [★★★] 69 70 71 72 73 76 77 78
74-acre Grand Cru between VOSNE-ROMANÉE and CLOS DE VOUGEOT. Superlative fragrant burgundy without great weight.

Edelzwicker Alsace w. [★] D.Y.A.
Light everyday white from mixture of grapes, often fruity and good.

Entre-Deux-Mers B'x. w. dr. [★] D.Y.A.
Standard dry white Bordeaux from between the Garonne and Dordogne rivers. Often a good buy.

Les Epenots B'y. r. ★★★
Famous Premier Cru v'yd. of POMMARD. Also spelt Epeneaux for the 12-acre Clos des Epeneaux owned by Comte Armand.

Eschenauer, Louis
Famous Bordeaux merchants, owners of Ch'x. OLIVIER, SMITH-HAUT-LAFITTE and LA GARDE in GRAVES, now controlled by the Lonrho group.

l'Etoile Jura (r.) (p.) or w. dr./sw./sp. ★★
Sub-region of the Jura with typically various wines, incl. VIN JAUNE like CHÂTEAU-CHALON.

Faiveley, J.
Family-owned growers (with 250 acres) and merchants at NUITS-ST-GEORGES, with v'yds. in CHAMBERTIN-CLOS-DE-BÈZE, CHAMBOLLE-MUSIGNY, CORTON, NUITS and MERCUREY (150 acres).

Faugères Midi (r.) (p.) or w. dr* 76 78
Isolated village of the COTEAUX DU LANGUEDOC making above-average wine.

Fitou Midi r. ✶✶ 71 73 75 76
Superior CORBIÈRES red; powerful and ages well.

Fixin B'y. r. ✶✶ 69 71 72 73 76
A worthy and under-valued neighbour to GEVREY-CHAMBERTIN. Often splendid reds.

Fleurie B'y. r. ✶✶✶ 76 78
The epitome of a Beaujolais cru: fruity, scented, silky, racy.

Frais
Fresh or cool.

French bottle shapes

1 Champagne 2 Loire 3 Burgundy 4 Alsace 5 Beaujolais "pot" 6 Bordeaux 7 Châteauneuf-du-Pape

---

Frappé
Ice-cold.

Froid
Cold.

Fronsac B'x. r. ✶→✶✶ 70 71 73 75 76 78
Pretty hilly area of good reds just w. of St-Emilion. CÔTES-CANON-FRONSAC and CÔTES DE FRONSAC are the appellations of the best wines. For ch'x see these entries.

Frontignan Midi br. sw. ✶ NV
Strong sweet and liquorous muscat wine.

Gaillac S.W. France r. p. or w. dr./sw. or sp. ✶ NV
Dull but usually adequate everyday wine.

Gamay
See Grapes for red wine

Geisweiler et Fils
One of the biggest merchant-houses of Burgundy. Cellars and 50 acres of v'yds. at NUITS-ST-GEORGES. Also 150 acres at Bevy in the HAUTES CÔTES DE NUITS and 30 in the CÔTE CHALONNAISE.

Gevrey-Chambertin B'y. r. ✶✶✶ 69 70 71 72 73 76 78
The village containing the great CHAMBERTIN and many other noble v'yds. as well as some more commonplace.

Gewürztraminer
The speciality grape of ALSACE: perfumed and spicy, whether dry or sweet.

Gigondas Rh. r. or p. ✶✶ 69 70 71 72 73 74 76 78
Worthy neighbour to CHÂTEAUNEUF-DU-PAPE. Strong full-bodied wine.

Gilbey, S.A.
British firm long-established as Bordeaux merchants at Ch. LOUDENNE. Now owned by International Distillers and Vintners.

Ginestet

Third-generation Bordeaux merchants and former owners of CH. MARGAUX.

Givry B'y. r. or w. dr. ★★ 76 78

Underrated village of the CÔTE CHALONNAISE: light but tasty and typical burgundy.

Gouges, Henri

Leading burgundy grower of NUITS-ST-GEORGES.

Goût

Taste, e.g. "goût anglais"—as the English like it i.e. (dry).

Grand Cru

One of the top Burgundy v'yds. with its own Appellation Controlée. Similar in Alsace but more "vague elsewhere.

Grand Roussillon Midi br. sw. ★★ NV

Broad appellation for muscat and other sweet fortified wines of e. Pyrenees.

Grands-Echézeaux B'y.r. ★★★★ 66 69 70 71 72 73 76 77 78

22-acre Grand Cru next to CLOS DE VOUGEOT. Superlative rich burgundy.

Graves B'x. r. or w. ★→★★★★

Large region s. of Bordeaux city. Its best wines are red, but the name is used chiefly for its dry or medium golden-whites.

Graves de Vayres B'x r. or w. ★

Part of ENTRE-DEUX-MERS; of no special character.

Les Gravières B'y. r. ★★★

Famous Premier Cru v'yd. of SANTENAY.

Griotte-Chambertin B'y. r. ★★★ 66 69 70 71 72 73 76 77 78

14-acre Grand Cru adjoining CHAMBERTIN. Similar wine, but less masculine and more "tender".

Gros Plant du Pays Nantais Lo. w. ★ D.Y.A.

Junior cousin of MUSCADET, sharper and lighter; made of the COGNAC grape also known as Folle Blanche, Ugni Blanc etc.

Haut Comtat Rh. r. or p. ★★ 72 73 74 76 78

Small appellation n. of Avignon. Sound strong wines.

Hautes-Côtes de Beaune B'y.r. or w. dr. ★★ 71 72 76 78

Appellation for a dozen villages in the hills behind the CÔTE DE BEAUNE. Light wines, worth investigating.

Hautes-Côtes de Nuits B'y. r. ★★ 71 72 76 78

The same for the CÔTE DE NUITS. Rarely seen outside France.

Haut-Médoc B'x. r. ★★→★★★ 66 70 71 73 75 76 77 78

Big appellation including all the best areas of the Médoc. Most wines have château names: those without should still be above average.

Haut-Montravel Dordogne w. sw. ★ 75 76 78

Medium-sweet BERGERAC.

Heidsieck, Charles NV and 66 69 70 71 73

Leading champagne house of Reims, family-owned, now merged with Champagne Henriot. Luxury brand: Prestige Royal Champagne.

Heidsieck, Dry Monopole NV and 66 69 71 73 75

Important champagne merchant and grower of Reims. Luxury brand: Diamant Bleu (1969).

Hérault Midi

The biggest v'yd. *département* in France with 400,000 hectares of vines. Chiefly vin ordinaire.

Hermitage Rh. r. or w. dr. ★★★ 66 67 69 70 71 72 73 76 78

The "manliest" wine of France. Dark, powerful and profound. Needs long ageing. The white is heady and golden.

Hospices de Beaune

15th-century charity hospital in BEAUNE, with excellent v'yds. in MEURSAULT, POMMARD, VOLNAY, BEAUNE, CORTON, etc. See panel on page 41.

Hugel Père et Fils

The best-known ALSACE growers and merchants. Founded at Riquewihr in 1639 and still in the family. Best wines: Cuvées Exceptionnelles.

Imperiale

Bordeaux bottle holding 8½ normal bottles.

Irancy B'y. r. or (p.) ****** 71 75 76 78

Good light red made near CHABLIS. The best vintages are long-lived and mature well.

Irouléguy S.W. France (r.) or w. dr. ** D.Y.A.

Agreeable local wine of the Basque country.

Jaboulet, Paul

Old family firm, leading growers of HERMITAGE etc.

Jaboulet-Vercherre et Cie

Well-known Burgundy merchant-house with v'yds. in POMMARD, etc., and cellars in Beaune.

Jadot, Louis

Much-respected Burgundy merchant-house with v'yds. in BEAUNE, CORTON, etc.

Jasnières Lo. (r.) (p.) or w. sw. *** 69 70 71 73 75 76 78

Rare VOUVRAY-like wine of n. Touraine.

Jeroboam

In England a 6-bottle bottle, or triple magnum; in Champagne a double magnum.

Juliénas B'y. r. *** 76 78

Leading cru of Beaujolais: vigorous fruity wine.

Jura

See Côtes de Jura

Jurançon S.W. France w. sw. or dr. ** 72 73 75 76 78

Unusual high-flavoured and long-lived speciality of Pau in the Pyrenean foothills. Ages well for several years.

Kressman, E. S. & Cie

Family-owned Bordeaux merchants and owners of CH. LATOUR-MARTILLAC in GRAVES.

Krug "Grande Réserve", Blanc de Blancs, NV 66 69 71 73

Small but very prestigious champagne house known for full-bodied very dry wine.

Labarde

Village just s. of MARGAUX and included in that appellation. Best ch.: GISCOURS.

La Cour Pavillon

Reliable branded red Bordeaux from GILBEY, SA.

Lalande de Pomerol B'x. r. ****** 70 71 73 75 76 78

Neighbour to POMEROL. Wines similar but considerably less fine. Ch. BEL-AIR is well known.

Lanson Père et Fils NV and 66 69 71

Important growers and merchants of Champagne, cellars at Reims. Luxury brand: Red Label.

Laroche, Domaine

Important growers of Chablis marketed by the house of Bacheroy-Josselin.

La Tâche

See Tâche

Latour, Louis

Top Burgundy merchant and grower with v'yds. in CORTON, BEAUNE, etc.

Latricières-Chambertin B'y. r. *** 66 69 70 71 72 73 76 78

17-acre Grand Cru neighbour of CHAMBERTIN. Similar wine, but lighter and "prettier".

Laurent-Perrier NV and rosé brut and 64 66 70 73

Well-known champagne house of Tours-sur-Marne. Luxury brand: Cuvée Grand Siécle.

Léognan B'x.

Leading village of the GRAVES appellation. Best ch'x.: DOMAINE DE CHEVALIER, MALARTIC-LAGRAVIÈRE and HAUT-BAILLY.

Leroy

Important burgundy merchants at MEURSAULT, part-owners and distributors of the DOMAINE DE LA ROMANÉE-CONTI.

Lichine, Alexis et Cie

Successful post-war Bordeaux merchants, proprietors of CH. LASCOMBES, now controlled by Bass Charrington Ltd.

Burgundy: a grower's own label

MISE EN BOUTEILLES AU DOMAINE NUITS ST GEORGES LES PRULIERS APPELLATION CONTROLÉE DOMAINE HENRI GOUGES A NUITS ST GEORGES, CÔTE D'OR	Domaine is the burgundy equivalent of château. The Appellation Controlée is Nuits St Georges. The individual v'yd. in Nuits is called Les Pruliers. The name and address of the grower/producer. (The word propriétaire is often also used.)

A merchant's label

SANTENAY LES GRAVIERES APPELLATION CONTROLÉE PROSPER MAUFOUX NEGOCIANT À SANTENAY	The village. The vineyard. The wine qualifies for the Appellation Santenay. Prosper Maufoux is a Négociant, or merchant, who bought the wine from the grower to mature, bottle and sell.

Lie, sur

"On the lees." Muscadet is often so bottled, for maximum freshness.

Limoux Nature Midi w. dr. ⭐ D.Y.A.

The non-sparkling version of BLANQUETTE DE LIMOUX.

Lirac Rh. r. p. or (w. dr.) ⭐⭐ 74 76 78

Neighbouring village to TAVEL. Similar wine; the red becoming more important than the rosé.

Listrac B'x. r. ⭐⭐

Village of HAUT-MÉDOC next to MOULIS. Best ch.: FOURCAS-HOSTEN and FOURCAS-DUPRÉ.

Loire

See under Wine names (Muscadet, etc.)

Loupiac B'x. w. sw. ⭐⭐ 67 70 71 75 76

Neighbour to SAUTERNES with similar but less good wine.

Ludon

HAUT-MÉDOC village s. of MARGAUX. Best ch.: LA LAGUNE.

Lupé-Cholet et Cie

Merchants and growers at NUITS-ST-GEORGES. Best estate wine: Château Gris.

Lussac-Saint-Emilion B'x. r. ⭐⭐ 70 71 75 76 78

North-eastern neighbour to ST-EMILION. Often good value. Ch. Co-operative makes "Roc de Lussac".

Macau

HAUT-MÉDOC village s. of MARGAUX. Best ch.: CANTEMERLE.

macération carbonique

Traditional Beaujolais technique of fermentation with whole bunches of unbroken grapes in an atmosphere saturated with carbon dioxide. Fermentation inside each grape eventually bursts it, giving vivid and very fruity mild wine for quick consumption. Now much used in the Midi.

Mâcon B'y. r. (p.) or w. dr. ** 73 74 75w. 76 77w. 78

Southern district of sound, usually unremarkable, reds and tasty dry whites. Wine with a village name (e.g. Mâcon-Prissé) is better. POUILLY-FUISSÉ is best appellation of the region. See also Mâcon-Villages.

Mâcon Supérieur

The same but slightly stronger from riper grapes.

Mâcon-Villages B'y. w. dr. ** 74 75 76 77 78

Increasingly well-made and excellent white burgundies. Mâcon-Prissé, MÂCON-VIRÉ are examples.

Mâcon-Viré

See Mâcon-Villages and Viré

Madiran S.W. France r. ** 69 70 71 72 73 75 76

Dark vigorous red from ARMAGNAC. Needs ageing.

Magnum

A double bottle.

Mähler-Besse

First-class Dutch wine-merchants in Bordeaux, with a majority shareholding in Ch. PALMER.

Maire, Henri

The biggest grower and merchant of JURA wines.

Marc

Grape skins after pressing; also the strong-smelling brandy made from them.

Margaux B'x. r. **→**** 66 67 70 71 73 75 76 78

Village of the HAUT-MÉDOC making the most "elegant" red Bordeaux. The name includes CANTENAC and several other villages as well. Top ch'x. include MARGAUX, LASCOMBES, etc.

Marque déposée

Trade mark.

Marsannay B'y. (r.) or p. *** 76 78

Village near Dijon with excellent light red and delicate rosé, perhaps the best rosé in France.

Martillac

Village in the GRAVES appellation, Bordeaux.

Maufoux, Prosper

Family firm of burgundy merchants at SANTENAY.

Mazis-Chambertin B'y. r. *** 66 67 69 70 71 72 73 76 78

30-acre Grand Cru neighbour of CHAMBERTIN. Lighter wine.

Médoc B'x. r. ** 70 73 75 76 78

Appellation for reds of the less good (n.) part of Bordeaux's biggest and best district. Typical but light wines. HAUT-MÉDOC is better.

Ménétou-Salon Lo. r. p. or w. dr. ** D.Y.A.

Attractive light wines from w. of SANCERRE. SAUVIGNON white; CABERNET red.

Mercier et Cie NV and 62 64 66 69 70 71

One of the biggest champagne houses, at Epernay.

Mercurey B'y. r. or w. dr. ** 71 72 76 78

Leading red-wine village of the CÔTE CHALONNAISE. Good middle-rank burgundy.

méthode champenoise

The traditional laborious method of putting the bubbles in champagne by refermenting the wine in its bottle.

Meursault B'y. (r.) w. dr. *** 69 70 71 72 73 74 75 76 77 78

CÔTE DE BEAUNE village with some of the world's greatest whites: rich, smooth, savoury, dry but mellow. Best v'yds. incl. Perrières, Genevrières, Charmes.

Meursault-Blagny

See Blagny

Midi

General term for the south of France. When used of wine is often derogatory, though standards have risen consistently in recent years.

Minervois Midi r. or (p.) [★→★★] 75 76

Hilly VDQS area with some of the best wines of the Midi: lively and full of flavour.

mise en bouteilles au château, au domaine

Bottled at the château, at the property or estate. N.B. dans nos caves (in our cellars) or dans la région de production (in the area of production) mean little.

Moët & Chandon NV and 64 66 69 70 71 73

The biggest champagne merchant and grower, with cellars in Epernay and branches in Argentina and California. Luxury brand: DOM PÉRIGNON.

Moillard Grivot

Big firm of growers and merchants in NUITS-ST-GEORGES.

Mommessin, J.

Major Beaujolais merchant and owner of CLOS DE TART.

Monbazillac Dordogne w. sw. [★★] 71 73 74 75 76 78

Golden SAUTERNES-style wine from BERGERAC. Ages well. Ch. Monbazillac is best known.

Monopole

V'yd. in single ownership.

Montagne-Saint-Emilion B'x. r. [★★] 70 71 73 75 76 78

North-east neighbour of ST-EMILION with similar wines.

Montagny B'y. w. dr. [★★] →★★★ 73 74 75 76 77 78

CÔTE CHALONNAISE village between MÂCON and MEURSAULT, both geographically and gastronomically.

Montée de Tonnerre B'y.

Famous and excellent PREMIER CRU of CHABLIS.

Monthélie B'y. r. [★★★] 71 72 73 76 78

Little-known neighbour and almost equal of VOLNAY. Excellent fragrant reds. Best estate: Château de Monthélie.

Montlouis Lo. w. sw./dr. ★★ 64 69 71 73 74 75 76 78

Neighbour of VOUVRAY. Similar sweet or dry long-lived wine.

Montrachet B'y. w. dr. ★★★★ 66 67 69 70 71 72 73 74 75 76 77 78

19-acre Grand Cru v'yd. in both PULIGNY and CHASSAGNE-MONTRACHET. The greatest white burgundy: strong, perfumed, intense, dry yet luscious. (The "ts" are silent.)

Montravel

See Côtes de Montravel

Mont-Redon, Domaine de

Famous estate in CHÂTEAUNEUF-DU-PAPE.

Morey-Saint-Denis B'y. r. [★★★] 66 69 70 71 72 73 76 77 78

Small village with four Grands Crus between GEVREY-CHAMBERTIN and CHAMBOLLE-MUSIGNY. Glorious wine, often overlooked.

Morgon B'y. r. ★★★ 71 76 77 78

The "firmest" cru of Beaujolais, needing time to develop its rich flavour.

Moueix, J-P et Cie

The leading proprietor and merchant of St-Emilion and Pomerol. Ch'x. incl. MAGDELAINE, LAFLEUR-PETRUS, and part of PETRUS.

Moulin-à-Vent B'y. r. ★★★ 71 76 77 78

The "biggest" and best wine of Beaujolais; powerful and long-lived when not unbalanced by too much added sugar

Moulis B'x. r. ★★→★★★

Village of the HAUT-MÉDOC with its own appellation and several good, not top-rank ch'x.: CHASSE-SPLEEN, POUJEAUX-THEIL, etc.

Mousseux
> Sparkling.

Mouton Cadet
> Best-selling brand of red Bordeaux.

Mumm, G. H. & Cie NV and **69 71 73 75 76**
> Major champagne grower and merchant owned by Seagram's. Luxury brand: Président René Lalou.

Muscadet Lo. w. dr. ****** D.Y.A.
> Popular, good-value, often delicious dry wine from round Nantes in s. Brittany. Perfect with fish.

Muscadet de Sèvre-et-Maine
> Wine from the central and usually best part of the area.

Muscat
> Distinctively perfumed grape and its (usually sweet) wine.

Muscat de Beaumes de Venise
> The best French muscat (see Beaumes de Venise).

Muscat de Lunel br. sw. ****** NV
> Sweet Midi muscat. A small area but good.

Muscat de Mireval br. sw. ****** NV
> Ditto, from near Montpellier.

Muscat de Rivesaltes br. sw. ***** NV
> Sweet muscat from a big zone near Perpignan.

Musigny B'y. r. ****** 66 69 70 71 72 73 76 77 78**
> 25-acre Grand Cru in CHAMBOLLE-MUSIGNY. Often the best, if not the most powerful, of all red burgundies. Best growers: DE VOGÜÉ, DROUHIN.

Nature
> Natural or unprocessed, esp. of still champagne.

Néac B'x. r. ******
> Little village n. of POMEROL. Sound wines, sold as LALANDE-DE-POMEROL.

Négociant-élèveur
> Merchant who "brings up" (i.e. matures) the wine.

Nicolas, Ets.
> Paris-based wholesale and retail wine merchants; one of the biggest in France and one of the best. Their Rhône and Midi wines are particularly good.

Nuits-St-Georges r. ****→*** 66 69 70 71 72 73** 76 77 78
> Important wine-town: wines of all qualities, typically sturdy and full-flavoured. Name can be shortened to "Nuits". Best v'yds. incl. Les St-Georges, Vaucrains, Les Pruliers, Clos des Corvées, Les Cailles, etc.

Ordinaire
> Commonplace, everyday: not necessarily pejorative.

Pacherenc-du-Vic-Bilh S.W. France w. sw. ***** NV
> Rare minor speciality of the ARMAGNAC region.

Palette Prov. r. p. or w. dr. ******
> Minor appellation area near Aix-en-Provence. Aromatic reds and good rosés, which improve with age.

Pasquier-Desvignes
> Very old firm of Beaujolais merchants at St Lager, BROUILLY, since the 15th century.

Patriarche
> Popular firm of burgundy merchants in BEAUNE.

Pauillac B'x. r. ****→**** 66 67** 70 **71 73** 75 76 78
> The only village in Bordeaux (HAUT-MÉDOC) with three first-growths (Ch'x. LAFITE, LATOUR, MOUTON-ROTHSCHILD) and many other fine ones, famous for high flavour and a scent of cedarwood.

Pécharmant Dordogne r. **** 75 76** 78
> Slightly better-than-typical l ght BERGERAC red.

Pelure d'oignon

"Onion skin"—tawny tint of certain rosés.

Perlant

Very slightly sparkling.

Pernand-Vergelesses B'y. r. or (w. dr.) ⭐⭐⭐ 69 70 71 72 73 76 78

Village next to ALOXE-CORTON containing part of the great CORTON and CORTON-CHARLEMAGNE v'yds. and one other top v'yd.: Ile des Vergelesses.

Perrier-Jouet NV, 69 71 73 75 76 Laudrofé brut 73 75

Excellent champagne-growers and makers at Epernay. Luxury brand: Belle Epoque.

Pétillant

Slightly sparkling.

Petit Chablis B'y. w. dr. ⭐⭐ 76 77 78

Wine from fourth-rank CHABLIS v'yds. Lacks great character but can be good value. But frost severely reduced '77 and '78.

Piat Père et Fils

Important growers and merchants of Beaujolais and Mâcon wines at MÂCON, now controlled by Grand Metropolitan Ltd. V'yds. in MOULIN-À-VENT, also CLOS DE VOUGEOT. BEAUJOLAIS and MÂCON-VIRÉ in Piat bottles are good value.

Picpoul-de-Pinet Midi w. dr. ⭐ NV

Rather dull very dry southern white.

Pineau Charentais

Strong sweet apéritif made of white grape juice and Cognac.

Pinot

See Grapes for white wine

Piper-Heidsieck NV, rosé 71 and 66 69 71 73

Champagne-makers of old repute at Reims. Luxury brand: Florens Louis Blanc de Blancs.

Pol Roger NV, rosé 71 and 66 69 71 73

Excellent champagne house at Epernay. Particularly good non-vintage White Foil.

Pomerol B'x. r. ⭐⭐➔⭐⭐⭐⭐ 66 70 71 73 75 76 78

The next village to ST-EMILION: similar but more "fleshy" wines, maturing sooner, on the whole reliable and delicious. Top ch.: PETRUS.

Pommard B'y. r. ⭐⭐⭐ 66 69 70 71 72 73 76 78

The biggest and best-known village in Burgundy. No superlative wines, but many warmly appealing ones. Best v'yds.: Rugiens, EPENOTS and HOSPICES DE BEAUNE Cuvées.

Pommery & Greno NV, NV rosé and 66 69 71

Very big growers and merchants of champagne at Reims.

Ponnelle, Pierre

Large-scale wine-merchants of BEAUNE.

Pouilly-Fuissé B'y. w. dr. ⭐⭐➔⭐⭐⭐ 72 74 75 76 77 78

The best white of the MÂCON area. Never great: at its best excellent, but often over-priced. Buy it domaine-bottled.

Pouilly-Fumé Lo. w. dr. ⭐⭐➔⭐⭐⭐ 75 76 78

Smoky-fragrant, fruity, often sharp pale white from the upper Loire, next to SANCERRE. Grapes must be SAUVIGNON BLANC. Good vintages improve for 2–3 yrs.

Pouilly-Loché B'y. w. dr. ⭐⭐

Neighbour of POUILLY-FUISSÉ. Similar wine.

Pouilly-Sur-Loire Lo. w. dr. ⭐ D.Y.A.

Inferior wine from the same v'yds. as POUILLY-FUMÉ, but different grapes (CHASSELAS).

Pouilly-Vinzelles B'y. w. dr. ⭐⭐

Neighbour of POUILLY-FUISSÉ. Similar wine.

Pradel

Well-known brand of Provençal wines, esp. a dry rosé.

Preiss Zimmer, Jean
> Old-established Alsace wine-merchants at Riquewihr.

Premières Côtes de Blaye
> Restricted appellation for better reds of **Blaye**. Ch'x. include Barbé, l'Escadre, Mendaudat, des Petits-Arnauds.

Premier Cru
> First-growth in Bordeaux, but the second rank of v'yds. (after Grand Cru) in Burgundy.

Premières Côtes de Bordeaux B'x. r. (p.) or w. dr. or sw. ★→★★
> Large area east of GRAVES: a good bet for quality and value, though never brilliant. Ch'x incl. Laffitte (sic).

"Noble rot" (in French pourriture noble, in German Edelfäule, in Latin Botrytis cinerea) is a form of mould that attacks the skins of ripe grapes in certain vineyards in warm and misty autumn weather.

Its effect, instead of rotting the grapes, is to wither them. The skin grows soft and flaccid, the juice evaporates though it, and what is left is a super-sweet concentration of everything in the grape except its water content.

The world's best sweet table wines are all made of nobly rotten grapes. They occur in good vintages in Sauternes, the Rhine, the Mosel (where wine made from them is called Trockenbeerenauslese), in Tokaji in Hungary, in Burgenland in Austria, and occasionally elsewhere—California included. The danger is rain on the pulpy grapes when they are already far gone in noble rot. All too often, particularly in Sauternes, the grower's hopes are dashed by a break in the weather.

Primeur
> Early wine, like early vegetables; esp. of BEAUJOLAIS.

Prissé
> See Mâcon-Villages

Propriétaire-récoltant
> Owner–manager.

Provence
> See Côtes de Provence

Puisseguin-Saint-Emilion B'x. r. ★★ 75 76 78
> Eastern neighbour of ST-EMILION; wines similar—not so fine but often good value. No famous ch'x. but a good co-operative.

Puligny-Montrachet B'y. w. dr. ★★★ 69 71 72 73 74 75 76 77 78
> Bigger neighbour of CHASSAGNE-MONTRACHET with equally glorious rich dry whites. Best v'yds.: MONTRACHET, CHEVALIER-MONTRACHET, BÂTARD-MONTRACHET, Bienvenue-Bâtard-Montrachet, Les Combettes, Clavoillon, Pucelles, Champ-Canet, etc.

Quarts de Chaume Lo. w. sw. ★★★ 69 70 71 73 75 76 78
> Famous 120-acre plot in COTEAUX DU LAYON, Anjou. CHENIN BLANC grapes. Long-lasting, intense, rich golden wine.

Quatourze Midi r. (p.) or w. dr. ★ 75 76 78
> Minor VDQS area near Narbonne.

Quincy Lo. w. dr. ★★ 76 78
> Small area making very dry SANCERRE-style wine of SAUVIGNON BLANC.

Ramonet-Prudhon
> One of the leading proprietors in CHASSAGNE-MONTRACHET.

Rasteau Rh. (r. p. w. dr.) or br. sw. ★★ NV
> Village of s. Rhône valley. Good strong sweet dessert wine is the local speciality.

Ratafia de Champagne
> Sweet apéritif made in Champagne of ⅔ grape juice and ⅓ brandy.

Récolte

    Crop or vintage.

Remoissenet Père et Fils

    Fine growers and merchants of burgundy at BEAUNE.

Rémy Pannier

    Important Loire-wine merchants at Saumur.

Reuilly Lo. w. dr. ** 76 78

    Neighbour of QUINCY with similar wine; also good PINOT GRIS.

Richebourg B'y. r. **** 66 67 69 70 71 72 73 76 77 78

    19-acre Grand Cru in VOSNE-ROMANÉE. Powerful, perfumed, fabulously expensive wine, among Burgundy's best.

Riesling

    See Grapes for white wine

Rivesaltes Midi br. sw. * NV

    Fortified sweet wine, some muscat-flavoured, none distinguished, from e. Pyrenees.

La Roche-aux-Moines Lo. w. dr./sw. *** 69 71 73 75 76 78

    60-acre v'yd. in Savennières, Anjou. Intense strong fruity/sharp wine ages well.

Roederer, Louis NV and 64 66 69 70 71 73 74

    One of the best champagne-growers and merchants at Reims. Excellent non-vintage wine. Luxury brand: Cristal Brut (in white glass bottles).

La Romanée B'y. r. **** 66 67 69 70 71 72 73 76 78

    2-acre Grand Cru in VOSNE-ROMANÉE just uphill from ROMANÉE-CONTI and in the same hands.

Romanée-Conti B'y. r. **** 66 67 69 70 71 72 73 76 78

    4½-acre Grand Cru in VOSNE-ROMANÉE. The most celebrated and expensive red wine in the world, though seldom the best.

Romanée-Conti, Domaine de la

    The grandest estate of Burgundy, owning the whole of ROMANÉE-CONTI and LA TÂCHE and major parts of RICHEBOURG, GRANDS ECHÉZEAUX, ECHÉZEAUX and ROMANÉE-ST-VIVANT (under Marey-Monge label). Also a small part of Le MONTRACHET.

Romanée-St-Vivant B'y. r. ****

    23-acre Grand Cru in VOSNE-ROMANÉE. Similar to ROMANÉE-CONTI in all respects.

Ropiteau

    Burgundy wine-growers and merchants at MEURSAULT. Specialists in Meursault and CÔTE DE BEAUNE wines.

Rosé d'Anjou Lo. p. * D.Y.A.

    Pale, often slightly sweet, rosé. Cabernet d'Anjou is better.

Rousseau, Domaine A.

    Major burgundy grower famous for CHAMBERTIN, etc.

Roussette de Savoie Savoie w. dr. [**] D.Y.A.

    Pleasant light fresh white from s. of Geneva.

Roussillon

    See Côtes du Roussillon

Ruchottes-Chambertin B'y. r. *** 66 67 69 70 71 72 73 76 77 78

    7½-acre Grand Cru neighbour of CHAMBERTIN. Similar splendid long-lasting wine.

Ruinart Père et Fils NV and 66 69 71

    The oldest champagne house, now belonging to MOËT & CHANDON. Luxury brand: Dom Ruinart.

Rully B'y. r. or w. dr. or (sp.) [**] 73 76 78

    Village of the CÔTE CHALONNAISE famous for sparkling burgundy. Still reds and white light but tasty and good value.

Sablant Lo. w. dr. sp. ** NV

    Brand name for high-quality CRÉMANT DE LOIRE.

Saint-Amour B'y. r. [**] 76 78

    Northernmost cru of BEAUJOLAIS: light, fruity, irresistible.

Saint-Aubin B'y. (r.) or w. dr. ⟦**★★**⟧ 71 72 73 74 75w. 76

Little-known neighbour of CHASSAGNE-MONTRACHET, up a side-valley. Not top-rank, but typical and good value. Also sold as CÔTE-DE-BEAUNE-VILLAGES.

Saint Bris B'y. w. dr. ⟦**★**⟧ D.Y.A.

Village w. of CHABLIS known for its fruity ALIGOTÉ, making good sparkling burgundy, and hillside cherry orchards. See also Sauvignon-de-St-Bris.

Saint Chinian Midi r. ⟦**★→★★**⟧ 76 78

Hilly VDQS area of growing reputation. Tasty reds.

Sainte Croix-du-Mont B'x. w. sw. ⟦**★★**⟧ 67 70 71 75 76

Neighbour to SAUTERNES with similar golden wine. No superlatives but well worth trying.

Sainte-Foy-Bordeaux B'x.

Part of ENTRE-DEUX-MERS.

Saint-Emilion B'x. r. ★★→★★★★ 66 67 70 **71** 73 75 76 78

The biggest top-quality Bordeaux district; solid, rich, tasty wines from scores of ch'x., incl. CHEVAL-BLANC, AUSONE, CANON, MAGDELAINE, FIGEAC, etc.

Saint-Estèphe B'x. r. ⟦**★★**⟧ →★★★ 66 67 70 71 **73** 75 77 78

Northern village of HAUT-MÉDOC. Solid, satisfying, occasionally superlative wines. Top ch'x.: CALON-SÉGUR, COS D'ESTOURNEL, MONTROSE, etc., and many good CRUS BOURGEOIS.

Saint-Georges-Saint-Emilion

Part of MONTAGNE-ST-EMILION. Best ch.: ST-GEORGES.

Saint-Joseph Rh. r. (p. or w. dr.) ⟦**★★**⟧ 71 72 73 76 78

Northern Rhône appellation of second rank but reasonable price. Substantial wine comparable to CROZES-HERMITAGE in quality and worth ageing.

Saint-Julien B'x. r. ★★★→★★★★ 66 70 71 **73** 75 76 77 78

Mid-Médoc village with a dozen of Bordeaux's best ch'x., incl. three LÉOVILLES, BEYCHEVELLE, DUCRU-BEAUCAILLOU, GRUAUD-LAROSE, etc. The epitome of well-balanced red wine.

Saint-Laurent

Village next to SAINT-JULIEN. Appellation Haut-Médoc.

Saint-Nicolas-de-Bourgueil Lo. r. ★★ 71 73 75 76 78

The next village to BOURGUEIL: the same light but lively and fruity CABERNET red.

Saint-Péray Rh. w. dr. or sp. ★★ NV

Rather heavy white from the n. Rhône, much of it made sparkling. A curiosity.

Saint Pourçain Central France r. p. or w. dr ⟦**★**⟧ D.Y.A.

The agreeable local wine of Vichy, becoming fashionable in Paris. Made from GAMAY and/or PINOT NOIR.

Saint-Sauveur

HAUT-MÉDOC village just w. of PAUILLAC.

Saint-Seurin-de-Cadourne

HAUT-MÉDOC village just n. of SAINT-ESTÈPHE.

Saint-Véran B'y. w. dr. ⟦**★★**⟧ 73 74 75 76 77 78

Next-door appellation to POUILLY-FUISSÉ. Similar but better value: dry white of real character from the best slopes of MÂCON-VILLAGES.

Sancerre Lo. (r. p.) or w. dr. ★★★ 75 76 78

Very fragrant and fresh SAUVIGNON white almost indistinguishable from POUILLY-FUMÉ, its neighbour over the Loire. Drink young. Also light PINOT NOIR red and a little rosé, best drunk very young.

Santenay B'y. r. or (w. dr.) ★★★ 66 69 70 71 72 73 76 78

Very worthy, rarely rapturous, sturdy reds from the s. of the CÔTE DE BEAUNE. Best v'yds.: Les Gravières, Clos de Tavannes.

Saumur Lo. r. p. or w. dr. and sp. ★★→ ★★

Big versatile district in Anjou, with fresh fruity whites, good-value sparklers, pale rosés and occasionally good CABERNET reds, the best from Saumur-Champigny.

Sauternes B'x. w. sw. ★★→ ★★★★ 67 69 70 71 75 76

District of 5 villages (incl. BARSAC) making France's best sweet wine: strong (14% alcohol) luscious and golden, improving with age. Top ch'x.: D'YQUEM, LA TOUR-BLANCHE, SUDUIRAUT, COUTET, CLIMENS, GUIRAUD, etc. Also a few heavy dry wines which cannot be sold as Sauternes.

Sauvignon Blanc

See Grapes for white wine

Sauvignon-de-St-Bris B'y. w. dr. ★★ D.Y.A.

A baby VDQS cousin of SANCERRE from near CHABLIS.

Sauzet, Etienne

Excellent white burgundy estate at PULIGNY-MONTRACHET.

Savennières Lo. w. dr./sw. ★★★ 67 69 70 71 72 73 75 76 78

Small ANJOU district of pungent long-lived whites, incl. COULÉE DE SERRANT, LA ROCHE AUX MOINES, Clos du Papillon.

Savigny-lès-Beaune B'y. r. or (w. dr.) ★★★ 69 71 72 73 76 77 78

Important village next to BEAUNE, with similar well-balanced middle-weight wines, often deliciously delicate and fruity. Best v'yds.: Marconnets, Dominode, Serpentières, Vergelesses.

Savoie E. France (r.) or w. dr. ★★ D.Y.A.

Alpine area with light dry wines like some Swiss wine or minor Loires. CRÉPY and SEYSSEL are best known.

Schlumberger et Cie

Excellent Alsace growers and merchants at Guebwiller.

Schröder & Schyler

Old family firm of Bordeaux merchants, owners of CH. KIRWAN.

Sec

Literally means dry, though champagne so-called is medium-sweet.

Sèvre-et-Maine

The *département* containing the central and best v'yds. of MUSCADET.

Seyssel Savoie w. dr. or sp. ★★ NV

Delicate pale dry white making admirable sparkling wine.

Sichel & Co.

Famous Bordeaux (and Burgundy and Germany) merchants, owners of CH. D'ANGLUDET and part-owners of CH. PALMER.

Soussans

Village just n. of MARGAUX, sharing its appellation.

Sylvaner

See Grapes for white wine

La Tâche B'y. r. ★★★★ 62 66 67 69 70 71 72 73 74 76 77 78

15-acre Grand Cru of VOSNE-ROMANÉE and one of the best v'yds. on earth: dark, perfumed and luxurious wine. Owned by the Domaine de la Romanée-Conti.

Taittinger NV, rosé 70 71 and 66 69 70 71 73

Fashionable champagne growers and merchants of Reims. Luxury brand: Comtes de Champagne.

Tastevin, Confrèrie du

Burgundy's colourful and successful promotion society. Wine carrying their Tastevinage label has been approved by them and will usually be good. A tastevin is the traditional shallow silver wine-tasting cup of Burgundy. See panel, page 46.

Tavel Rh. p. ★★★ D.Y.A.

France's most famous rosé, strong, dry and slightly orange in colour.

Tête de Cuvée

Term vaguely used of the best wines of an appellation.

Thorin, J.

Fine grower and major merchant of BEAUJOLAIS, at Pontanevaux.

Tokay d'Alsace

See Pinot Gris under Grapes for white wine

Tollot-Beaut

Excellent burgundy grower with some 20 hectares in the Côte de Beaune, incl. Corton, Beaune Grèves, Savigny (Les Champs Chevrey) and at Chorey-lès-Beaune.

Touraine Lo. r. p. w. dr./sw./sp.

Big mid-Loire province with immense range of wines, incl. dry white SAUVIGNON, dry and sweet CHENIN BLANC (e.g. Vouvray), red CHINON and BOURGUEIL, light red CABERNETS, GAMAYS and rosés. Cabernets, Sauvignons and Gamays of good years are bargains.

Trimbach, F. E.

Distinguished ALSACE grower and merchant at Ribeauvillé. Best wines incl. Riesling Clos Ste. Hune.

Vacqueyras Rh. r. [★★] 71 72 73 74 76 78

Up-and-coming village of s. CÔTES-DU-RHÔNE, neighbour to GIGONDAS; comparable with CHÂTEAUNEUF-DU-PAPE but less heavy.

Valençay Lo. w. dr. ★ D.Y.A.

Neighbour of CHEVERNY: similar pleasant sharpish wine.

Varichon & Clerc

Principal makers and shippers of SAVOIE sparkling wines.

Varoilles, Domaine des

Excellent estate in GEVREY-CHAMBERTIN.

Vaudésir B'y. w. dr. [★★★★] 69 71 74 75 76 77 78

Arguably the best of the 7 Grands Crus of CHABLIS.

VDQS

Vin Délimité de Qualité Supérieure (see Introduction).

Vendange

Vintage.

Vendange tardive

Late vintage. In ALSACE equivalent to German AUSLESE.

Veuve Clicquot NV and 64 66 69 70 73

Historic champagne house of the highest standing. Cellars at Reims. Luxury brand: La Grande Dame.

Vidal-Fleury, J.

Long-established shippers and growers of top-quality Rhône wines.

Vieilles Vignes

"Old vines" – therefore the best wine. Used as a trade name by BOLLINGER and DE VOGÜE.

Viénot, Charles

Grower and merchant of good burgundy, at NUITS-ST-GEORGES. 70 acres in Nuits, CORTON, RICHEBOURG, etc.

Vignoble

Area of v'yds.

Vin de garde

Wine that will improve with keeping.

Vin de l'année

This year's wine. See Beaujolais.

Vin de paille

Wine from grapes dried on straw mats, consequently very sweet, like Italian passito. Especially in the JURA.

Vin de Pays

The junior rank of country wines (see Introduction).

Vin Doux Naturel ("VDN")
>Sweet wine fortified with alcohol, so far from "natural".
>Common in ROUSSILLON.

Vin Gris
>"Grey" wine is very pale pink, made of red grapes pressed
>before fermentation begins, unlike rosé, which ferments
>briefly before pressing.

Vin Jaune Jura w. dr. ★★★
>Speciality of ARBOIS: odd yellow wine like fino sherry. Ready
>when bottled.

Vin nouveau
>See Beaujolais Nouveau

Vin vert
>A very light, acidic, refreshing white wine, a speciality of
>ROUSSILLON.

---

*Paris has one wine school that offers individual amateur as well as
professional courses. L'Académie du Vin, 25 rue Royale/24 rue Boissy-
D'Anglas, was founded by an English wine merchant, Stephen
Spurrier, in a little mews house near La Madeleine in 1973. It has
become a centre for the fashionable pursuit of comparing the best
wines of California with those of France.*

Vinsobres Rh. r. (p. or w. dr.) ★★ 72 76 78
>Contradictory name of good s. Rhône village. Strong sub-
>stantial reds which mature well.

Viré
>See Mâcon-Villages

Visan Rh. r. p. or w. dr. ★★ 74 76 78
>One of the better s. Rhône villages. Reds better than white.

Viticulteur
>Wine-grower.

Vogüé, de
>First-class burgundy domaine at CHAMBOLLE-MUSIGNY.

Volnay B'y. r. ★★★ 66 69 71 72 73 76 78
>Village between POMMARD and MEURSAULT: the best reds of
>the CÔTE DE BEAUNE, not strong or heavy but fragrant and
>silky. Best v'yds.: Caillerets, Clos des Ducs, Champans, Clos
>des Chênes, etc.

Volnay-Santenots B'y. r. ★★★
>Excellent red wine from MEURSAULT is sold under this name.
>Indistinguishable from VOLNAY.

Vosne-Romanée B'y. r. ★★★→★★★★ 66 67 69 70 71 72 73 76 77 78
>The village containing Burgundy's grandest Crus (ROMANÉE-
>CONTI, LA TÂCHE, etc.). There are (or rather should be) no
>common wines in Vosne.

Vougeot
>See Clos de Vougeot

Vouvray Lo. w. dr./sw./sp. ★★→★★★★ 64 67 69 70 71 73 75 76 78
>Small district of TOURAINE with very variable wines, at their
>best intensely sweet and almost immortal. Good dry
>sparkling.

"Y" (Pronounced ygrec)
>Brand name of powerful dry wine occasionally made at CH.
>D'YQUEM.

Germany

Germany has the most complicated labelling system in the world—a fact that has put most people off tackling it seriously and driven them to settle for pleasantly innocuous blended wines: Liebfraumilch and the like.

Yet those who funk its complications will never experience the real beauty of the style of wine which is Germany's unique contribution.

The secret of the style is the balance of sweetness against fruity acidity. A great vintage in Germany is one in which the autumn weather allows the late-ripening Riesling—the grape which makes virtually all the great German wines—to develop a high sugar content. What is so special about the Riesling is that as it ripens it also develops a concentration of fragrant acids and essences to balance the increasing sweetness. The resulting wine is tense and thrilling with this sugar/acid balance.

It smells and tastes extraordinarily flowery, lively and refreshing while it is young. But because of its internal equilibrium it also has the ability to live and mature for a remarkable length of time. As good Riesling matures all sorts of subtle scents and flavours emerge. Straight sweetness gives way to oily richness. Suggestions of countless flowers and fruits, herbs and spices develop.

These are the rewards for anyone who can be bothered to master the small print. They lead into realms of sensation where Liebfraumilch (with all the respect due to a perfectly decent drink) can never follow. The great German growers make wine for wine's sake. Food is irrelevant, except in so far as it gets in the way.

The Labels and the Law

German wine law is based on the ripeness of the grapes at harvest time. Recent vintages have been exceptionally kind to growers, but as a general rule most German wine needs sugar added to make up for the missing warmth and sunshine of one of the world's northernmost vineyards.

The exceptional wine, from grapes ripe enough not to need sugar, is kept apart as Qualitätswein mit Prädikat or QmP. Within this top category its natural sugar-content is expressed by traditional terms—in ascending order of ripeness: Kabinett, Spätlese, Auslese, Beerenauslese, Trockenbeerenauslese.

But reasonably good wine is also made in good vineyards from grapes that fail to reach the natural sugar-content required for a QmP label. The authorities allow this, within fairly strict controls, to be called Qualitätswein as well, but with the different qualification of bestimmter Anbaugebiete (i.e. QbA) instead of mit Prädikat. mP is therefore a vitally important ingredient of a fine-wine label.

Both levels are officially checked, tested and tasted at every bottling. Each batch is given an identifying test ("prüfungs") number. No other country has quality control approaching this. It can't make dull wine exciting, but it can and does make all "quality" wine a safe bet.

Moselle Saar Ruwer **M-S-R**

R. Moselle

Ruwer

Saar

Mittel-Mosel **M-M**

Rheingau **Ring**

Frankfurt

Mainz

Rheinhessen **Rhh**

R. Nahe

Nahe **Na**

R. Main

Franken **Frank**

Mannheim

R. Neckar

Stuttgart

Saarbrucken

Rheinpfalz **Rhpf**

R. Rhine

R. Rhine

Abbreviations of regional names
shown in bold type are used in
the text.

Karlsruhe

Württemburg **Wurtt**

Baden **Bad**

•Freiburg

The third level, Tafelwein, has no pretentions to quality
and is not allowed to give itself airs beyond the name of the
village or the general region it comes from.

Though there is very much more detail in the laws this is
the gist of the quality grading. Where it differs completely
from the French system is in ignoring geographical difference. There are no Grands Crus, no VDQS. In theory all any
German vineyard has to do to make the best wine is to grow
the ripest grapes.

The law distinguishes only between degrees of geographical exactness. In labelling quality wine the grower or merchant is given a choice. He can (and always will) label the
relatively small quantities of his best wine with the name of
the precise vineyard or Einzellage where it was grown.
Germany has about 3,000 Einzellage names. Obviously only
particularly good ones are famous enough to help sell the
wine. Therefore the law has created a second class of vineyard name: the Grosslage. A Grosslage is a group of neighbouring Einzellages of supposedly similar character and
standing. Because there are fewer Grosslage names, and far
more wine from each, Grosslages have a better chance of
building reputations, brand-name fashion.*

Thirdly the grower or merchant (more likely the latter) may choose to sell his wine under a regional name: the word is Bereich. To cope with the vast demand for "Bernkasteler" or "Niersteiner" or "Johannisberger" these world-famous names have been made legal for considerable districts. "Bereich Johannisberg" is the whole of the Rheingau; "Bereich Bernkastel" the whole of the Mittel-Mosel.

As with all wine names, in fact, the better the wine the more precise the labelling. The trick with German labels is to be able to recognize which is the most precise. Finally, though, and above all, it is to recognize the grower and his vineyard.

The basic German label

The order of wording on German quality wine labels follows a standard pattern.

TRIERER
ABSTBERG

RIESLING AUSLESE

QmP
A.P. NR. 12345678
ERZEUGERABFÜLLUNG
WINZERVEREIN TRIER

The first name is the town or parish, with the suffix -er. The second is the vineyard (either Einzellage or Grosslage—see introduction). The third (optional) is the grape variety. The fourth is the quality in terms of ripeness. For QmP see page 74.
For A.P. Nr. see page 66.
Erzeugerabfüllung means bottled by the grower, in this case the grower's co-operative of Trier. For other words appearing on German labels see the Germany A–Z.

*Where the law is less than candid, however, is in pretending to believe that the general public will know a Grosslage name from an Einzellage name, when the two are indistinguishably similar (see any entry on the following pages). It is actually against the law to indicate on the label whether the name in question is that of a particular plot or a wider grouping. The names of all relevant Grosslages are given in this book. Note that Grosslage wines are very rarely of the stature of Einzellage wines.

N.B. on vintage notes opposite

Vintage notes after entries in the German section are given in a different form from those elsewhere, to show the style of the vintage as well as its quality.
Three styles are indicated:
The classic, super-ripe vintage with a high proportion of natural (QmP) wines, including Spätleses and Ausleses. By a freakish chance three of the seven vintages shown, an unprecedented proportion, come into this category.
Example: 71
The "normal" successful vintage with plenty of good wine but no great preponderance of sweeter wines. Example: 77
The cool vintage with generally poor ripeness but a fair proportion of reasonably successful wines, tending to be over-acid. Such wines sometimes mature better than expected. Example: 78
Where no mention is made the vintage is generally not recommended.

Recent vintages

Mosel

Mosels (including Saar and Ruwer wines) are so attractive young that their keeping qualities are not often enough explored, and wines older than seven years or so are unusual. But well-made wines of Kabinett class gain from two or three years in bottle, Spätleses by a little longer, and Ausleses and Beerenausleses by anything from 10 to 20 years, depending on the vintage.

As a rule, in poor years the Saar and Ruwer fare worse than the Middle Mosel and make sharp, thin wines, but in the best years they can surpass the whole of Germany for elegance and "breed".

1978	A similar vintage to '77, though very late and rather small. Very few sweet wines.
1977	Big vintage of serviceable quality, mostly QbA.
1976	Very good small vintage, with some superlative sweet wines and almost no dry. Kabinetts and Spätleses can lack balance.
1975	Superb; many Spätleses and Ausleses. Perfect balance will give them long life.
1974	Most wine needed sugaring; few Kabinetts, but some well-balanced wines which have kept well.
1973	Very large, attractive, but low acid and extract will mean a short life. Good eiswein.
1972	Large; medium to poor; few late-picked wines, many with unripe flavour. Should be drunk by now.
1971	Superb, with perfect balance. Many top wines still need keeping for years.
1970	Large; good to average. Quite soft, not for keeping.
1969	Some very fine wines; most merely good. Best in the Saar and Ruwer. Now mature.

Older fine vintages: '67, '64, '59, '53, '49, '45.

Rhine/Nahe/Palatinate

Even the best wines can be drunk with pleasure after two or three years, but Kabinett, Spätlese and Auslese wines of good vintages gain enormously in character and complexity by keeping for longer. Rheingau wines tend to be longest-lived, often improving for 10 years or more, but wines from the Nahe and the Palatinate can last nearly as long. Rheinhessen wines usually mature sooner, and dry Franconian wines are best young.

The Riesling, predominant in the Rheingau, benefits most from hot summers; Palatinate wines can taste almost overripe.

1978	Satisfactory vintage saved by late autumn. 25% QmP, but very few Spätleses.
1977	Big and useful; few Kabinett wines or better. Not to keep. Rheinpfalz best.
1976	The richest vintage since 1921 in places. Very few dry wines. Balance less consistent than 1975.
1975	A splendid Riesling year, a high percentage of Kabinetts and Spätleses. Needs time to mature.
1974	Variable; the best fruity and good; many Kabinetts.
1973	Very large, consistent and attractive, but not for long keeping.
1972	Excess acidity was the problem; no exciting wines, but some presentable. Should be drunk now.
1971	A superlative vintage with perfect balance. Still needs time to show its true quality.
1970	Very pleasant wines, but no more. Huge crop. Not for keeping.
1969	All above average; the best great. Nahe and Palatinate specially good.
1968	Poor; a wet summer. The Palatinate made some good light wines.
1967	Marvellous; the best of the '60s; Rheinhessen made great wines.

Older fine vintages: '66, '64, '59, '57, '53, '49, '45.

Achkarren Bad. (r.) w. ★→★★

Well-known wine village of the KAISERSTUHL.

Adelmann, Graf

Famous grower with 125 acres at Kleinbottwar, WÜRTTEM-BERG. Uses the name Brussele. Light reds; good RIESLINGS.

Ahr Ahr r. ★→★★★ 71 75 76 77

Germany's best-known red-wine area, s. of Bonn. Very light pale SPÄTBURGUNDERS.

Amtliche Prüfungsnummer

See Prüfungsnummer.

Anbaugebiet

Wine-region. See QbA.

Anheuser

Name of two distinguished growers of the NAHE.

Annaberg Rhpf. w. ★★★ 71 75 76 77 78

Thirty-two-acre estate at DÜRKHEIM famous for sweet and pungent wines, esp. SCHEUREBE.

A.P.Nr.

Abbreviation of Amtliche Prüfungsnummer.

Assmannshausen Rhg. r. ★→★★★ 71 75 76 77 78

RHEINGAU village known for its pale reds. Top v'yd.: Höllenberg. Grosslage: Steil.

The German Wine Academy runs regular courses of wine-instruction at all levels for both amateurs and professionals, in German and English. The Academy is based at the glorious 12th-century Cistercian monastery of Kloster Eberbach in the Rheingau. The course normally includes tasting-tours of Germany's wine regions. Particulars can be obtained from the Academy, P. O. Box 1705, D-6500 Mainz, West Germany.

Auslese

Late-gathered wine with high natural sugar content.

Avelsbach M-S-R (Ruwer) w. ★★★ 71 75 76 77 78

Village near TRIER. Supremely delicate wines. Growers: Staatliche Weinbaudomäne (see Staatsweingut), BISCHÖF-LICHE WEINGÜTER. Grosslage: Trierer Römerlay.

Ayl M-S-R (Saar) w. ★★★ 71 75 76 77 78

One of the best villages of the SAAR. Top v'yds.: Kupp, Herrenberger. Grosslage: Scharzberg.

Bacchus

Modern highly perfumed grape variety.

Bacharach (Bereich)

District name for the s. Mittelrhein v'yds. downstream from the RHEINGAU. No great or famous wines; some pleasant.

Baden

Huge area of scattered wine-growing. Few classic wines: most are heavy or soft. Best areas are KAISERSTUHL and ORTENAU.

Badische Bergstrasse/Kraichgau (Bereich)

Principal district name of n. BADEN.

Bad Dürkheim

See Dürkheim.

Badisches Frankenland (Bereich)

Minor district name of n. BADEN.

Bad Kreuznach Na. w. ★★→★★★ 71 75 76 77 78

Main town of the NAHE with some of its best wines. Many fine v'yds., incl. Brückes, St. Martin, Kauzenberg. Grosslage: Kronenberg.

Balbach Erben

One of the best growers of NIERSTEIN.

Basserman-Jordan
> 100-acre MITTEL-HAARDT family estate with many of the best v'yds. in DEIDESHEIM, FORST, RUPPERTSBERG, etc.

Beerenauslese
> Extremely sweet and luscious wine from very late-gathered individual bunches.

Bereich
> District within a Gebiet (region). See under Bereich names, e.g. Bernkastel (Bereich).

Bergzabern, Bad Rhpf. (r.) w. *→*** 75 76 77 78
> Town of SÜDLICHE-WEINSTRASSE. Pleasant sweetish wines. Grosslage: Liebfrauenberg.

Bernkastel M-M w. **→***** 71 75 76 77 78
> Top wine-town of the Mosel; the epitome of RIESLING. Best v'yds.: Doktor, Bratenhöfchen, etc. Grosslages: Badstube (***) and Kurfürstlay (**).

Bernkastel (Bereich)
> Wide area of mixed quality but decided flowery character. Includes all the Mittel-Mosel.

Bingen Rhh. w. **→*** 71 75 76 77 78
> Town on Rhine and Nahe with fine v'yds., incl. Scharlachberg. Grosslage: Sankt Rochuskapelle.

Bingen (Bereich)
> District name for w. Rheinhessen.

Bischöfliche Weingüter
> Outstanding M-S-R estate at TRIER, a union of the Cathedral properties with two famous charities. 230 acres of top v'yds. in AVELSBACH, WILTINGEN, SCHARZHOFBERG, AYL, KASEL, EITELSBACH, PIESPORT, TRITTENHEIM, ÜRZIG, etc.

Blauburgunder
> A form of PINOT NOIR.

Blue Nun
> The best-selling brand of LIEBFRAUMILCH, from SICHEL.

Bodensee (Bereich)
> Minor district of s. BADEN, on La. Constance.

Boxbeutel
> Flask-shaped bottle used for FRANKEN wines.

Brauneberg M-M w. *** 71 75 76 77 78
> Village near BERNKASTEL with 100 acres making excellent full-flavoured wine. Best v'yd.: Juffer. Grosslage: Kurfürstlay.

Breisgau (Bereich)
> Minor district of BADEN, just n. of KAISERSTUHL.

Brentano, von
> 20-acre old family estate in WINKEL, Rheingau.

Bühl, von
> Great RHEINPFALZ family estate. 200+ acres in DEIDESHEIM, FORST, RUPPERTSBERG, etc. In the very top class.

Bullay M-S-R *→ ** 75 76 77 78
> Lower Mosel village. Good light wine to drink young.

Bundesweinprämierung
> The top German Wine Award: a gold, silver or bronze medal on bottles of remarkable wines.

Burgerspital zum Heiligen Geist
> Ancient charitable estate at WÜRZBURG. 185 acres in WÜRZBURG, RANDERSACKER, etc., make rich dry wines.

Bürklin-Wolf
> Great RHEINPFALZ family estate. 222 acres in WACHENHEIM, FORST, DEIDESHEIM and RUPPERTSBERG, with rarely a dull, let alone poor, wine.

Crown of Crowns
> Popular brand of LIEBFRAUMILCH from LANGENBACH & CO.

Deidesheim Rhpf. w. (r.) [★★] →★★★★ 71 74 75 76 77 78
Biggest top-quality wine-village of RHEINPFALZ with 1,000
acres. Rich, high-flavoured, lively wines. V'yds. incl. Hohen-
morgen, Kieselberg, Grainhübel, Leinhöhle, Herrgottsacker,
etc. Grosslages: Hofstück, Mariengarten.

Deinhard
Famous old Koblenz merchants and growers in Rheingau (see
Wegeler), Mittel-Mosel (27 acres in Bernkastel, incl. part of
Doktor v'yd., and Graach) and Rheinpfalz.

Deutscher Tafelwein
TAFELWEIN from Germany (only).

Deutsches Weinsiegel
A quality "seal" (i.e. neck label) for wines which have passed a
stiff tasting test.

Deutsches Weintor
See Schweigen

Diabetiker Wein
Wine with minimal residual sugar (less than 4gms/litre).
Suitable for diabetics—or those who like very dry wine.

Dhron
See Neumagen-Dhron

Dienheim Rhh. w. ★★→★★★ 77 78
Southern neighbour of OPPENHEIM. Mainly run-of-the-mill
wines. Top v'yds.: Kreuz, Herrenberg, Schloss. Grosslages:
Guldenmorgen, Krötenbrunnen.

Dom
German for Cathedral. Wines from the famous TRIER
Cathedral properties have "Dom" before the v'yd. name. But
"Domgarten" is a brand name of HALLGARTEN.

Domäne
German for "domain" or "estate". Sometimes used alone to
mean the "State domain" (Staatliche Weinbaudomäne).

Durbach Baden w. (r.) ★→★★★★ 75 76 77 78
150 acres of the best v'yds. of BADEN. Top growers: Schloss
Staufenberg, Wolf-Metternich, von Neveu. Choose their
RIESLINGS.

Dürkheim, Bad Rhpf. w. or (r.) [★★] →★★★
Main town of the MITTEL-HAARDT. Top v'yds.: Hochbenn,
Michelsberg. Grosslages: Feuerberg, Schenkenböhl.

Edel
Means "noble". Edelfäule means "noble rot": the condition
which gives the greatest sweet wines (see p. 52).

Egon Müller-Scharzhof
Top Saar estate of 24 acres at WILTINGEN. SCHARZHOFBERGERS
are supreme in top years.

Eiswein
Wine made from frozen grapes with the ice (e.g. water con-
tent) rejected, thus very concentrated in flavour and sugar.
Rare and expensive. Sometimes produced as late as the
January or February following the vintage.

Eitelsbach Ruwer w. ★★→★★★★ 71 75 76 77 78
RUWER village now part of TRIER, incl. superb Karthäuserhof-
berg estate. Grosslage: Trierer Römerlay.

Elbling
Inferior grape widely grown on upper Mosel.

Eltville Rhg. w. [★★] →★★★ 71 75 76 77 78
Major wine-town with cellars of the Rheingau State domain,
SCHLOSS ELTZ and VON SIMMERN estates. Excellent wines. Top
v'yds.: Sonnenberg, Taubenberg. Grosslage: Heiligenstock.

Eltz, Schloss
Superb 98-acre Rheingau estate with v'yds. in ELTVILLE,
KIEDRICH, RAUENTHAL, RÜDESHEIM.

Enkirch M-M w. ∗∗→ ⟨∗∗∗⟩ 71 75 76 77 78
> Minor middle-Mosel village, often overlooked but with lovely light tasty wine. Grosslage: Schwarzlay.

Erbach Rhg. w. ∗∗∗→∗∗∗∗ 71 75 76 77 78
> One of the best parts of the Rheingau with powerful, perfumed wines, incl. the great MARCOBRUNN; other top v'yds.: Schlossberg, Siegelsberg, Hönigberg, Michelmark. Grosslage: Mehrhölzchen. Major estates: SCHLOSS REINHARTSHAUSEN, von SCHÖNBORN.

Erden M-M w. ∗∗∗→∗∗∗ 71 75 76 77 78
> Village between Urzig and Kröv with full-flavoured vigorous wine. Top v'yds.: Prälat, Treppchen. Leading grower: Beeres. Grosslage: Schwarzlay.

Erzeugerabfüllung
> Bottled by the grower.

Escherndorf Franc. w. ∗∗→∗∗∗ 71 75 76 77 78
> Important wine-town near WÜRZBURG. Similar tasty dry wine. Top v'yds.: Lump, Berg. Grosslage: Kirchberg.

Feine, feinste, hochfeinste
> Terms formerly used to distinguish a good grower's best barrels. Now, unfortunately, illegal.

Forst Rhpf. w. ∗∗∗→∗∗∗∗ 71 75 76 77 78
> MITTEL-HAARDT village with 500 acres of Germany's best v'yds. Ripe, richly fragrant but subtle wines. Top v'yds.: Kirchenstück, Jesuitengarten, Ungeheuer, etc. Grosslages: Mariengarten, Schnepfenflüg.

Franken
> Franconia: region of excellent distinctive dry wines. The centre is WÜRZBURG. BEREICH names: MAINVIERECK, MAINDREIECK, STEIGERWALD.

Friedrich Wilhelm Gymnasium
> Superb 104-acre charitable estate with v'yds. in BERNKASTEL, ZELTINGEN, GRAACH, TRITTENHEIM, OCKFEN, etc., all M-S-R.

Geisenheim Rhg. w. ∗∗→∗∗∗ 71 75 76 77 78
> Village famous for Germany's leading wine-school. Best v'yds. incl. Rothenberg, Kläuserweg, Fuchsberg. Grosslage: Burgweg.

Gemeinde
> A commune or parish.

Gewürztraminer
> Spicy grape of Alsace, used a little in s. Germany, esp. Rheinpfalz.

Gimmeldingen Rhpf. w. ∗→ ⟨∗∗⟩ 75 76 77 78
> Village just s. of MITTEL-HAARDT. Similar wines. Grosslage: Meerspinne.

Goldener Oktober
> Popular Rhine-wine and Mosel blend from the firm of St. Ursula, BINGEN.

Graach M-M w. ∗∗→ ⟨∗∗∗⟩ 71 75 76 77 78
> Small village between BERNKASTEL and WEHLEN. Top v'yds.: Himmelreich, Domprobst, Abstberg, Josephshöfer. Grosslage: Münzlay.

Grosslage
> See Introduction, p. 59

Guntersblum Rhh. w. ∗→∗∗ 75 76 77 78
> Big wine-town s. of OPPENHEIM. Grosslages: Krötenbrunnen, Vogelsgarten.

Guntrum, Louis
> 130-acre family estate in RHINEHESSEN. Fine v'yds. in NIERSTEIN, OPPENHEIM, etc.

Gutedel
> German for the low-quality Chasselas grape.

Hallgarten Rhg. w. **➔*** 71 75 76 77 78
> Important little wine-town behind HATTENHEIM. Robust full-bodied wines. Top v'yds. incl. Schönhell, Jungfer. Grosslage: Mehrhölzchen.

Hallgarten, House of
> Well-known London-based wine-merchant.

Hanns Christof
> Top brand of LIEBFRAUMILCH from DEINHARD'S.

Hattenheim Rhg. w. **➔**** 71 75 76 77 78
> Superlative 500-acre wine-town. V'yds. incl. STEINBERG, MARCOBRUNN, Nüssbrunnen, Mannberg, etc. Grosslage: Deutelsberg.

Hessische Bergstrasse Rhh. w. **➔*** 75 76 77 78
> Minor (700-acre) region s. of Frankfurt. Pleasant Riesling wines from State domain v'yds. in Heppenheim and Bensheim.

Hessische Forschungsanstalt für Wein- Obst- & Gartenbau
> Germany's top wine-school and research establishment, at GEISENHEIM.

Heyl zu Herrnsheim
> Fine 50-acre estate at NIERSTEIN.

Hochfeinste
> "Very finest." Traditional label-term, now illegal.

Hochheim Rhg. w. **➔*** 71 75 76 77 78
> 500-acre wine-town 15 miles e. of RHEINGAU. Similar fine wines. Top v'yds.: Domdechaney, Kirchenstück, Hölle, Königin Viktoria Berg. Grosslage: Daubhaus.

Hock
> English term for Rhine-wine, derived from HOCHHEIM.

Huxelrebe
> Modern very fruity grape variety.

Ihringen Bad. (r.) w. *➔** 75 76 77 78
> One of the best villages of the KAISERSTUHL, BADEN. Heavy dryish wines.

Ilbesheim Rhpf. w. *➔ ** 75 76 77 78
> Base of important growers co-operative of SÜDLICHE WEIN-STRASSE. See also Schweigen.

Ingelheim Rhh. r. or w. * 75 76 77
> Village on Rhine known for red wine.

Iphofen Franc. w. **➔ ⬚ *** 71 75 76 77 78
> Village e. of WÜRZBURG. Top v'yd.: Julius-Echter-Berg. Grosslage: Burgweg.

Jesuitengarten
> V'yd. in FORST. One of Germany's best.

Johannisberg Rhg. w. **➔**** 71 75 76 77 78
> 260-acre village with superlative subtle wine. Top v'yds. incl. SCHLOSS JOHANNISBERG, Hölle, Klaus, etc. Grosslage: Erntebringer.

Johannisberg (Bereich)
> District name of the entire RHEINGAU.

Josephshöfer
> Fine v'yd. at GRAACH, the property of von KESSELSTATT.

Juliusspital
> Ancient charity at WÜRZBURG with top FRANKEN v'yds.

Kabinett
> The term for the driest and least expensive natural unsugared (QmP) wines.

Kaiserstuhl-Tuniberg (Bereich)
> Best v'yd. area of BADEN. Villages incl. IHRINGEN, ACHKARREN.

Kallstadt Rhpf. w. (r.) **➔*** 71 75 76 77 78
> Village just n. of MITTEL-HAARDT. Fine rich wines. Top v'yd.: ANNABERG. Grosslages: Kobnert, Feuerberg.

Kanzem M-S-R (Saar) w. ★★→★★★ 71 75 76 77 78

>   Small but excellent neighbour of WILTINGEN. Top v'yds.: Sonnenberg, Altenberg. Grosslage: Scharzberg.

Kasel M-S-R (Ruwer) w. ★★ 71 75 76 77 78

>   Village with attractive light wines. Grosslage: Römerlay.

Keller

>   Wine-cellar or winery.

Kerner

>   Modern very flowery grape variety.

Kesselstatt, von

>   The biggest private Mosel Estate, 600 years old. 150 acres in GRAACH, PIESPORT, KASEL, MENNIG, WILTINGEN, etc.

Kesten M-W w. ★→★★★ 71 75 76 77 78

>   Neighbour of BRAUNEBERG. Best wines (from Paulinshofberg v'yd.) similar. Grosslage: Kurfürstlay.

Kiedrich Rhg. w. ★★→★★★★ 71 75 76 77 78

>   Neighbour of RAUENTHAL; almost as splendid and high flavoured. Top v'yds.: Gräfenberg, Wasseros, Sandgrub. Grosslage: Heiligenstock.

Most German wine is bottled in tall narrow sloping-shouldered bottles: invariably brown glass for Rhine wines (including Nahe and Palatinate wines) and green for Mosel-Saar-Ruwer. The glass may be said to epitomize the respective qualities of the wines: the Rhine full and gold, the Mosel fresh and green (often literally so). In any case it is useful to remember when you are asked by malicious friends to give an opinion. Franconian wine is alone in being bottled in flagon-shaped "Boxbeuteln".

Kloster Eberbach

>   Glorious 12th-century Abbey at HATTENHEIM, Rheingau, now State domain property and H.Q. of the German Wine Academy. See panel, p. 66.

Klüsserath M-M w. ★★→ ★★★ 71 75 76 77 78

>   Minor Mosel village worth trying in good vintages. Best v'yds.: Brüderschaft, Königsberg. Grosslage: St. Michael.

Kreuznach (Bereich)

>   District name for the entire northern NAHE. See also Bad Kreuznach.

Kröv M-M w. ★→★★★ 75 76 77 78

>   Popular tourist resort famous for its Grosslage name: Nacktarsch, meaning "bare bottom".

Landgräflich Hessisches Weingut

>   75-acre estate in JOHANNISBERG, WINKEL, etc.

Langenbach & Co.

>   Well-known merchants of London and WORMS.

Lauerburg

>   One of the three owners of the famous Doktor v'yd. in BERNKASTEL, with THANISCH and DEINHARD.

Liebfrauenstift

>   26-acre v'yd. in the city of WORMS, said to be the origin of the name LIEBFRAUMILCH.

Liebfraumilch

>   Legally defined as a QbA "of pleasant character" from RHEINHESSEN, RHEINPFALZ, NAHE or RHEINGAU, blended from RIESLING, SYLVANER or MÜLLER-THURGAU. Most is mild semi-sweet wine from Rheinhessen and Rheinpfalz.

Lieser M-M w. ★→ ★★ 71 75 76 77 78

>   Little-known neighbour of BERNKASTEL. Grosslages: Beerenlay, Kurfürstlay.

Lorch Rhg. w. (r.) ★→★★★ 71 75 76 77 78

> At extreme w. end of Rheingau. Secondary quality. Best grower: von Kanitz.

Löwenstein, Fürst

> 70-acre FRANKEN estate: classic dry wines.

Maindreieck (Bereich)

> District name for central part of FRANKEN, incl. WÜRZBURG.

Mainviereck (Bereich)

> District name for minor w. part of FRANKEN.

Marcobrunn

> See Erbach

Markgräflerland (Bereich)

> Minor district s. of Freiburg (BADEN). GUTEDEL wine. Drink very young.

Martinsthal Rhg. w. ★★→ ★★★ 71 75 76 77 78

> Little-known neighbour of RAUENTHAL. Top v'yds.: Langenberg, Wildsau. Grosslage: Steinmacher.

Matuschka-Greiffenklau, Graf

> Owner of the ancient SCHLOSS VOLLRADS estate.

Maximin Grünhaus M-S-R (Ruwer) w. ★★★★ 71 75 76 77 78

> Supreme RUWER estate of 52 acres at Mertesdorf.

German wine bottles are too tall for most ice-buckets to cool the whole bottle. To make sure that the top of the bottle (your first glass) is properly cooled, put the bottle upside down in the bucket for the final five minutes before opening it.

Mennig M-S-R (Saar) w. ★★ 71 75 76 77 78

> Village between TRIER and the SAAR. Its Falkensteiner v'yd. is famous.

Mertesdorf

> See Maximin Grünhaus

Mittelheim Rhg. w. ★★→ ★★★ 71 75 76 77 78

> Minor village between WINKEL and OESTRICH. Top grower: WEGELER. Grosslage: Honigberg.

Mittel-Haardt

> The n., best part, of RHEINPFALZ, incl. FORST, DEIDESHEIM, etc.

Mittel-Mosel

> The central and best part of the Mosel, incl. BERNKASTEL, PIESPORT, etc.

Mittelrhein

> Northern Rhine area of secondary quality, incl. BACHARACH.

Morio Muskat

> Stridently aromatic grape variety.

Moselblümchen

> The "LIEBFRAUMILCH" of the Mosel, but on a lower quality level: TAFELWEIN not QbA.

Mosel-Saar-Ruwer

> Huge wine area, incl. MITTEL-MOSEL, SAAR, RUWER and lesser areas.

Müller-Thurgau

> Fruity, low-acid grape variety; the commonest in RHEINPFALZ and RHEINHESSEN, but increasingly planted in all areas.

Mumm, von

> 111-acre estate in JOHANNISBERG, RUDESHEIM, etc.

Munster Nahe w. ★→★★★ 71 75 76 77 78

> Best village of n. NAHE, with fine delicate wines. Top grower: State Domain. Grosslage: Schlosskapelle.

Nackenheim Rhh. w. ★→★★★ 71 75 76 77 78

> Neighbour of NIERSTEIN; best wines (Engelsberg, Rothenberg) similar. Grosslages: Spiegelberg, Gutes Domtal.

Nahe

Tributary of the Rhine and quality wine region. Balanced, fresh and clean but full-flavoured wines. Two Bereiche: KREUZNACH and SCHLOSS BÖCKELHEIM.

Neef M-S-R w. *→ ☐****** 71 75 76 77 78

Village of lower Mosel with one fine v'yd.: Frauenberg.

Neipperg, Graf

62-acre top WÜRTTEMBERG estate at Schwaigern.

Nell, von

40-acre family estate at TRIER and AYL, etc.

Neumagen-Dhron M-M w. ****→***** 71 75 76 77 78

Neighbour of PIESPORT. Top v'yd.: Hofberger. Grosslage: Michelsberg.

Neustadt

Central city of Rheinpfalz, with famous wine school.

Niederhausen Na. w. ****→** ☐******** 71 75 76 77 78

Neighbour of SCHLOSS BÖCKELHEIM and H.Q. of Nahe State Domain. Wines of grace and power. Top v'yds. incl. Hermannshöhle, Steinberg. Grosslage: Burgweg.

Niedermennig

See Mennig

Niederwalluf

See Walluf

Nierstein (Bereich)

Large e. RHEINHESSEN district of very mixed quality.

Nierstein Rhh. w. *→*** 71 75 76 77 78

Famous but treacherous name. 1,300 acres incl. superb v'yds.: Hipping, Orbel, Pettenthal, etc., and their Grosslages Rehbach, Spiegelberg, Auflangen: ripe, racy wines. But beware Grosslage Gutes Domtal: no guarantee of anything.

Norheim Nahe w. *→*** 71 75 76 77 78

Neighbour of NIEDERHAUSEN. Top v'yds.: Klosterberg, Kafels, Kirschheck. Grosslage: Burgweg.

Oberemmel M-S-R (Saar) w. ****→***** 71 75 76 77 78

Next village to WILTINGEN. Very fine wines from Rosenberg, Hütte, etc. Grosslage: Scharzberg.

Obermosel (Bereich)

District name for the upper Mosel above TRIER. Generally poor wines from the Elbling grape.

Oberwalluf

See Walluf

Ockfen M-S-R (Saar) w. ****→***** 71 75 76 77 78

200-acre hill with superb fragrant austere wines. Top v'yds.: Bockstein, Herrenberg. Grosslage: Scharzberg.

Oechsle

Scale for sugar-content of grape-juice.

Oestrich Rhg. w. ****→***** 71 75 76 77 78

Big village; good but rarely top grade. V'yds. incl. Doosberg, Lenchen. Grosslage: Gottesthal.

Oppenheim Rhh. w. *→*** 71 75 76 77 78

Town just s. of NIERSTEIN, best wines (Kreuz, Sackträger, etc.) similar. Grosslages: Guldenmorgen (***) Krotenbrunnen (**).

Originalabfüllung

Bottled by the grower. An obsolete term.

Ortenau (Bereich)

District just s. of Baden-Baden. Soft wines to drink young. Best village DURBACH.

Palatinate

English for RHEINPFALZ.

Pfalz

See Rheinpfalz

Perlwein

Semi-sparkling wine.

Piesport M-M w. ✶✶→✶✶✶✶ 71 75 76 77 78

Tiny village with famous amphitheatre of vines giving fine gentle fruity wine. Top v'yds.: Goldtröpfchen, Gunterslay, Falkenberg. Treppchen is on flatter land and inferior. Grosslage: Michelsberg.

Plettenberg, von

Fine 100-acre Nahe estate at BAD KREUZNACH.

Pokalwein

Café wine. A pokal is a big glass.

Portugieser

Second-rate red-wine grape.

Prädikat

Special attributes or qualities. See QmP.

Prüfungsnummer

The official identifying test-number of a quality wine.

Prüm, J. J.

Superlative 35-acre Mosel estate in WEHLEN, GRAACH, BERNKASTEL.

Qualitätswein bestimmter Anbaugebiete (QbA)

The middle quality of German wine, with added sugar but strictly controlled as to grape areas, etc.

Qualitätswein mit Prädikat (QmP)

Top category, incl. all wines ripe enough to be unsugared, from KABINETT to TROCKENBEERENAUSLESE.

Randersacker Franc. w. ✶✶→✶✶✶ 71 75 76 77 78

Leading village for distinctive dry wine. Top v'yds. incl. Teufelskeller. Grosslage: Ewig Leben.

Rauenthal Rhg. w. ✸✸✸ →✶✶✶✶ 71 75 76 77 78

Supreme village for powerful spicy wine. Top v'yds. incl. Baiken, Gehrn, Wulfen. Grosslage: Steinmacher. The State Domain is an important grower.

Rautenstrauch Erben

Owners of the splendid Karthäuserhof, EITELSBACH.

Rheinburgengau (Bereich)

District name for the v'yds. of the MITTELRHEIN round the famous Rhine gorge. Moderate quality only.

Rheingau

The best v'yd. region of the Rhine, near Wiesbaden. 5,000 acres. Classic, subtle but substantial RIESLING. Bereich name, JOHANNISBERG.

Rheinhessen

Vast region (30,000 acres of v'yds.) between Mainz and the NAHE, mostly second-rate, but incl. NIERSTEIN, OPPENHEIM, etc.

Rheinpfalz

Even vaster 35,000-acre v'yd. region s. of Rheinhessen. Wines inclined to sweetness. (See Mittel-Haardt and Südliche Weinstrasse.) This and the last are the chief sources of LIEBFRAUMILCH.

Rhodt

Village of SÜDLICHE WEINSTRASSE with well-known co-operative. Agreeable fruity wines. Grosslage: Ordensgut.

Riesling

The best German grape: fine, fragrant, fruity.

Ritter zu Groenesteyn, Baron

Fine 37-acre estate in KIEDRICH and RÜDESHEIM.

Roseewein

Rosé wine.

Rotenfelser Bastei

See Traisen

Rotwein

Red wine.

Rüdesheim Rhg. w. ★★→★★★ 71 75 76 77 78

Rhine resort with 650 acres of excellent v'yds.; the three best called Berg. . . . Full-bodied wines. Grosslage: Burgweg.

Rüdesheimer Rosengarten

Rüdesheim is also the name of a NAHE village near BAD KREUZNACH. Do not be misled by the ubiquitous blend going by this name. It has nothing to do with the great Rheingau RÜDESHEIM.

Ruländer

The PINOT GRIS: grape giving soft heavy wine.

Ruppertsberg Rhpf. w. ★★→ ★★★ 71 75 76 77 78

Southern village of MITTEL-HAARDT. Top v'yds. incl. Gaisbohl, Hoheburg. Grosslage: Hofstück.

Ruwer

Tributary of Mosel near TRIER. Very fine delicate wines. Villages incl. EITELSBACH, MERTESDORF, KASEL.

Saar

Tributary of Mosel s. of RUWER. Brilliant austere wines. Villages incl. WILTINGEN, AYL, OCKFEN, SERRIG.

Saar-Ruwer (Bereich)

District incl. the two above.

St. Ursula

Well-known merchants at BINGEN.

Scharzberger

Grosslage name of WILTINGEN and neighbours.

Scharzhofberger Saar w. ★★★★ 71 75 76 77 78

Superlative 30-acre SAAR v'yd.: austerely beautiful wines, the perfection of RIESLING. Do not confuse with the last.

Schaumwein

Sparkling wine.

Scheurebe

Fruity aromatic grape used in RHEINPFALZ.

Schillerwein

Light red or rosé QbA from WÜRTTEMBERG.

Schlossabzug

Bottled at the Schloss (castle).

Schloss Böckelheim Nahe w. ★★→★★★★ 71 75 76 77 78

Village with the best NAHE v'yds., incl. Kupfergrübe, Felsenberg. Firm yet delicate wine. Grosslage: Burgweg.

Schloss Böckelheim (Bereich)

District name for the whole s. NAHE.

Schloss Johannisberg

Famous RHEINGAU estate of 66 acres belonging to the Metternich family. Polished, elegant wine.

Schloss Reinhartshausen

Fine 99-acre estate in ERBACH, HATTENHEIM, etc.

Schloss Vollrads Rhg. w. ★★★→★★★★ 71 75 76 77 78

Great estate at WINKEL, since 1300. 81 acres producing classical RHEINGAU RIESLING.

Schmitt, Gustav Adolf

Fine old 124-acre family estate at NIERSTEIN.

Schmitt, Franz Karl

Even older 74-acre ditto.

Schönborn, Graf von

One of the biggest and best Rheingau estates, based at HATTENHEIM.

Schoppenwein

Café wine: i.e. wine by the glass.

Schubert, von

Owner of MAXIMIN GRÜNHAUS.

Schweigen Rhpf. w. ★→ ★★ 75 76 77 78
Southernmost Rheinpfalz village with big co-operative. DEUTSCHES WEINTOR: Grosslage: Guttenberg.

Sekt
German (QbA) sparkling wine.

Serrig M-S-R (Saar) w. ★★→★★★ 71 75 76 77 78
Village known for "steely" wine, excellent in hot years. Top growers: VEREINIGTE HOSPITIEN and State Domain. Grosslage: Scharzberg.

Sichel H., Söhne
Famous wine-merchants of London and Mainz.

Silvaner
Common German white grape, best in FRANKEN.

Simmern, von
94-acre family estate at HATTENHEIM since 1464 and in ELTVILLE, RAUENTHAL, etc.

Sonnenuhr
"Sun-dial." Name of several famous v'yds., esp. one at WEHLEN.

Every wine district has its own favourite pattern of glass for bringing out the character of the local product. For practical purposes at home, however, three shapes/sizes are enough. These three were designed by Professor Lord Queensberry of the Royal College of Art and the author for Ravenhead Glass as ideal glasses for, respectively, sherry/port, white wine/general purpose, fine red wines.

Spätburgunder
PINOT NOIR: the best red-wine grape in Germany.

Spätlese
"Late gathered." One better (stronger or sweeter) than KABINETT.

Spindler
Fine 33-acre family estate at FORST, Rheinpfalz.

Staatsweingut (or Staatliche Weinbaudomäne)
The State wine estate or domain.

Steigerwald (Bereich)
District name for e. part of FRANKEN.

Steinberg Rhg. w. ★★★→★★★★ 71 75 76 77 78
Famous 62-acre v'yd. at HATTENHEIM walled by Cistercians 700 yrs. ago. Now property of the State.

Steinwein
Wine from WÜRZBURG's best v'yd., Stein. Loosely used for all Franconian wine.

Stuttgart
Chief city of WÜRTTEMBERG, producer of some pleasant wines, not exported.

Südliche Weinstrasse (Bereich)
District name for the s. RHEINPFALZ.

Tafelwein
"Table wine." The vin ordinaire of Germany. Can be blended with other EEC wines. But Deutscher Tafelwein must come from Germany alone.

Thanisch, Dr.
32-acre BERNKASTEL family estate, incl. part of Doktor v'yd.

Traben-Trarbach M-W w. **★★** 75 76 78
Secondary wine-town, some good light wines. Top v'yds. incl. Schlossberg, Ungsberg. Grosslage: Schwarzlay.

Traisen Na. w. **★★★** 71 75 76 77 78
Small village incl. superlative Bastei v'yd., making wine of great concentration and class.

Traminer
See Gewürztraminer

Trier M-S-R w. ★★→★★★★
Important wine city of Roman origin, on the Mosel, adjacent to RUWER, now incl. AVELSBACH and EITELSBACH. Grosslage: Römerlay.

Trittenheim M-M w. **★★** →★★★ 71 75 76 77 78
Attractive light wines. Top v'yds.: Apotheke, Altärchen. Grosslage: Michelsberg.

Trocken
Dry. On labels Trocken *alone* means dry enough for diabetics. But see next entry.

Trockenbeerenauslese
The sweetest and most expensive category of wine, made from selected withered grapes. See also Edelfäule.

Trollinger
Common red grape of WÜRTTEMBERG: poor quality.

Ürzig M-M w. **★★★** 71 75 76 77 78
Village famous for lively spicy wine. Top v'yd.: Würzgarten. Grosslage: Schwarzlay.

Vereinigte Hospitien
"United Hospitals." Ancient charity with large holdings in SERRIG, WILTINGEN, TRIER, PIESPORT, etc.

Verwaltung
Property.

Villa Sachsen
75-acre BINGEN estate belonging to ST. URSULA Weingut.

Wachenheim Rhpf. w. **★★★** →★★★★ 71 75 76 77 78
840 acres, incl. exceptionally fine Rieslings. V'yds. incl. Gerümpel, Böhlig, Rechbächel, etc. Top grower: Bürklin-Wolf. Grosslages: Schenkenbohl, Schnepfenflug, Mariengarten.

Waldrach M-S-R (Ruwer) w. **★★** 75 76 77 78
Some charming light wines. Grosslage: (Trierer) Römerlay.

Walluf Rhg. w. **★★** 73 75 76 77
Neighbour of ELTVILLE; formerly Nieder- and Ober-Walluf. Good but not top wines. Grosslage: Steinmacher.

Walporzheim-Ahrtal (Bereich)
District name for the whole AHR valley.

Wawern M-S-R (Saar) w. ★★→★★★ 71 75 76 77 78
Small village with fine Rieslings. Grosslage: Scharzberg.

Wegeler Erben
138-acre Rheingau estate owned by DEINHARD'S. V'yds. in OESTRICH, MITTELHEIM, WINKEL, GEISENHEIM, RÜDESHEIM, etc.

Wehlen M-M w. **★★★** →★★★★ 71 75 76 77 78
Neighbour of BERNKASTEL with equally fine, somewhat richer, wine. Best v'yd.: Sonnenuhr. Top growers: Prüm family. Grosslage: Münzlay.

Weil, Dr.
45-acre private estate at KIEDRICH. Very fine wines.

Weingut
Wine estate.

Weinkellerei
Wine cellars or winery.

Weinstrasse

"Wine road." Scenic route through v'yds. Germany has several, the most famous in RHEINPFALZ.

Weintor

See Schweigen

Weissherbst

Rosé of QbA standard, speciality of BADEN and WÜRTTEMBERG.

Werner, Domdechant

Fine 32-acre family estate at HOCHHEIM.

Wiltingen Saar w. ★★→★★★★ 71 75 76 77 78

The centre of the Saar. 330 acres. Beautiful subtle austere wine. Top v'yds. incl. SCHARZHOFBERG, Braune Kupp, Braunfels, Klosterberg. Grosslage (for the whole Saar): Scharzberg.

If anything is stable in a changing world it seems to be the business of making and selling refreshment. According to The Guinness Book of the Business World seven of the twelve oldest companies on earth are either brewers or wine-growers. The oldest company is an Assyrian bank, Egibi and Son, founded in 700 BC. Then come two Bavarian breweries dating from 1040 and 1119. Sixth and seventh come Clerget-Buffet et Fils and Raoul Clerget et Fils, both wine-growers at Beaune, in Burgundy, both founded in 1270. Tenth comes the Burgerspital zum Heiligen Geist, Würzburg wine-growers, founded in 1319.

Winkel Rhg. w. ★★★→★★★★ 71 75 76 77 78

Village famous for fragrant, elegant wine, incl. SCHLOSS VOLLRADS. Other v'yds. incl. Hasensprung, Jesuitengarten. Grosslage: Hönigberg.

Wintrich M-M w. ★★→★★★★ 71 75 76 77 78

Neighbour of PIESPORT; similar wines. Top v'yds.: Grosser Herrgott, Ohligsberg, Sonnenseite. Grosslage: Kurfürstlay.

Winzergenossenschaft

Wine-growers' co-operative, often making good and reasonably priced wine.

Winzerverein

The same as the last.

Wonnegau (Bereich)

District name for S. RHEINHESSEN.

Worms Rhh. w. ★★

City with the famous LIEBFRAUENSTIFT v'yd.

Württemberg

Vast s. area with scattered v'yds. of secondary quality.

Würzburg Frank. ★★→★★★★ 71 75 76 77 78

Great baroque city on the Main, centre of Franconian (FRANKEN) wine: fine, full-bodied and dry. Top v'yds.: Stein, Leiste, Schlossberg. No Grosslage. See also Maindreieck (Bereich).

Zell M-S-R w. ★→★★ 75 76 77 78

Lower Mosel village famous for its Grosslage name Schwartze Katz ("Black Cat"). No fine wines.

Zell (Bereich)

District name for the whole lower Mosel from Zell to Koblenz.

Zeltingen-Rachtig M-M w. ⟦★★⟧ →★★★★ 71 75 76 77 78

Important Mosel village next to WEHLEN. Typically lively but full-bodied wine. Top v'yds.: Sonnenuhr, Schlossberg. Grosslage: Münzlay.

Switzerland

Switzerland has some of the world's most efficient and productive vineyards. Costs are high and nothing less is viable. All the most important are lined along the south-facing slopes of the upper Rhône valley and Lake Geneva, respectively the Valais and the Vaud. Wines are known both by place-names, grape-names, and legally controlled type-names. All three, with those of leading growers and merchants, appear in the following list. On the whole, D.Y.A.

Aigle   Vaud w. dr. ★★
> Principal town of CHABLAIS, between La. Geneva and the VALAIS. Dry whites of transitional style: at best strong and well balanced.

Amigne
> Traditional white grape of the VALAIS. Heavy but tasty wine, usually made dry.

Arvine
> Another old VALAIS white grape, similar to the last; perhaps better. Makes good dessert wine.

Auvernier   Neuchâtel r. p. w. dr. (sp.) ★★
> Village s. of NEUCHÂTEL known for PINOT NOIR, CHASSELAS and ŒIL DE PERDRIX.

Blauburgunder
> One of the names given to the form of PINOT NOIR grown in German Switzerland.

Bonvin
> Old-established growers and merchants at SION.

Chablais   Vaud (r.) w. dr. ★★
> The district between Montreux on La. Geneva and Martigny where the Rhône leaves the VALAIS. Good DORIN wines. Best villages: AIGLE, YVORNE, Bex.

Chasselas
> The principal white grape of Switzerland, neutral in flavour but taking local character. Known as FENDANT in VALAIS, DORIN in VAUD and PERLAN round Geneva.

Clevner (or Klevner)
> Another name for BLAUBURGUNDER.

Cortaillod   Neuchâtel r. (p. w.) ★★
> Village near NEUCHÂTEL specializing in light PINOT NOIR reds.

Côte, La
> The n. shore of La. Geneva between Geneva and Lausanne. Pleasant DORIN and SALVAGNIN. Best villages incl. Féchy and Rolle.

Dézaley Vaud w. dr. ★★★

Best-known village of LAVAUX, between Lausanne and Montreux. Steep s. slopes to the lake make fine fruity DORIN. Dézaley-Marsens is equally good.

Domaine Château Lichten

Property making first-class VALAIS wines at Loèche Ville.

Dôle Valais r. ★★

Term for red VALAIS wine of PINOT NOIR or GAMAY or both grapes, reaching a statutory level of strength and quality.

Dorin Vaud w. dr. ★→★★

The name for CHASSELAS wine in the VAUD, the equivalent of FENDANT from the VALAIS.

Epesses Vaud w. dr. ★★

Well-known lakeside village of LAVAUX. Good dry DORIN.

Ermitage

VALAIS name for white wine from MARSANNE grapes. Rich, concentrated and heavy; usually dry.

Fendant Valais w. dr. ★→★★★

The name for CHASSELAS wine in the VALAIS, where it reaches its ripest and strongest. SION is the centre.

Flétri

Withered grapes for making sweet wine, often MALVOISIE.

Glacier, vin du

Almost legendary long-matured white stored at high altitudes. Virtually extinct today.

Goron Valais r. ★

Red VALAIS wine that fails to reach the DÔLE standard.

Herrschaft Grisons r. (w. sw.) ★→★★★

District near the border of Austria and Liechtenstein. Small amount of light PINOT NOIR reds and a few sweet whites.

Humagne

Rare old VALAIS grape. Some red Humagne is sold: decent country wine. Apparently there was formerly white as well.

Johannisberg

The Valais name for SYLVANER, which makes pleasant soft dry wine here.

Lavaux Vaud r. w. dr. ★→★★★

The n. shore of La. Geneva between Lausanne and Montreux. The e. half of the VAUD. Best villages incl. DÉZALEY, EPESSES, Villette, Lutry, ST-SAPHORIN.

Légèrement doux

Most Swiss wines are dry. Any with measurable sugar must be labelled thus or as "avec sucre résiduel".

Malvoisie

VALAIS name for PINOT GRIS.

Mandement Geneva r. (p.) w. dr. ★

Wine district just w. of Geneva, (see Vin-Union-Genève). Very light reds, chiefly GAMAY, and whites (PERLAN).

Marsanne

The white grape of Hermitage on the French Rhône, used in the VALAIS to make ERMITAGE.

Merlot

Bordeaux red grape (see Grapes for red wine) used to make the better wine of Italian Switzerland (TICINO). See also Viti.

Mont d'Or, Domaine du Valais w. dr. sw. ★★★★

The best wine estate of Switzerland: 60 acres of steep hillside near SION. Good FENDANT, JOHANNISBERG, AMIGNE, etc., and real Riesling. Very rich concentrated wines.

Neuchâtel Neuchâtel r. p. w. dr. sp. ★→★★★

City of n.w. Switzerland and the wine from the n. shore of its lake. Pleasant light PINOT NOIR and attractive sometimes sparkling CHASSELAS.

Nostrano

Word meaning "ours" applied to the lesser red wine of the TICINO, made from a mixture of native and Italian grapes, in contrast to MERLOT from Bordeaux.

Oeil de Perdrix

Pale rosé of PINOT NOIR.

Orsat

Important and reliable wine firm at Martigny, VALAIS.

Perlan Geneva w. dr. ★

The MANDEMENT name for the ubiquitous CHASSELAS, here at its palest, driest and least impressive.

Premier Cru

Any wine from the maker's own estate can call itself this.

Provins

One of the best-known producers of VALAIS wine.

Rèze

The grape, now rare, used for VIN DU GLACIER.

Rivaz Vaud r. w. dr. ★★

Well-known village of LAVAUX.

St-Saphorin Vaud w. dr. ★★

One of the principal villages of LAVAUX: wines drier and more austere than DÉZALEY OR EPESSES.

Salvagnin Vaud r. ★→★★

Red VAUD wine of tested quality: the equivalent of DÔLE.

Savagnin

Swiss name for the TRAMINER, called Païen in the VALAIS.

Schafiser Bern (r.) w. dr. ★→★★

The n. shore of La. Bienne (Bielersee) is well known for light CHASSELAS sold as either Schafiser or Twanner.

Sion Valais w. dr. ★→★★★

Centre of the VALAIS wine region, famous for its FENDANT.

Spätburgunder

PINOT NOIR: by far the commonest grape of German Switzerland, making very light wines.

Testuz

Well-known growers and merchants at Cully, LAVAUX.

Ticino

Italian-speaking s. Switzerland. See Merlot, Viti, Nostrano.

Twanner

See Schafiser

Valais

The Rhône valley between Brig and Martigny. Its n. side is an admirable dry sunny and sheltered v'yd., planted mainly, alas, to the second-rate CHASSELAS grape, which here makes its best wine.

Vaud

The region of La. Geneva. Its n. shore is Switzerland's biggest v'yd. and in places as good as any. DORIN and SALVAGNIN are the main wines.

Vétroz Valais (r.) w. dr. ★★

Village near SION in the best part of the VALAIS.

Vevey

Town near Montreux with a famous wine festival once every 30-odd years. The last was in 1977.

Vin-Union-Genève

Big growers' co-operative at Satigny in the MANDEMENT. Light reds and white PERLAN are Geneva's local wine.

Viti Ticino r. ★★

Legal designation of better-quality TICINO red, made of MERLOT and with at least 12% alcohol.

Yvorne

Village near AIGLE with some of the best CHABLAIS v'yds.

Italy

Italy is the world's biggest wine producer with the biggest per capita consumption: 130 bottles a year. She is so at home with wine that she can seem alarmingly casual about it. A sense of humour is as important as a corkscrew to anyone who steps off the well-beaten track.

The chief clue to Italian wine is the DOC system, an approximate equivalent of France's Appellations Controlées, which has been taking shape since the 1960s. Most of Italy's worthwhile wines now have defined areas and standards under the new system. A few, like Chianti Classico, it must be said, had them long before. A few, however, have not—and DOCs have been granted to many areas of only local interest: so the mere existence of a DOC proves little. The entries in this book ignore a score of unimportant DOCs and include a score or so non-DOCs.

They also include a large number of grape-name entries. Italian wines are named in a variety of ways: some geographical like French wines, some historical, some folklorical, and many of the best from their grapes. These include old "native" grapes such as Barbera and Sangiovese and more and more imported "international" grapes from France and Germany. Many of the DOCs, particularly in the north-east, are area names applying to widely different wines from as many as a dozen different varieties. No overall comment on the quality of such a diversity is really possible, except to say that general standards are rising steadily and a small number of producers are emerging as outstanding by international standards.

Another rather disconcerting aspect of Italian wine is clear from the following pages: in many cases the same name applies to wine which can be red or white or in between, sweet or dry or in between, still or sparkling or in between. This must be taken into account when interpreting the necessarily cryptic grades of quality and vintage notes. Vintage notes are given when specific information has been available. Where there is no comment the best plan is to aim for the youngest available white wine and experiment with the oldest available red . . . within reason.

The map is the key to the province names used for locating each entry.

Abbreviations of province names shown in bold type are used in the text.

The following abbreviations are used in the Italian section
Pa.   passito
Pr.   Province
Com.   commune
f.   fortified
See also key to symbols opposite
Contents

Abboccato
Semi-sweet.

Aglianico del Vulture Bas. DOC r. (s/sw. sp.) ✶✶✶ 75 77
Among the best wines of s. Italy. Ages well. Called Vecchio after 3 yrs., Riserva after 5 yrs.

Alba
Major wine-centre of PIEMONTE.

Albana di Romagna Em-Ro. DOC w. dr. s/sw. (sp.) ✶✶ 76 77
Produced for several centuries in Romagna from Albana grapes. The dry slightly tannic, the semi-sweet fruity.

Aleatico
Red muscat-flavoured grape.

Most Italian wines have a simple name, in contrast to the combination village and vineyard names of France and Germany.

> SOAVE
> CLASSICO
>
> VINO A DENOMINAZIONE DI
> ORIGINE CONTROLLATA
>
> IMBOTTIGLIATO DAL
> PRODUTTORE ALL'ORIGINE
> CANTINA SOCIALE DI SOAVE

Soave is the name of this wine. It is qualified only by the word Classico, a legal term for the central (normally the best) part of many of the long-established wine regions.
"Denominazione di Origine Controllata" is the official guarantee of authenticity. Imbottigliato . . . all origine means bottled by the producer. Cantina Sociale di Soave means the growers' co-operative of Soave.

Aleatico di Gradoli Lat. DOC r. sw. or f. ✶✶
Aromatic, fresh, fruity, alcohol 12–15%, made in the Pr. of Viterbo.

Aleatico di Puglia Apu. DOC r. sw. or f. ✶✶
Aleatico grapes make good dessert wine over a large area. 14% alcohol or more, aromatic and full.

Allegrini
Well-known producers of Valpolicella and other Veronese wines.

Alto Adige Tr-AAd. DOC r. p. w. dr. sw. sp. ✶✶
A DOC covering some 17 different wines named after their grape varieties in 33 villages round Bolzano.

Amabile
Semi-sweet, but usually sweeter than ABBOCCATO.

Amaro Bitter.

Amarone
See Recioto

Antinori
A long-established Tuscan house of repute producing CHIANTI and ORVIETO.

Asti
Major wine-centre of PIEMONTE.

Asti Spumante Piem. DOC w. sp. ✶✶✶ NV
Famous sweet and very fruity muscat sparkling wine. Low in alcohol.

Badia a Coltibuono
Fine Chianti-maker at Gaiole with a restaurant and remarkable collection of old vintages.

Barbacarlo (Oltrepo' Pavese) Lomb. DOC r. dr. or sw. ✶✶ 73 76 77
Delicately flavoured with bitter after-taste, made in the Com. of Broni in the Pr. of Pavia.

Barbaresco Piem. DOC r. dr. ∗∗∗ 68 69 70 71 74
>   Neighbour of BAROLO from the same grapes but lighter, ageing sooner. At best subtle and fine. At 3 yrs. becomes Riserva.

Barbera
>   Dark acidic red grape, a speciality of Piemonte also used in Lombardy, Veneto, Friuli and other n. provinces. Its best wines are:

Barbera d'Alba Piem. DOC r. dr. ∗∗ 71 73 74
>   Round ALBA other grapes are added. Clean, tasty, fragrant red improves for 3–4 yrs.

Barbera d'Asti Piem. DOC r. dr. (s/sw.) ∗∗ 71 73 74
>   The best of the Barberas; all Barbera grapes; dark, grapy and appetizing. Ages up to 7–8 yrs.

Barbera del Monferrato Piem. DOC r. dr. (s/sw.) ∗ 73 74 76 77
>   From a large area in the Pr. of Alessandria and ASTI. Pleasant, slightly fizzy, sometimes sweetish.

Bardolino Ven. DOC r. dr. (p.) ∗∗ D.Y.A.
>   Pale, light, slightly bitter red from e. shore of La. Garda. Sometimes quickly taken off the skins to make v. pale B. Chiaretto.

Barolo Piem. DOC r. dr. ∗∗∗ 65 67 68 70 71 74
>   Small area s. of Turin with one of the best Italian red wines, dark, rich, alcoholic (minimum 12°), dry but deep in flavour. From NEBBIOLO grapes. Ages for up to 15 yrs.

Bertani
>   Well-known producers of quality Veronese wines (VAL-POLICELLA, SOAVE, etc.).

Bertolli, Francesco
>   Among the best-known producers of CHIANTI CLASSICO. Cellars at Castellina in Chianti, n. of Siena.

Bianco
>   White.

Bianco di Pitigliano Tusc. DOC w. dr ∗ D.Y.A.
>   A soft, fruity, lively wine made near Grosseto.

Bigi
>   Famous producers of ORVIETO and other wines of Umbria and Tuscany.

Biondi-Santi
>   One of the leading producers of BRUNELLO with cellars in Montalcino (Siena).

Boca Piem. DOC r. dr. ∗∗ 69 70 71 74 75 76
>   From same grape as BAROLO in n. of PIEMONTE, Pr. of Novara.

Bolla
>   Famous Veronese firm producing VALPOLICELLA, SOAVE, etc.

Bonarda
>   Minor red grape widely grown in PIEMONTE and Lombardy.

Bonarda (Oltrepo' Pavese) Lomb. DOC r. dr. ∗∗ 73 74 75 76 77
>   Soft, fresh, pleasant red from s. of Pavia.

Bosca
>   Wine-producers from PIEMONTE known for their ASTI SPUMANTE and Vermouths.

Botticino Lomb. DOC r. dr. ∗ 73 74 76 77
>   Strong, full-bodied red from Brescia.

Brachetto d'Acqui Piem. DOC r. sw. (sp.) ∗ 71 74 76
>   Sweet sparkling red with pleasant muscat aroma.

Brolio
>   The oldest (c. 1200) and most famous CHIANTI CLASSICO estate.

Brunello di Montalcino Tusc. DOC r. dr. ∗∗∗∗ 64 66 67 70 73 75 77
>   Italy's most expensive wine. Strong, full-bodied, high-flavoured and long-lived. After 5 yrs. is called Riserva. Produced for over a century 15 miles s. of Siena.

Cabernet

Bordeaux grape much used in n.e. Italy. See place names, e.g.:

Cabernet di Pramaggiore Ven. DOC r. dr. ** 73 75 77

Good, herb-scented, rather tannic, middle-weight red. Riserva after 3 yrs.

Calcinaia

First-class CHIANTI CLASSICO estate for centuries in the Caponi family.

Caldaro or Lago di Caldaro Tr-AAd. DOC r. dr. ** 74 75 76 77

Light, soft, slightly bitter-almond red. Classico from a smaller area is better. From s. of Bolzano.

Calissano

A long-established House of PIEMONTE producing ASTI SPUMANTE, Vermouths and red wines of that region.

Caluso Passito Piem. DOC w. sw. (f.) ** 70 71 74 75

Made from selected Erbaluce grapes left to partly dry; delicate scent, velvety taste. From a large area in the Pr. of Turin and Vercelli.

Cannonau di Sardegna Sard. DOC r. dr. or s/sw. (f.) ** 72 73 74 76 77

One of the good wines of the island capable of ageing.

Cantina

1. Cellar or winery. 2. Cantina Sociale = growers' co-op.

Capena Lat. DOC w. dr. s/sw ★ D.Y.A.

A sound wine for daily drinking from n. of Rome.

Capri

Widely abused name of the famous island in the Bay of Naples. No guarantee of quality.

Carema Piem. DOC r. dr. ** 71 73 74 75

Old speciality of Val d'Aosta. NEBBIOLO grapes fermented Beaujolais-style before crushing. (See France: Macération carbonique.)

Carmignano Tusc. DOC r. dr. **→ [★★★]

Section of CHIANTI using CABERNET to make good wine.

Casa fondata nel ...

Firm founded in ...

Castel del Monte Apu. DOC r. p. w. dr. ** 73 74 75 76 77

Dry, fresh, well-balanced southern wines. The red becomes Riserva after 3 yrs.

Castel S. Michele

A good red made of Cabernet and Merlot grapes by the Trentino Agricultural College near Trento.

CAVIT

CAntina VITicultori, a second degree co-operative (a co-operative of co-operatives) near Trento, producing large quantities of table wine.

Cellatica Lomb. DOC r. dr. ** 73 75 76 77

Light red with slightly bitter after-taste, from the Pr. of Brescia.

Cerveteri Lat. DOC w. dr. ★

Sound wines produced n.w. of Rome between Lake Bracciano and the Tyrrhenian Sea.

Chianti Tusc. DOC r. dr. [★★] 71 74 75 76 77

The lively local wine of Florence. Fresh but warmly fruity when young, usually sold in straw-covered flasks. Ages moderately. Montalbano, Rufina and Colli Fiorentini, Senesi, Aretini, Colline Pisane are sub-districts.

Chianti Classico Tusc. DOC r. dr. [★★★] 70 71 74 75 76 77

Senior Chianti from the central area. Many estates make fine powerful scented wine. Riservas (after 3 yrs.) often have the bouquet of age in oak.

Cinque Terre Lig. DOC w. dr. or sw. or pa. ★★★
  Fragrant, fruity white made for centuries near La Spezia. The PASSITO is known as Sciacchetra.

Cinzano
  A Vermouth company also known for its ASTI SPUMANTE from PIEMONTE.

Ciro Cal. DOC r. (p. w.) dr. ★★ 71 73 74 75 77
  The wine of the ancient Olympic games. Very strong red, fruity white (to drink young).

Classico
  Term for wines from a restricted, usually central, area within the limits of a DOC. By implication, and often in practice, the best of the region.

Clastidio Lomb. r. (p.) w. dr. ★★ 71 73 74 75 76 77
  Pleasant, sour touch to the white. Full, slightly tannic to the red.

Collavini, Cantina
  High-quality producers of GRAVE DEL FRIULI wines: PINOT GRIGIO, RIESLING, MERLOT, PINOT NERO, etc.

Colli
  Means "hills" in many wine-names.

Colli Albani Lat. DOC w. dr. or s/sw. (sp.) ★★ 76 77
  Soft fruity wine of the Roman hills.

Colli Euganei Ven. DOC r. w. dr. or s/sw. (sp.) ★★ 73 75 76 77
  A DOC applicable to 3 wines produced s.w. of Padua. The red is scarcely memorable, the white soft and pleasant. The table wine of Venice.

Colli Orientali del Friuli Fr-VG. DOC r. w. dr. or sw. ★ 73 74 75 77
  12 different wines are produced under this DOC on the hills e. of Udine and named after their grapes.

Collio Goriziano Fr-VG. DOC r. w. dr. ★★ 72 74 76 77
  Ten different wines named after their grapes from a small area w. of Gorizia nr. the Yugoslav border.

Contratto
  Piemonte firm known for BAROLO, ASTI SPUMANTE, etc.

Cora
  A leading House producing ASTI SPUMANTE and Vermouth from PIEMONTE.

Cori Lat DOC w. r. dr./sw. ★
  Soft and well-balanced wines made 30 miles s. of Rome, in the province of Latina.

Cortese di Gavi Piem. DOC w. dr. (sp.) ★★ D.Y.A.
  Delicate fresh white from between Alessandria and Genoa.

Cortese (Oltrepo' Pavese) Lomb. DOC w. dr. ★ D.Y.A.
  The same from w. Lombardy.

Corvo Sic. r. w. dr. ★★
  Popular Sicilian wines. Sound dry red, pleasant soft white.

D'Ambra
  Well-known producer of Elba and other wines of that island.

Dolce Sweet.

Dolceacqua
  See Rossese di Dolceacqua

Dolcetto
  Common red grape of PIEMONTE, giving its name to:

Dolcetto d'Acqui Piem. DOC r. dr. ★ D.Y.A.
  Good standard table wine from s. of ASTI.

Dolcetto d'Alba Piem. DOC r. dr. ★★ 71 74
  Among the best Dolcetti, with a trace of bitter-almond.

Dolcetto d'Asti Piem. DOC r. dr. ★ D.Y.A.

Donnaz Vd'A. DOC dr. ★★
  A mountain NEBBIOLO, fragrant, pale and faintly bitter. Aged for a statutory 3 yrs.

Donnici Cal. DOC r. (p.) dr. ★

Middle-weight southern red from Cosenza.

Elba Tusc. r. w. dr. (sp.) ☆ ★ 71 73 76 77

The island's white is better: admirable with fish.

Enfer d'Arvier Vd'A. DOC r. dr. ★★

An Alpine speciality: pale, pleasantly bitter, light red.

Enoteca

Italian for "wine library", of which there are many in the country, the most comprehensive being the Enoteca Italica Permanente of Siena.

Erbaluce di Caluso Piem. DOC w. dr. ★ 74 75 76

Pleasant fresh hot-weather wine.

Est! Est!! Est!!! Lat. DOC w. dr. or s/sw. ★★ D.Y.A.

Famous soft fruity white from La. Bolsena, n. of Rome. The name is more remarkable than the wine.

Etna Sic. DOC r. p. w. dr. ☆★★ 70 73 74 75 77

Wine from the volcanic slopes. The red is warm, full, balanced and ages very well; the white is delicate and distinctly grapy.

Fabiano

Producers of Veronese wines with cellars in Sona, near Verona.

Falerio dei Colli Ascolani Mar. DOC w. dr. ★

Made in the Pr. of Ascoli Piceno, pleasant, fresh, fruity; a wine for the summer.

Falerno Camp. r. w. dr. ★

One of the best-known wines of ancient times, but nothing special today. Strong red, fruity white.

Fara

Piem. DOC r. dr. ★★ 70 71 74 75 76

Good NEBBIOLO wine from Novara, n. PIEMONTE. Fragrant; worth ageing. Small production.

Faro Sic. r. dr. ★★ 73 75 77

Sound strong Sicilian red, made in sight of the Straits of Messina.

Fazi-Battaglia

Well-known producer of VERDICCHIO, etc.

Ferrari

Firm making Italy's best dry sparkling wine by the champagne method nr. Trento, Trentino-Alto Adige.

Folonari

Leading producers of quality Veronese wines as well as other table wines from various parts of Italy.

Fontana Candida

One of the best producers of FRASCATI.

Fontanafredda

Leading producer of Piemontese wines, incl. BAROLO.

Fracia Lomb. DOC r. dr. ★★ 71 73 75 76

Good light but fragrant red from Valtellina.

Franciacorta Pinot Lomb. DOC w. dr. (sp.) ★★

Agreeable soft white made of PINOT BIANCO.

Franciacorta Rosso Lomb. DOC r. dr. ★★ 73 74 75 76 77

Lightish red of mixed CABERNET and BARBERA from Brescia.

Frascati Lat. DOC w. dr. s/sw. sw. (sp.) ★★ 75

Best-known wine of the Roman hills: soft, ripe, golden, tasting of whole grapes. The sweet is known as Cannellino.

Frecciarossa Lomb. r. w. dr. ★★ 70 71 73 76 77

Sound wines produced nr. Casteggio in the Oltrepo' Pavese; the white is better known.

Freisa d'Asti Piem. DOC r. s/sw. or sw. (sp.) ★★ 70 71 73 74

Sweet, often sparkling red, said to taste of raspberries and roses.

Frizzante

Semi-sparkling or "pétillant", a word used to describe wines such as LAMBRUSCO.

Gambellara Ven. DOC w. dr. or s/sw. (sp.) ⋆ 72 75 76 77

Neighbour of SOAVE. Dry wine similar. Sweet (known as RECIOTO DI GAMBELLARA), agreeably fruity.

Gancia

Famous Vermouth House from PIEMONTE, also produces ASTI SPUMANTE.

Gattinara Piem. DOC r. dr. ⌜ ⋆⋆⋆ ⌝ 69 70 74 75 76

Excellent big-scale BAROLO-type red from n. PIEMONTE. Made from NEBBIOLO, locally known as Spanna.

Gavi Piem. w. dr. ⋆⋆→ ⋆⋆⋆

At best almost burgundian dry white. Gavi dei Gavi from Rovereto di Gavi Ligure is best. Needs two or three years aging.

Ghemme Piem. DOC r. dr. ⋆⋆ 70 71 73 74

Neighbour of GATTINARA, a shade less full and fine.

Giacobazzi

Well-known producers of Lambrusco wines with cellars in Nonantola and Sorbara, near Modena.

Giacosa, Bruno

Old family business making excellent Barolo and other Piemonte wines at Neive (Cuneo).

Gradi

Degrees (of alcohol) i.e. percent by volume.

Grave del Friuli Fr-VG. DOC r. w. dr. ⋆⋆ 73 75 76 77

A DOC covering 7 different wines named after their grapes, from near the Yugoslav border.

Greco di Tufo Camp. DOC w. dr. s/sw. ⋆⋆ 74 75 76 77

One of the best whites of the south, fruity and slightly bitter.

Grignolino d'Asti Piem. DOC r. dr. ⋆ 73 74 76

Pleasant lively standard wine of PIEMONTE.

Grumello Lomb. DOC r. dr. ⋆⋆ 71 73 75 76

NEBBIOLO wine from Valtellina, can be delicate and fine.

Gutturnio dei Colli Piacentini Em-Ro. DOC r. dr. (s/sw.) ⋆⋆ 64 70 71 74 77

Full-bodied wine of character from the hills of Piacenza. Named after a large Roman drinking cup.

Inferno Lomb. DOC r. dr. ⌜ ⋆⋆ ⌝ 70 73 75 76

Similar to GRUMELLO and like it classified as VALTELLINA Superiore.

Ischia Camp. DOC (r.) w. dr. ⋆ 71 75 77

The wine of the island off Naples. The slightly sharp white is best; ideal with fish.

Isonzo Fr-VG. DOC r. w. dr. ⋆

DOC covering 10 varietal wines in the extreme n.e.

Kalterersee German name for LAGO DI CALDARO.

Kretzer

German term for rosé used in the Italian Tyrol.

Lacrima Cristi del Vesuvio Camp. r. p. w. (f.) dr. (sw.) ⋆ 73 74 77

Famous but frankly ordinary wines in great variety from the slopes of Mount Vesuvius.

Lago di Caldaro

See Caldaro

Lagrein del Trentino Tr-AAd. DOC r. dr. ⋆⋆ 74 75 76 77

Lagrein is a Tyrolean grape with a bitter twist. Good fruity light wine.

Lamberti

Producers of SOAVE, VALPOLICELLA and BARDOLINO at Lazise on the e. shore of La. Garda.

Lambrusco di Sorbara Em-Ro. DOC r. dr. or s/sw. sp. ★★★ 75 76 77
  Bizarre but popular fizzy red from near Modena.

Lambrusco Grasparossa di Castelvetro Em-Ro. DOC r. dr. or s/sw. sp. ★★ 75 76 77
  Similar to above. Highly scented, pleasantly acidic; often drunk with rich food.

Lambrusco Salamino di Santa Croce Em-Ro. DOC r. dr. or s/sw. sp. ★ 75
  Similar to above. Fruity smell, high acidity and a thick "head".

Langhe
  The hills of central PIEMONTE.

Latisana Fr-VG. DOC r. w. dr. ★★
  DOC for 7 varietal wines from some 50 miles n.e. of Venice.

Lessona Piem. DOC r. d. ★
  Full-bodied wine produced in the province of Vercelli from Nebbiolo grapes.

Liquoroso
  Strong and usually sweet, e.g. like Tuscan Vinsanto.

Locorotondo Apu. DOC w. dr. ★ D.Y.A.
  A pleasantly fresh southern white.

Lugana Lomb. DOC w. dr. ★★★ 76 77 78
  One of the best white wines of s. La. Garda: fragrant and delicate.

Lungarotti
  Leading producers of TORGIANO wine, with cellars and an outstanding Wine Museum near Perugia.

Malvasia
  Important white or red grape for luscious wines, incl. Madeira's Malmsey. Used all over Italy.

Malvasia di Bosa Sard. DOC w. dr. sw. or f. ★★
  A wine of character. Strong and aromatic with a slightly bitter after-taste. A liquoroso (fortified) version is best.

Malvasia di Cagliari Sard. DOC w. dr. s/sw. or sw. (f. dr. s.) ★★
  Interesting strong Sardinian wine, fragrant and slightly bitter.

Malvasia di Casorzo d'Asti Piem. DOC r. p. sw. sp. ★★ 71 74 76
  Fragrant grapy sweet red, sometimes sparkling.

Malvasia di Castelnuovo Don Bosco Piem. DOC r. sw. (sp.) ★★
  Peculiar method of interrupted fermentation gives very sweet aromatic red.

Malvasia delle Lipari Sic. DOC w. sw. (pa. f.) ★★★ 73 76 77
  Among the very best Malvasias, aromatic and rich, produced on the Lipari or Aeolian Islands n. of Sicily.

Malvasia di Nus Vd'A. w. dr. ★★★
  Rare Alpine white, with a deep bouquet of honey. Small production and high reputation. Can age remarkably well.

Mamertino Sic. w. s/sw. ★★ 73 74 75 76 77
  Made near Messina since Roman times. Sweet-scented, rich in glycerine. Mentioned several times by Caesar in *De Bello Gallico*.

Manduria (Primitivo di) Apu. DOC r. s/sw. (f. dr. or sw.) ★★
  Heady red, naturally strong but often fortified. From nr. Taranto. Primitivo is a southern grape.

Mantonico Cal. w. sw. f. ★★
  Fruity deep amber dessert wine from Reggio Calabria. Can age remarkably well. Named from the Greek for "prophetic".

Marino Lat. DOC w. dr. or s/sw. ★ 76 77 78
  A neighbour of FRASCATI with similar wine.

Marsala Sic. DOC br. dr. s/sw. or sw. f. ∗∗∗ NV
> Dark sherry-type wine invented by the Woodhouse Brothers from Liverpool in 1773; excellent apéritif or for dessert. The dry ("virgin") made by the solera system.

Marsala Speciali
> These are Marsalas with added flavours of egg, almond, strawberry, etc.

Martinafranca Apu. DOC w. dr. ∗ D.Y.A.
> Agreeable but rather neutral southern white.

Martini & Rossi
> Well-known vermouth House also famous for its fine wine museum in Pessione, PIEMONTE.

Marzemino (del Trentino) Tr.-AAd. DOC r. dr. ∗ 74 75 76 77
> Pleasant local red of Trento. Fruity fragrance; slightly bitter taste.

Masi, Cantina
> Well-known specialist producers of VALPOLICELLA, RECIOTO, SOAVE, etc., incl. fine red Campo Fiorin.

Mastroberardino
> Leading wine-producer of Campania, incl. TAURASI and LACRIMA CRISTI DEL VESUVIO.

Meleto
> Another CHIANTI CLASSICO estate of Barone Ricasoli, proprietor of the famous BROLIO.

Melini
> Long-established and important producers of CHIANTI CLASSICO at Pontassieve. Inventors of the standard *fiasco*, or litre flask.

Melissa Cal. r. dr. ∗∗ 74 75 77
> Mostly made from Gaglioppo grapes in the Pr. of Catanzaro. Delicate, balanced, ages rather well.

Meranese di Collina Tr-AAd. DOC r. dr. ∗ 75 76 77
> Light red of Merano, known in German as Meraner.

Merlot
> Adaptable red Bordeaux grape widely grown in n.e. Italy and elsewhere.

Merlot (del Trentino) Tr-AAd. DOC r. dr. ⌐∗⌐ 74 75 76
> Full flavour, slightly grassy scent, improves for 2–3 yrs.

Merlot di Aprilia Lat. DOC r. dr. ∗ 75 77
> Harsh at first, softer after 2–3 yrs.

Merlot Colli Berici Ven. DOC r. dr. ∗ D.Y.A.
> Pleasantly light and soft.

Merlot Colli Orientali del Friuli Fr-VG. DOC r. dr. ∗
> Pleasant herby character, best at 2–3 yrs.

Merlot Collio Goriziano Fr-VG. DOC r. dr. ∗
> Grassy scent, slightly bitter taste. Best at 2–3 yrs.

Merlot Grave del Friuli Fr-VG. DOC r. dr. ∗
> Pleasant light wine, best at 1–2 yrs.

Merlot del Piave Ven. DOC r. dr. ∗∗ 71 72 75 77
> Sound tasty red, best at 2–3 yrs.

Merlot (Isonzo) Fr-VG. DOC r. dr. ∗
> A DOC in Gorizia. Dry, herby, agreeable wine.

Merlot di Pramaggiore Ven. DOC r. dr. ∗∗ 74 75 76 77
> A cut above other Merlots; improves in bottle. Riserva after 3 yrs.

Monica di Cagliari Sard. DOC r. dr. or sw. (f. dr. or sw.) ∗ 72 73 77
> Strong spicy red, often fortified. Monica is a Sardinian grape.

Monica di Sardegna Sard. DOC r. sw. ∗ NV
> Commoner form of above, not fortified.

Montecarlo Tusc. DOC w. dr. ∗∗ D.Y.A.
> One of Tuscany's best whites, smooth and delicate. From near Lucca.

Montecompatri-Colonna Lat. DOC w. dr. or s/sw. ★
    A neighbour of FRASCATI. Similar wine.

Montepaldi
    Well-known producers and merchants of CHIANTI CLASSICO at
    San Casciano Val di Pesa. Owned by the Corsini family.

Montepulciano d'Abruzzo Abr&M. DOC r. p. dr. ★★★ 73 74 75 77
    One of Italy's best reds, from Adriatic coast round Pescara.
    Soft, slightly tannic, reminiscent of MARSALA when aged. Best
    from Francavilla al Mare, Sulmona, Pratola Peligna.

Monterosso (Val d'Arda) Em-Ro. DOC w. dr. or sw. (sp.) ★ D.Y.A.
    Agreeable and fresh minor white from Piacenza.

Moscato
    Fruitily fragrant grape grown all over Italy.

Moscato d'Asti Piem. DOC w. sw. sp. ★ NV
    Low-strength sweet fruity sparkler made in bulk. ASTI
    SPUMANTE is the superior version.

Moscato dei Colli Euganei Ven. DOC w. sw. (sp.) ★★ 75 77
    Golden wine, fruity and smooth, from nr. Padua.

Moscato Naturale d'Asti Piem. DOC w. sw. ★ D.Y.A.
    The light and fruity base wine for Moscato d'Asti.

Moscato di Noto Sic. DOC w. s/sw. or sw. or sp. or f. ★ NV
    Light sweet still and sparkling versions, or strong Liquoroso.
    Noto is near Siracuse.

Moscato (Oltrepo' Pavese) Lomb. DOC w. sw. (sp.) ★★ 76 77 78
    The Lombardy equivalent of Moscato d'Asti.

Moscato di Pantelleria Sic. DOC w. sw. (sp.) (f. pa.) ★★★
    Italy's best muscat, from the island of Pantelleria close to the
    Tunisian coast; rich, fruity and aromatic. Ages well.

Moscato di Siracusa Sic. DOC w. sw. ★★ NV
    Strong amber dessert wine from Siracuse. Can be superb.

Moscato di Sorso Sennori Sard. DOC w. sw. (f.) ★
    Strong golden dessert wine from Sassari, n. Sardinia.

Moscato di Trani Apu. DOC w. sw. or f. ★ 74 76 77
    Another strong golden dessert wine, sometimes fortified,
    with "bouquet of faded roses".

Moscato (Trentino) Tr-AAd. DOC w. sw. ★
    Typical muscat: high strength for the north.

Nasco di Cagliari Sard. DOC w. dr. or sw. (f. dr. or sw.) ★ 72 73 74
    Sardinian speciality, delicate bouquet, light bitter taste, high
    alcoholic content.

Nebbiolo
    The best red grape of PIEMONTE and Lombardy.

Nebbiolo d'Alba Piem. DOC r. dr. s/sw. (sp.) ★★ 74 76 77
    Like light-weight BAROLO; often good. Barolo that fails to
    reach the statutory 12° alcohol is sold under this name. Some
    prefer it so.

Negri, Nino
    Famous house of VALTELLINA known for its excellent reds.

Nipozzano, Castello di
    The most important CHIANTI producer outside the Classico
    zone, to the n. near Florence.

Nuraghe Majore Sard. w. dr. ★★ D.Y.A.
    North Sardinian white: delicate, fresh, among the best wines
    of the island.

Nuragus di Cagliari Sard. DOC w. dr. ★ 72 73 74 77
    Lively Sardinian white, not too strong.

Oliena Sard. r. dr. ★★
    Interesting strong fragrant red; a touch bitter.

Oltrepo' Pavese Lomb. DOC r. w. dr. sw. sp. ★→★★
    DOC applicable to 7 wines produced in the Pr. of Pavia,
    named after their grapes. The name means the part of Pavia
    beyond the river Po.

Orvieto   Umb. DOC w. dr. or s/sw. $\boxed{**\rightarrow***}$ 75 77 78

The classical Umbrian golden-white, smooth and substantial. O. Classico is superior.

Ostuni   Apu. DOC w. dr. **

Rather delicate, dry, balanced; produced in the Pr. of Brindisi.

Parrina   Tusc. r. or w. dr. ** D.Y.A.

Light red and fresh appetizing white from n. Tuscany.

Passito

Strong sweet wine from grapes dried either in the sun or indoors.

Per' e' Palummo   Camp. r. dr. **

Excellent red produced on the island of Ischia; delicate, slightly grassy, a bit tannic, balanced.

Piave   DOC r. or w. dr. ** 75 76 77

DOC covering 4 wines, 2 red and 2 white, named after their grapes.

Pieropan

Outstanding producers of SOAVE.

Picolit (Colli Orientali del Friuli)   Fr-VG. DOC w. s/sw. or sw. **** 64 69 71 71 72 73 74 75 77

Known as Italy's Château d'Yquem. Delicate bouquet, well balanced, high alcoholic content. Ages very well.

Piemonte

The most important Italian region for quality wine. Turin is the capital, Asti the wine-centre. See Barolo, Barbera, Grignolino, Moscato, etc.

Pinot Bianco

Good rather neutral grape popular in n.e., good for sparkling wine.

Pinot Bianco (dei Colli Berici)   Ven. DOC w. dr. **

Straight satisfying dry white.

Pinot Bianco (Colli Orientali del Friuli)   Fr-VG. DOC w. dr. ** 75 76 77

Good white; smooth rather than showy.

Pinot Bianco (Collio Goriziano)   Fr-VG. DOC w. dr. ** 76 77 78

Similar to the above.

Pinot Bianco (Grave del Friuli)   Fr-VG. DOC w. dr. **

Same again.

Pinot Grigio

Tasty, low-acid white grape popular in n.e.

Pinot Grigio (Collio Goriziano)   Fr-VG. DOC w. dr. ** 76 77 78

Fruity, soft, agreeable dry white. The best age well.

Pinot Grigio (Grave del Friuli)   Fr-VG. DOC w. dr. ** 75 76 77

Hardly distinguishable from the above.

Pinot Grigio (Oltrepo' Pavese)   Lomb. DOC w. dr. (sp.) $\boxed{**}$ 74 75 77

Lombardy's P.G. is considered best.

Pinot Nero Trentino   Tr-AAd. DOC r. dr. $\boxed{**}$ 73 75 76 77

Pinot Nero (Noir) gives lively burgundy-scented light wine in much of n.e. Italy, incl. Trentino.

Pio Cesare

A producer of quality red wines of PIEMONTE, incl. outstanding BAROLO.

Primitivo di Apulia   Apu. r. dr. $\boxed{**}$

One of the best southern reds. Fruity when young, soft and full-flavoured with age. Primitivo is the grape. (See also Manduria.)

Prosecco di Conegliano   Ven. DOC w. dr. or s/sw. (sp.) *** 75 77

Popular sparkling wine of the n.e. Slight fruity bouquet, the dry pleasantly bitter, the sw. fruity; the best are known as Superiore di Cartizze. Best producer: Carpene-Malvolti.

Raboso del Piave   Ven. r. dr. ✶✶ 71 73 74 75 76
>   Powerful but sharp country red; needs age.

Ramandolo
>   See Verduzzo Colli Orientali del Friuli

Ravello   Camp. r. p. w. dr. ✶✶
>   Among the best wines of Campania: full dry red, fresh clean
>   white. Caruso is the best-known brand.

Recioto
>   Wine made of half-dried grapes. Speciality of Veneto.

Italian bottle shapes

1 Orvieto 2 Chianti 3 Verdicchio 4 Barolo

Recioto di Gambellara   Ven. DOC w. s/sw. sp. ✶
>   Sweetish golden wine, often half-sparkling.

Recioto di Soave   Ven. DOC w. s/sw. (sp.) ✶✶
>   Soave made from selected half-dried grapes; sweet, fruity,
>   fresh, slightly almondy: high alcohol.

Recioto della Valpolicella   Ven. DOC r.s/sw. sp. ✶✶ 73 74 77
>   Strong rather sweet red, sometimes sparkling. Popular in
>   Verona.

Recioto Amarone della Valpolicella   Ven. DOC r. dr. ✶✶✶✶ 64 66
68 71 74 77
>   Dry version of the above; strong concentrated flavour, rather
>   bitter. Impressive and expensive.

Refosco (Colli Orientali del Friuli)   Fr-VG. DOC r. dr. ✶✶ 74 75 77
>   Full-bodied dry red; Riserva after 2 yrs. Refosco is a grape of
>   little character.

Refosco (Grave del Friuli)   Fr-VG. DOC r. dr. ✶✶
>   Similar to above but slightly lighter.

Regaleali   Sic. w. r. p. [✶]
>   Among the better Sicilian table wines, produced between
>   Caltanissetta and Palermo.

Ribolla (Colli Orientali del Friuli)   Fr-VG. DOC w. dr. ✶ D.Y.A.
>   Clean and fruity n.e. white.

Ricasoli
>   Famous Tuscan family whose CHIANTI is named after their
>   BROLIO estate and castle.

Riesling
>   Normally refers to Italian (R. Italico). German Riesling,
>   uncommon, is R. Renano.

Riesling Italico (Collio Goriziano)   Fr-VG. DOC w. dr. ✶✶ 76 77 78
>   Pleasantly fruity, fairly full-bodied n.e. white.

Riesling (Oltrepo' Pavese)   Lomb. DOC w. dr. (sp.) ✶✶
>   The Lombardy version, quite light and fresh. Occasionally
>   sparkling. Keeps well.

Riesling (Trentino)   Tr-AAd. DOC w. dr. ✶✶ D.Y.A.
>   Delicate, slightly acid, very fruity.

Riserva
>   Wine aged for a statutory period in barrels.

Riunite
>   Cantine Sociali, a Co-operative cellar near Reggio Emilia
>   producing large quantities of Lambrusco.

Rivera

Important and reliable wine-makers at Andria, near Bari, with good red and CASTEL DEL MONTE rosé.

Riviera Rosso Stravecchio   Apu. r. dr. ** 67 70 73 74 75 76

Good dry full-bodied red from Castel del Monte. Ages well.

Riviera del Garda Chiaretto   Ven. DOC p. dr. ** D.Y.A.

Charming cherry-pink, fresh and slightly bitter, from s.w. Garda.

Riviera del Garda Rosso   Ven. DOC r. dr. ** 73 75 76 77

Red version of the above; ages surprisingly well.

Rosato

Rosé.

Rosato del Salento   Apu. DOC p. dr. * D.Y.A.

Strong but refreshing southern rosé from round Brindisi.

Rossese di Dolceacqua   Lig. DOC r. dr. ** 73 75 76

Well-known fragrant light red of the Riviera with typical touch of bitterness. Superiore is stronger.

Rosso

Red.

Rosso delle Colline Lucchesi   Tusc. DOC r. dr. ** 72 75 77

Produced round Lucca but not greatly different from CHIANTI.

Rosso Conero   Mar. DOC r. dr. ** 73 74 75 77

Substantial CHIANTI-style wine from the Adriatic coast.

Rosso Piceno   Mar. DOC r. dr. * 74 75 77

Unremarkable Adriatic red.

Rubesco

See Torgiano

Rubino di Cantavenna   Piem. DOC r. dr. **

Lively red, principally BARBERA, from a well-known co-operative s.e. of Turin.

Rufina

A sub-region of CHIANTI.

Ruffino

Well-known CHIANTI merchants.

Runchet (Valtellina)   Lomb. DOC r. dr. **

Small production, soft bouquet, slightly tannic, drink relatively young.

Sangiovese

Principal red grape of CHIANTI, used alone for:

Sangiovese d'Aprilia   Lat. DOC p. dr. * 74 75 77

Strong dry rosé from s. of Rome.

Sangiovese di Romagna   Em-Ro. DOC r. dr. ** 75

Pleasant standard red; gains character with a little age.

Sangue di Giuda (Oltrepo' Pavese)   Lomb. DOC r. dr. **

"Judas' blood": Strong rather tannic red of w. Lombardy.

San Severo   Apu. DOC r. p. w. dr. * 74 75 77

Sound neutral southern wine; not particularly strong.

Santa Maddalena   Tr-AAd. DOC r. dr. ** 71 73 75

Perhaps the best Tyrolean red. Round and warm, slightly almondy. From Bolzano.

Sassella

A CHIANTI CLASSICO estate of Melini producing an excellent single vineyard wine.

Sassella (Valtellina)   Lomb. DOC r. dr. *** 71 73 75

Considerable NEBBIOLO wine, tough when young. Known since Roman times, mentioned by Leonardo da Vinci.

Sassicaia   Tusc. D.O.C. r. dr. ****

Perhaps Italy's best red wine, produced in the Tenuta San Guido of the Incisa family, at Bolgheri near Livorno. In the manner of first-growth claret. Tiny production.

Sauvignon

The Sauvignon Blanc: excellent white grape used in n.e.

Sauvignon (Colli Berici) Ven. DOC w. dr. ∗∗ D.Y.A.

Delicate, slightly aromatic, fresh white from near Vicenza.

Sauvignon (Colli Orientali del Friuli) Fr-VG. DOC w. dr. ∗∗ 75 77 78

Full, smooth, freshly aromatic n.e. white.

Sauvignon (Collio Goriziano) Fr-VG. DOC w. dr. ∗∗ 76 77

Very similar to the last; slightly higher alcohol.

Savuto Cal. DOC r. p. dr. ∗∗

The ancient Savuto produced in the Pr. of Cosenza and Catanzaro. Big juicy wine.

Sciacchetra d'

See Cinque Terre

Secco

Dry.

Sella & Mosca

Major Sardinian growers and merchants at Alghero.

Sforzato (Valtellina) Lomb. DOC r. dr. ∗∗∗ 67 68 70 71 75

Valtellina equivalent of RECIOTO AMARONE made with partly dried grapes. Velvety, strong, ages remarkably well. Also called Sfursat.

Sizzano Piem. DOC r. dr. ∗∗ 71 74 75 76

Attractive full-bodied red produced at Sizzano in the Pr. of Novara, mostly from NEBBIOLO.

Soave Ven. DOC w. dr. ∗∗∗ 76 77 78 D.Y.A.

Famous, if not very characterful, Veronese white. Fresh with attractive texture. Classico is more restricted and better.

Solopaca Camp. DOC r. w. dr. ∗

Comes from nr. Benevento, rather sharp when young, the white soft and fruity.

Sorni Tr-AAd. r. w. dr. ∗∗ 74 75 76

Made in the Pr. of Trento. Light, fresh and soft. Drink young.

Spanna

See Gattinara

Spumante

Sparkling.

Squinzano Apu. r. p. dr. ∗

Strong southern red from Lecce.

Stravecchio

Very old.

Sylvaner

German white grape successful in ALTO ADIGE and elsewhere.

Sylvaner (Alto Adige) Tr-AAd. DOC w. dr. ∗∗ 76 77 78

Pleasant grapy well-balanced white.

Sylvaner (Terlano) Tr-AAd. DOC w. dr. ∗∗ 76 77

Attractive lively and delicate wines.

Sylvaner (Valle Isarco) Tr-AAd. DOC w. dr. ∗∗

Similar to the last.

Taurasi Camp. DOC r. dr. ∗∗ 70 71 73 75 77

The best Campanian red, from Avellino. Bouquet of cherries. Harsh when young, improves with age. Riserva after 4 yrs.

Terlano Tr-AAd. DOC w. dr. ∗∗ 76 77 78

A DOC applicable to 6 white wines from the Pr. of Bolzano, named after their grapes. Terlaner in German.

Termeno Tr-AAd. r. w. dr. ∗∗

Village nr. Bolzano. Tramin in German, reputedly the origin of the TRAMINER. Its red is light and slightly bitter.

Teroldego Rotaliano Tr-AAd. DOC r. dr. ∗∗ 73 75 76 77

The attractive local red of Trento. Blackberry-scented, slight bitter after-taste, ages moderately.

Tignanello Tusc. r. dr. ∗∗∗

One of the new style of Bordeaux-inspired Tuscan reds, made by ANTINORI. Small production.

Tocai
>North-east Italian white grape; no relation of Hungarian or Alsace Tokay.

Tocai di Lison Ven. DOC w. dr. ** 76 77
>From Treviso, delicate smoky/fruity scent, fruity taste. Classico is better.

Tocai (Colli Berici) Ven. DOC w. dr. *
>Less character than the last.

Tocai (Grave del Friuli) Fr-VG. DOC w. dr. **
>Similar to TOCAI DI LISON, generally rather milder.

Tocai di S. Martino della Battaglia Lomb. DOC w. dr. ** D.Y.A.
>Small production s. of La. Garda. Light, slightly bitter.

Torbato Sard. w. dr. (pa.) **
>Good n. Sardinian table wine, also PASSITO of high quality.

Torgiano, Rubesco di Umb. DOC r. w. dr. *** 70 71 73 75 77
>Excellent red from near Perugia comparable with CHIANTI CLASSICO. Small production. White also good, but not as outstanding as the red.

Traminer Aromatico (Trentino) Tr-AAd. DOC w. dr. ** D.Y.A.
>Delicate, aromatic, rather soft Traminer.

Trebbiano
>The principal white grape of Tuscany and most of central Italy. Ugni Blanc in French.

A new top category, DOCG, Denominazione Controllata e Garantita, is to be added to the Italian wine classification in due course. It will be awarded only to certain wines from top-quality zones-within-zones which have been bottled and sealed with a government seal by the producer. So far no wine has been classified as DOCG. Barolo will probably be the first.

Trebbiano d'Abruzzo Abr&M. DOC w. dr. * D.Y.A.
>Gentle, rather neutral, slightly tannic. From round Pescara.

Trebbiano d'Aprilia Lat. DOC w. dr. * D.Y.A.
>Heady, mild-flavoured, rather yellow. From s. of Rome.

Trebbiano di Romagna Em-Ro. DOC w. dr or s/sw. (sp.) * 75 77 78
>Clean, pleasant white from near Bologna.

Trentino Tr-AAd. DOC r. w. dr. or sw. *→**
>DOC applicable to 10 wines named after their grapes.

Uzzano
>Fine old estate at Greve. First-class CHIANTI CLASSICO.

Valcalepio Lomb. DOC r. w. dr. * 70 74 77
>From nr. Bergamo. Pleasant red; lightly scented, fresh white.

Valdadige Tr-AAd. DOC r. w. dr. or s/sw. *
>Name for the ordinary table wines of the Adige valley—in German Etschtal.

Valgella (Valtellina) Lomb. DOC r. dr. ** 73 74 75 76
>One of the VALTELLINA NEBBIOLOS: good dry red growing nutty with age. Riserva at 4 yrs.

Valle Isarco Tr-AAd. DOC w. dr. *→**
>A DOC applicable to 5 varietal wines made n.e. of Bolzano.

Valpolicella Ven. DOC r. dr. *** 74 76 77
>Attractive light red from nr. Verona. Delicate nutty scent, slightly bitter taste. Classico more restricted; Superiore has 12% alcohol and 1 yr. of age.

Valtellina Lomb. DOC r. dr. **→***
>A DOC applicable to wines made principally from Chiavennasca (NEBBIOLO) grapes in the Pr. of Sondrio, n. Lombardy. V. Superiore is better.

Velletri Lat. DOC r. w. dr. or s/sw. **
>Agreeable Roman dry red and smooth white. Drink young.

Vendemmia
> Vintage.

Venegazzu'   Fr-VG. r. dr. ★★★
> Little-known red produced nr. Treviso. Rich bouquet, soft, warm taste, 13.5% alcohol, ages well.

Verdicchio dei Castelli di Jesi   Mar. DOC w. dr. (sp.) ★★★ D.Y.A.
> Ancient, famous and very pleasant fresh pale white from nr. Ancona. Goes back to the Etruscans. Classico is more restricted. Comes in amphora-shaped bottles.

Verdicchio di Matelica   Mar. DOC w. dr. (sp.) ★★
> Similar to the last, though less well known.

Verdiso
> Native white grape of n.e., used for PROSECCO.

Verduzzo (Colli Orientali del Friuli)   Fr-VG. DOC w. dr. s/sw. or sw. ★★
> Full-bodied white from a native grape. The sweet is called Ramandolo.

Verduzzo (Del Piave)   Ven. DOC w. dr. ★★
> Similar to the last but dry.

Vermentino   Lig. w. dr.   ★★   D.Y.A.
> The best dry white of the Riviera: good clean seafood wine made at Pietra Ligure and San Remo.

Vermentino di Gallura   Sard. DOC w. dr. ★★
> Soft, dry, rather strong white from n. Sardinia.

Vernaccia di Oristano   Sard. DOC w. dr. (f.)   ★★★   72 74 75 76 77
> Sardinian speciality, like light sherry, a touch bitter, full-bodied and interesting. Superiore with 15.5% alcohol and 3 yrs. of age.

Vernaccia di San Gimignano   Tosc. DOC w. dr. (f.) ★★ 75 77
> Distinctive strong high-flavoured wine from nr. Siena. Michelangelo's favourite.

Vernaccia di Serrapetrona   Mar. DOC r. dr. s/sw. sw. sp. ★★
> Comes from the Pr. of Macerata; aromatic bouquet, pleasantly bitter after-taste.

Vignamaggio
> Historic and beautiful CHIANTI CLASSICO estate.

Villa Terciona
> Important CHIANTI CLASSICO estate.

Vino da arrosto
> "Wine for roast meat," i.e. good dry red.

Vino da pasto
> Table wine: i.e. nothing special.

Vino Nobile di Montepulciano   Tusc. DOC r. dr. ★★★ 67 70 73 75 77
> Impressive traditional Tuscan red with bouquet and style. Aged for 3 yrs. Riserva; for 4 yrs. Riserva Speciale.

Vinsanto
> Term for certain strong sweet wines esp. in Tuscany: usually PASSITI.

Vinsanto di Gambellara   Ven. DOC w. sw. ★★
> Powerful, velvety, golden: made between Vicenza and Verona.

Vinsanto Toscano   Tusc. w. s/sw. ★★
> Made in the Pr. of Siena. Aromatic bouquet, rich and smooth. Aged in very small barrels known as Carratelli.

VPQRD
> Often found on the labels of D.O.C. wines to signify "Vini di Qualita Prodotti in Regioni Delimitate", or quality wines produced in restricted areas in accordance with E.E.C. regulations.

Zagarolo   Lat. DOC w. dr. or s/sw. ★★
> Neighbour of FRASCATI, similar wine.

Spain & Portugal

Abbreviations of regional names shown in bold type are used in the text.

The following additional abbreviations are used in the Spanish section (see p. 104):
R'a.A.   Rioja Alta
R'a.Al.   Rioja Alavesa
Res.   Reserva
g. see Vino generoso

The very finest wines of Spain and Portugal are respectively sherry and port and madeira, which have a section to themselves on pages 150 to 154.

Spain's table wines divide naturally into those from the Mediterranean climate of the centre, south and east and those from the Atlantic climate of the north and west. The former are strong and with rare exceptions dull. The latter include the very good wines of Rioja, certainly the most important quality table-wine region of the peninsula.

Rainy north-west Spain and northern Portugal make their very similar "green" wines. Central Portugal has an excellent climate for wines like full-bodied Bordeaux.

The Portuguese system of controlled appellation is old and unrealistic today: it includes areas of dwindling interest and excludes several good new areas. The Spanish system is new (since 1971) and for the moment over-optimistic, delimiting some areas of purely local interest.

The listing here includes the best and most interesting types and regions of each country, whether legally delimited or not. Geographical references (see map) are to the traditional division of Spain into the old kingdoms, and the major provinces of Portugal.

Spain

Albariño del Palacio Gal. w. dr. **

Flowery "green wine" from FEFIÑANES near Cambados, made with the Albariño grape, the best of the region.

Alella Cat. r. (p.) w. dr. or sw. **

Small demarcated region just n. of Barcelona. Makes pleasantly fresh and fruity wines in limited amounts. (See Marfil.)

Alicante Lev. r. (w.) *

Demarcated region. Its wines tend to be "earthy", high in alcohol and heavy.

Almansa Lev. r. *

Demarcated region w. of ALICANTE, producing heavy wines high in alcohol.

Aloque N. Cas. r. ⟦*⟧

A light (though not in alcohol) variety of VALDEPEÑAS, made by fermenting together red and white grapes.

Almendralejo Ext. r. w. *

Commercial wine centre of the Extremadura. Much of its produce is distilled to make the spirit for fortifying sherry.

Ampurdán

See Perelada.

Año

4° Año (or Años) means 4 years old when bottled.

Benicarló Lev. r. *

Town on the Mediterranean. Its strong red wines were formerly used for adding colour and body to Bordeaux.

Berberana, Bodegas R'a.A. r. (w. dr.) *→***

Best are the fruity, full-bodied reds: the 3° año Carta de Plata, the 5° año Carta de Oro and the smooth velvety reservas.

Bilbainas, Bodegas R'a.A. r. (p.) w. dr. sw. or sp. res. ⟦**⟧ →***

Large bodega in HARO, making a wide range of reliable wines, including "Royal Carlton" by the champagne method.

Blanco

White.

Bodega

1. a wineshop; 2. a concern occupied in the making, blending and/or shipping of wine.

Campanas, Las Nav. r. (w.) ⟦**⟧

Small wine area near Pamplona. Clarete Campanas is a sturdy red. Mature 5° año Castillo de Tiebas is like a heavy Rioja Reserva.

Cañamero Ext. w. *

Remote village near Guadalupe whose wines grow FLOR and acquire a sherry-like taste.

Caralt, Cavas Conde de Cat. sp. ***

Good sparkling wines from SAN SADURNÍ DE NOYA, made by the champagne method.

Cariñena Ara. r. (p.w.) ⟦*⟧

Demarcated region and large-scale supplier of strong wine for everyday drinking.

Carlos Primero And. Brandy ***

Spanish favourite among the more expensive and delicate brandies.

Castillo Ygay

See Marques de Murrieta.

Cava

1. an establishment making sparkling wines by the champagne method; 2. a Spanish name for such wines.

Cenicero

Wine township in the RIOJA ALTA.

Cepa

Wine or grape variety.

Chacolí Gui. (r.) w. *
> Alarmingly sharp "GREEN WINE" from the Basque coast, containing only 8% to 9% alcohol.

Champaña
> "Champagne": i.e. Spanish sparkling wine.

Cheste Lev. r. w. *
> Demarcated region inland of VALENCIA. Blackstrap wines with 13% to 15% alcohol.

Clarete
> Light red wine (occasionally dark rosé).

Codorníu, S.A. Cat. sp. `***`
> Best known of the firms in SAN SADURNÍ DE NOYA making good sparkling wines by the champagne method. Ask for the *bruto* (extra dry).

Compañía Vinícola del Norte de España (C.V.N.E.) R'a.A. r. (p.) w. dr. or sw. `**→****`
> The 3° año is among the best of young red Riojas and Monopol one of the best dry whites. Excellent red Imperial reservas.

Consejo Regulador
> Official organization for the defence, control and promotion of a DENOMINACIÓN DE ORIGEN.

Cosecha
> Crop or vintage.

Criado y embotellado por . . .
> Grown and bottled by . . .

Cumbrero
> See Montecillo, Bodegas.

Domecq Domain R'a.A. r. **
> A reliable red Rioja made by Pedro Domecq in their new bodega near Laguardia.

Denominación de origen
> Officially regulated wine region. (See introduction p. 4.)

Dulce
> Sweet.

Elaborado y añejado por . . .
> Made and aged by . . .

Elciego
> Village in the Rioja Alavesa surrounded by vineyards.

Espumoso
> Sparkling.

Fefiñanes Palacio Gal. w. res. ***
> Best of all the ALBARIÑO wines, though hardly "green", since it is aged for 2–6 years.

Ferrer, José L. Mallorca r. res. **
> His wines, made in Binisalem, are the only ones of any distinction from Mallorca.

Flor
> A wine yeast peculiar to sherry and certain other wines that oxidize slowly and tastily under its influence.

Franco-Españolas, Bodegas R'a.A. r. w. dr. or sw. res. *→***
> Reliable wines from LOGROÑO. The sweet white Diamante is a favourite in Spain.

Freixenet, S.A., Cavas Cat. sp. `**→****`
> Cava, next in size to CODORNIU, making a range of good sparkling wines by the champagne method.

Fuenmayor
> Wine township in the RIOJA ALTA.

Fundador And. Brandy **
> One of the drier of the large-selling brandies.

Gaseoso
> A cheap sparkler made by pumping carbon dioxide into wine.

Gonzalez y Dubosc, S.A. Cavas Cat. sp. ★★→★★★
> Cavas making pleasant sparkling wines by the champagne method.

Gran Vas
> Pressurized tanks (*cuvés closes*) for making inexpensive sparkling wines; also used to describe this type of wine.

Green Wines
> See under Portugal, p. 107.

Haro
> The wine centre of the RIOJA ALTA.

Huelva And. r. w. br. ★→★★
> Demarcated region w. of Cadiz. The best of its wine is not on sale, since it goes to JEREZ for blending.

Jerez de la Frontera
> The city of sherry. (See p. 152.)

Jumilla Lev. r. ★
> Demarcated region in the mountains north of MURCIA. Its full-bodied wines may approach 18% alcohol.

Laguardia
> Picturesque walled town at the centre of the wine-growing district of LA RIOJA ALAVESA.

Lan, Bodegas R'a.A. r. (p.w.) ★★→★★★
> A huge new bodega, lavishly equipped and making red Riojas of quality.

La Rioja Alta, Bodegas R'a.A. r. (p.) w. dr. or sw. res. ★★→★★★
> Excellent Riojas, esp. the red 5° año Ardanza, 6° año Arana (a Marks and Spencer house wine) and Reserva 904, also the dry white Metropol Extra.

León O.Cas. r. p. w. ★→★★
> Its wines, particularly those from the unfortunately named V.I.L.E. (Planta de Elaboración y Embotellado de Vinos) are light, bone-dry and refreshing.

Lepanto And. Brandy ★★★
> Delicate and expensive, perhaps the best of Spanish brandies.

Logroño
> Principal town of the RIOJA region.

López de Heredia, S.A. R'a.A. r. (p.) w. dr. or sw. res. ★★→ ★★★
> Old established bodega in HARO with typical and good dry red Viña Tondonia of 6° año or more. Tondonia whites are also impressive, like old-fashioned Graves.

Malaga And. br. sw. ★★→★★★
> Demarcated region around the city of Malaga. At their best, its dessert wines yield nothing to tawny port.

Mallorca
> No wine of interest except from José FERRER.

Mancha/Manchuela N.Cas. r. w. ★
> Large demarcated region n. and n.e. of VALDEPEÑAS, but wines without the light and fresh flavour of the latter.

Marqués de Caceres, Bodegas R'a.A. r. ★→★★★
> Good red Riojas of various ages.

Marqués de Monistrol, Bodegas Cat. w. r. (dr. or sw.) res. ★★→★★★
> A family firm, just taken over by Martini and Rossi. It makes refreshing white wines, esp. the Vin nature, blanc de blancs and Blanco reserva, a good red and an odd sweet red wine.

Marqués de Murrieta, S.A. R'a.A. r. w. dr. ★★→ ★★★★
> Highly reputed bodega near LOGROÑO. Makes the 4° año Etiqueta Blanca, the superb red Castillo Ygay and a dry fruity white.

Marqués de Riscal, S.A. R'a.Al. r. (p. and w.) res. ★→ ★★★
> The best bodega of the RIOJA ALAVESA. Its red wines are relatively light and dry.

Masía Bach   Cat. r. p. w. dr. or sw. ★★
> Extrísimo Bach from SAN SADURNÍ DE NOYA, flowery and refined, is one of the best sweet white wines of Spain.

Marfil   Cat. r. (p.) w. ★★
> Brand name of Alella Vinícola (Bodegas Cooperativas), best known of the producers in ALELLA. Means "ivory".

Medellín   Ext. r. (p.) w. ★
> The Castillo de Medellín from this town near Mérida is of better quality than the local plonk.

Méntrida   N.Cas. r. w. ★
> Demarcated region w. of Madrid, supplying everyday wine to the capital.

Monopole
> See Compania Vinícola del Norte de España.

Montánchez   Ext. r. g. ★
> Village near Mérida, interesting because its red wines grow FLOR yeast like FINO sherry.

Montecillo, Bodegas   R'a.A. r. w. (p.) ★★
> Rioja bodega owned by Osborne (see Sherry), best known for its red and dry white Cumbrero, most reasonably priced and currently among the best of the 3° año wines.

Monterrey   Gal. r. ★
> Demarcated region near the n. border of Portugal, making wines like those of VERIN.

Montilla-Moriles   And. g. ★★★
> Demarcated region near Cordoba. Its crisp, sherry-like FINO and AMONTILLADO contain 14% to 17.5% natural alcohol and remain unfortified and singularly toothsome.

Muga, Bodegas   R'a.A. r. (w.) ★★★★
> Small family firm in HARO, making some of the best red Rioja now available by strictly traditional methods in oak. Its wines are fruity, intensely aromatic, with long complex finish.

Navarra   Nav. r. (w.) ★→★★
> Demarcated region, but little better than sturdy wine for everyday drinking.

Olarra, Bodegas   R'a.A. r. (w. p.) ★★→★★★
> A new and vast bodega near LOGROÑO, one of the show-pieces of the RIOJA, making good red wines.

Paternina, S.A., Bodegas   R'a.A. r. (p.) w. dr. or sw. res. ★→★★★★
> Bodega at Ollauri and a household name. Its best wines are the red Viña Vial, the Gran Reserva 1967 and the magnificent older reservas.

Pazo   Gal. r. p. w. dr. ★
> Brand name of the co-operative at RIBEIRO, making "GREEN WINES". The rasping red is the local favourite. The pleasant fizzy white is safer.

Peñafiel   O.Cas. r. and w. dr. ★★
> Sturdy red wine and well-made white, "Peñascal", from the village of the same name on the R. Duero near Valladolid.

Penedès   Cat. r. w. dr. sp. ★→★★★
> Demarcated region including Vilafranca del Penedès, SAN SADURNÍ DE NOYA and SITGES. See also Torres.

Perelada   Cat. (r. p.) w. sp. ★★
> In the demarcated region of AMPURDAN on the Costa Brava. Best known for a sparkling wine made by the tank or *cuve close* system.

Priorato   Cat. br. sw. ★★★ r. (w.) ★
> Demarcated region, an enclave in that of TARRAGONA, known for its good dessert wines and also for strong dark full-bodied reds, often used for blending. Lighter Priorato is a good carafe wine in Barcelona restaurants.

Reserva

Good-quality wine matured for long periods in cask.

Ribeiro Gal. r. (p.) w. dr. ★→★★

Demarcated region on the n. border of Portugal — the heart of the "GREEN WINE" country.

Rioja O.Cas.

This upland region along the R. Ebro in the n. of Spain produces most of the country's best table wines in some 50 BODEGAS DE EXPORTACION. It is sub-divided into:

Rioja Alavesa

North of the R. Ebro, the R'a.Al. produces fine red wines, mostly the lighter CLARETES.

Rioja Alta

South of the R. Ebro and w. of LOGROÑO, the R'a.A. grows fine red and white wines and also makes some rosé.

Rioja Baja

Stretching e. from LOGROÑO, the Rioja Baja makes coarser red wines, high in alcohol and often used for blending.

Riojanas, Bodegas R'a.A. r. w. (p.) ★★→★★★

One of the older bodegas, making good traditional Riojas. Its Monte Real reservas are big, mellow wines above average.

Rioja Santiago, S.A. R'a.A. r. w. dr. or sw. p. res. ★→★★★

Bodega at HARO with well-known wines. The flavour sometimes suffers from pasteurization, but the red RESERVAS can be first rate. Makes the biggest-selling bottled SANGRIA.

Rosado

Rosé.

Rueda O.Cas. w. ★→★★

Village-name given to the golden FLOR-growing wines with sherry-like taste and up to 17% alcohol, grown w. of Valladolid.

Rumasa

The great Spanish conglomerate, which has absorbed Williams and Humbert, Garvey, Paternina, Franco-Españolas and, in England, Augustus Barnett.

Salvatierra de Barros Ext. r. ⋆

Village near Zafra. Peasant-made wines with a certain extra something.

Sangre de Toro

1. Red wine from TORO. 2. Brand name for a soft, rich-flavoured red wine from TORRES S.A.

Sangria

Cold red wine cup made by adding ice, citrus fruit, fizzy lemonade and brandy to red wine.

Sanlúcar de Barrameda

Centre of the Manzanilla district. (See Sherry p. 153.)

San Sadurní de Noya Cat. sp. ★★→★★★

Town s. of Barcelona, hollow with cellars where dozens of firms produce sparkling wine by the champagne method. Standards are high, even if the ultimate finesse is lacking.

Sarría, Senorio de Nav. r. (p.) w. dr. ★★→★★★

The model winery of H. Beaumont y Cia. near Pamplona produces wines up to RIOJA standards.

Scholtz, Hermanos, S.A. And. br. ★→ ★★★

Makers of the best MALAGA, notably Solera Scholtz 1885.

Seco

Dry.

Sitges Cat. w. sw. ★★

Coastal resort s. of Barcelona noted for sweet dessert wine made from Moscatel and Malvasia grapes.

Soberano And. Brandy ★★

One of the driest of the popular Spanish brandies.

Tarragona Cat. r. w. dr. or sw. br. ⋆

1. The demarcated region produces little wine of note. 2. The town makes vermouth and exports cheap wine.

Terry And. Brandy ⋆

Highly caramelized brandy—definitely for those with a sweet tooth.

Tierra del Vino O.Cas. w. ⋆→⋆⋆

Area w. of Valladolid including the wine villages of La Nava and RUEDA.

Tinto

Red.

Toro O.Cas. r. ⋆

Town from which the strong red SANGRE DE TORO takes its name.

Torres, Bodegas Cat. r. w. dr. or semi-sw. res. ⋆⋆→⋆⋆⋆⋆

Distinguished family firm making the best wines of Penedés, esp. the flowery white Viña Sol and Gran Viña Sol, the red Tres Torres and Gran Sangredetoro, the beautiful Gran Coronas reservas, and the red Santa Digna from the Pinot Noir grape.

Utiel-Requeña Lev. r. (w.) ⋆

Demarcated region w. of Valencia. The CLARETES from the mountainous hinterland are best.

Valbuena O.Cas. r. ⋆⋆⋆

Made with the same grapes as VEGA SICILIA but sold as 3° año or 5° año.

Valdeorras Gal. r. w. dr. ⋆→⋆⋆

Demarcated region e. of Orense, making dry and refreshing wines, some slightly fizzy.

Valdepeñas N.Cas. r. (w.) ⋆→⋆⋆

Demarcated region near the border of Andalucia. The supplier of most of the carafe wine to Madrid. Its wines, though high in alcohol, are surprisingly light in flavour.

Valencia Lev. r. w. ⋆

Demarcated region producing earthy high-strength wine.

Vega Sicilia O.Cas. r. res. ⋆⋆⋆⋆ 41 48 53 59 61

One of the very best Spanish wines, full-bodied, fruity and almost impossible to find. Containing up to 16% alcohol.

Vendimia

Vintage.

Verín Gal. r. ⋆

Town near n. border of Portugal. Its wines are the strongest from Galicia, without a bubble, and up to 14% alcohol.

Vicente, Suso y Pérez, S.A. Ara. r. ⋆⋆

A bodega s. of Sarragossa producing superior Cariñena.

Viña

Vineyard.

Vino Blanco

White wine.

commun/corriente Ordinary wine.

clarete Light red wine.

dulce Sweet wine.

espumoso Sparkling wine.

generoso Aperitif or dessert wine rich in alcohol.

rancio Maderized (brown) white wine.

rosado Rosé wine.

seco Dry wine.

tinto Red wine.

verde See Green wine under Portugal.

Yecla Lev. r. w. ⋆

Demarcated region n. of Murcia. Its co-operative-made wines, once heavy-weight champions, have been much improved.

Portugal

For Port and Madeira see pages 150 to 154.

Adega

A cellar or winery.

Aguardente

The Portuguese word for brandy, made by a multiplicity of firms. Safest to ask for one from a port concern.

Algarve Alg. r. w. ★

Lagoa is the wine centre of the holiday area. It is nothing to write home about.

Amarante

Sub-region in the VINHOS VERDES area. Rather heavier and stronger wines than those from farther n.

Aveleda Douro w. dr. ★★

A first-class "GREEN WINE" made on the Aveleda estate of the Guedes family, proprietors of SOGRAPE. Sold dry in Portugal but sweetened for export.

Bagaceira

A potent spirit made like the Spanish *aguardiente*. One of the best is CEPA VELHA from MONÇÃO.

Bairrada Bei. Lit. r. and sp. ★★

Undemarcated region supplying much of Oporto's (often good) carafe wine. Also makes good-quality sparkling wines by the champagne method.

Basto

A sub-region of the VINHOS VERDES area on the R. Tamega, producing more astringent red wine than white.

Borba Alen. r. ★

Small enclave near Evora, making the only wine of any class from Alentejo (s. of the R. Tagus).

Braga

Sub-region of the VINHOS VERDES area, good for both red and white.

Bual

A type of sweet dessert MADEIRA; less sweet and more smoky than MALMSEY.

Buçaco B'a.Al. r. (w.) ★★★

The speciality of the luxury Buçaco hotel near Coimbra, not seen elsewhere.

Bucelas Est'a. w. dr. ★★★

Tiny demarcated region just n. of Lisbon. João Camilo Alves Lda. and Caves Velhas make delicate, perfumed wines with 11% to 12% alcohol.

Carcavelos Est'a. br. sw. ★★★

Minute demarcated region w. of Lisbon. Its excellent sweet wines average 19% alcohol and are drunk cold as an apéritif or with dessert. ★

Cartaxo Rib. r. w. ★

Brand name of adequate carafe wine from the Ribatejo n. of Lisbon, popular in the capital.

Casal García Douro w. dr. ★★

One of the biggest-selling "GREEN WINES" in Portugal, made by SOGRAPE.

Casal Mendes M'o. w. dr. ★★

The "GREEN WINE" from Caves Aliança.

Casaleiro

Trade mark of Caves Dom Teodosio—João T. Barbosa, who make a variety of reliable wines: DÃO, VINHOS VERDES, etc.

Cepa Velha M'o. (r.) w. dr. ★★★

Brand name of Vinhos de Monção, Lda. Their Alvarinho, from the grape of that name, is the best of all "GREEN WINES".

Clarete

Light red wine.

Colares Est'a. r. ★★★

Small demarcated region on the coast w. of Lisbon. Its classical dark red wines, rich in tannin, are from vines which survived the phylloxera epidemic. Drink the oldest available.

Dão B'a.Al. r. w. ★→ ★★

Demarcated region round Viseu on the R. Mondego. Produces some of Portugal's best table wines: solid reds of some subtlety with age: substantial dry whites. All are sold under brand names.

Douro

The n. river whose valley produces port and more than adequate (though undemarcated) table wines.

White table wines have recently come into fashion as an apéritif, an end-of-the-day or any-time drink, taking the place of hard liquor in many households. German wines are riding high on the new wave, but in almost all countries the shift of emphasis from red wine to white is noticeable. Whoever coined the phrase "the thinking man's martini" summed up the arguments for wine: it provides refreshment and stimulus without stopping you thinking.

Evel Trás-os-M. r. ·✱·

Reliable middle-weight red made near VILA REAL by Real Companhia Vinícola do Norte de Portugal.

Faisca Est'a. p. ★

Big-selling sweet carbonated rosé from J. M. da Fonseca.

Ferreirinha Trás-os-M. r. res. ★★★★

One of Portugal's best wines, made in very limited quantity by the port firm of Ferreira. Fruity and fine with deep bouquet.

Gaeiras Est'a. r. ★★

Dry, full-bodied and well-balanced red made in the neighbourhood of Óbidos.

Gatão M'o. w. dr. ★★

Reliable "GREEN WINE" from the firm of Borges & Imão.

Grão Vasco B'a.A. r. w. res. ★★

One of the best brands of DÃO, blended and matured at Viseu by SOGRAPE.

Green Wine (Vinho verde)

Wine made from barely ripe grapes and undergoing a special secondary fermentation, which leaves it with a slight sparkle. Ready for drinking in the spring after the harvest. It may be white or red.

Lagoa

See Algarve.

Lagosta M'o. w. dr. ★★

Well-known "GREEN WINE" from the Real Companhia Vinícola do Norte de Portugal.

Lancers Est'a. p. ★

Sweet carbonated rosé extensively shipped to the USA by J. M. da Fonseca.

Lima

Sub-region in the n. of the VINHOS VERDES area making mainly harsh red wines.

Madeira Island br. dr./sw. ★★→★★★★

Producer of the famous apéritif and dessert wines. See Bual, Malmsey, Sercial, Verdelho and pages 150 to 154.

Malmsey

The sweetest and most unctuous dessert madeira.

Mateus Rosé Trás-os-M. p. ★

World's biggest-selling medium-sweet carbonated rosé, made by SOGRAPE at VILA REAL.

Monção

    Sub-region of the VINHOS VERDES area on the R. Minho, producing the best of the "GREEN WINES" from the ALVARINHO grape.

Moscatel de Setubal Est'a. br. ★★★

    Small demarcated region s. of the R. Tagus, where J. M. da Fonseca make an aromatic dessert muscat, 6 and 25 years old.

Palmela Est'a. r. ★★

    Reliable CLARETES made by J. M. da Fonseca at Azeitão, s. of Lisbon.

Penafiel

    Sub-region in the s. of the VINHOS VERDES area.

Periquita Est'a. r. ★★

    One of Portugal's more robust reds, made by J. M. da Fonseca at Azeitão s. of Lisbon from a grape of that name.

Pinhel B'a.Al. r. ★

    Undemarcated region e. of the DÃO, making similar wine.

Quinta de S. Claudio M'o. w. dr. ★★★

    Estate at Esposende and maker of the best "GREEN WINE" outside MONÇÃO.

Quinta do Corval Trás-os-M. r. ★★

    Estate near Pinhão making good light CLARETES.

Raposeira B'a.Al. sp. ★★

    One of the best-known Portuguese sparkling wines, made by the champagne method at Lamego. Ask for the *bruto* (extra dry).

Ribeiros D'o. w. dr. ★★

    "GREEN WINE" from the firm of Ribeiro & Irmão.

Sercial

    The driest of madeiras, drunk as an apéritif. Made from a grape thought to have originated from the Riesling.

Serradayres Est'a. r. (w.) ★★

    Blended table wines from Carvalho, Ribeiro & Ferreira, Lda. Sound and very drinkable.

Setubal

    See Moscatel.

Sogrape

    Sociedad Comercial dos Vinhos de Mesa de Portugal. Largest wine concern in the country, making VINHOS VERDES, DÃO, MATEUS ROSÉ, VILA REAL red, etc.

Terras Altas B'a.Al. r. w. res. ★★

    Good DÃO wines made by J. M. da Fonseca.

Verdelho

    A semi-sweet madeira, drunk either at the beginning of a meal or with Madeira cake.

Vila Real Trás-os-M. r. ★→ ★★

    Town in the upper DOURO now making some good undemarcated red table wine.

Vinho branco White wine.

    consumo Ordinary wine.

    doce Sweet wine.

    espumante Sparkling wine.

    generoso Apéritif or dessert wine rich in alcohol.

    maduro A normal, mature table wine—as opposed to a VINHO VERDE.

    rosado Rosé wine.

    seco Dry wine.

    tinto Red wine.

    verde See under Green Wines.

Vinhos Verdes M'o. and D'o. r. ★ w. dr. ★→★★★

    Demarcated region between R. Douro and n. frontier with Spain, producing "GREEN WINES".

North Africa & Asia

Algeria

The massive v'yds. of Algeria have dwindled in the last ten years from 860,000 acres to under 600,000. Red wines of some quality are made in the coastal hills of Tlemcen, Mascara, Haut-Dahra, Zaccar and Ain-Bessem. Most goes for blending today. The Soviet Union is the biggest buyer.

Israel

Israeli wine, since the industry was re-established by a Rothschild in the 1880s, has been primarily of Kosher interest until recently, when CABERNET, SAUVIGNON BLANC, SEMILLON and GRENACHE of fair quality have been introduced. Carmel is the principal brand.

Lebanon

The small Lebanese wine industry, based on Ksara, has made red wine of real vigour and quality. Château Musar has the character of fine Burgundy.

Morocco

Morocco today makes North Africa's best wine from v'yds. along the Atlantic coast and round Meknes. In ten years the v'yds. have declined from 190,000 to 170,000 acres. Sidi Larbi and Dar Bel Amri are the best reds; Gris de Boulaouane a very dry pale rosé.

Tunisia

Tunisia now has 90,000 acres compared with 120,000 ten years ago. Her speciality is sweet muscat, but reasonable reds come from Carthage, Grombalia and Cap Bon.

Turkey

Most of Turkey's huge v'yds. produce table grapes. But her wines, from Thrace, Anatolia and the Aegean, are remarkably good. Trakya (Thrace) white and Buzbag red are the well-known standards of the State wineries. Doluca and Kavaklidere are private firms of good quality. Villa Doluca red is remarkable: dry, full-bodied, deep-flavoured and vigorous.

USSR

With over 3 million acres of v'yds. the USSR is the world's fourth-biggest wine-producer—but almost entirely for home consumption. The Ukraine (incl. the Crimea) is the biggest v'yd. republic, followed by Moldavia, the Russian Republic and Georgia. The Soviet consumer has a sweet tooth, for both table and dessert wines. Of the latter the best come from the Crimea (esp. Massandra). Moldavia and the Ukraine use the same grapes as Romania, plus Cabernet, Riesling, Pinot Gris, etc. The Russian Republic makes the best Rieslings (esp. Arbau, Beshtau, Anapa) and sweet sparkling Tsimlanskoye "Champanski". Georgia uses mainly traditional grapes (esp. white Tsinandali and red Mukuzani) for good table wines.

Soviet wines are classified as ordinary (unmatured), "named" (matured in cask or vat) or "kollektsionye" (which are matured both in cask and bottle).

Japan

Japan has a small wine industry in Yamanashi Prefecture, w. of Tokyo. Standard wines are mainly blended with imports from Argentina, E. Europe, etc. Premium wines of Semillon, Cabernet and the local white grape, Koshu, are light but can be good, though expensive. Remarkable sweet wines with noble rot have been made in an area with high humidity. The main producers are Suntory, Mercian, Mann's. '77 was a good vintage.

Central & South-east Europe

The huge range of wines from the countries covered by this G map offers some of the best value for money in the world today. Quality is moderate to high, tending to improve, and reliability on the whole is excellent.

The references are arranged country by country, with all geographical references back to the map on this page.

Labelling in all the countries involved except Greece is based on the German, now international, pattern of place-name plus grape-variety. The main grape-varieties are therefore included alongside areas and other terms in the alphabetical listings. Quality ratings in this section are given where there is enough information to warrant it.

Tokay

Moldavia

Transylvania

ROMANIA

Focsani

Dragasani

Dealul Mare

Banat

Bucharest ●

Dobruja

Belgrade

R. Danube

Serbia

Karlovo

BULGARIA

● Sofia

Macedonia

Melnik

Thrace

R. Euros

GREECE

Attica

● Athens

Samos

Peloponnese

Santorin

Rhodes

Crete

Austria

Austria is new to the international wine trade — her domestic market has hitherto absorbed her whole crop — and consequently is still undervalued. Most of her practices and terms are similar to the German; the basic difference is a higher alcoholic degree in almost all her wine. New legislation is in force to control names and qualities. The Austrian Wine Quality Seal (Weingutesiegel or WGS), in the form of a red, white and gold disc on the bottle, means the wine has met fixed standards, been officially tested and approved.

Recent vintages:

1977 Average quantity; very good quality.
1976 Big; good average quality.
1975 Big, high quality, alcoholic. Some wines lack acid.
1974 Small, light wines, the best delicate.
1973 Excellent quality.

Apetlon Burgenland w. s./sw. or sw. ★→ ★★
    Village of the SEEWINKEL making tasty whites on sandy soil, incl. very good sweet wines.

Ausbruch
    Means "syrupy"; specifically used for very sweet wines between Beerenauslese and Trockenbeerenauslese (see Germany) in richness.

Baden Vienna (r.) w. dr. or sw. ★→★★★
    Town and area s. of VIENNA incl. GUMPOLDSKIRCHEN. Good lively high-flavoured wines, best from ROTGIPFLER and ZIERFÄNDLER grapes.

Blaufränkisch
    The GAMAY grape.

Bouvier
    Native Austrian grape giving soft but aromatic wine.

Burgenland Burgenland r. w. dr. sw. ★→ ★★★★
    Region on the Hungarian border with ideal conditions for sweet wines. "Noble rot" occurs regularly and Ausleses are abundant. (See Rust, etc.)

Dürnstein w. dr. sw. ★★→★★★
    Wine centre of the WACHAU with a famous ruined castle and important Winzergenossenschaft (co-op.). Some of Austria's best whites, esp. Rheinriesling and GRÜNER VELTLINER.

Eisenstadt Burgenland (r.) w. dr. or sw. ★★→★★★★
    Town in BURGENLAND and historic seat of the ESTERHAZY family and their splendid cellars.

Esterhazy
    Quasi-royal family whose AUSBRUCH and other BURGENLAND wines are of superlative quality.

Grinzing Vienna w. ★★ D.Y.A.
    Suburb of VIENNA with delicious lively HEURIGE wines.

Grüner Veltliner
    Austria's most characteristic white grape (26% of her white v'yds.) making short-lived but marvellously spicy and flowery, racy and vital wine.

Gumpoldskirchen Vienna (r.) w. dr. or sw. ★★→★★★
    Pretty resort s. of VIENNA with wines of great character.

Heiligenkreuz, Stift
    Cistercian Monastery at THALLERN making some of Austria's best wine, particularly from a fine steep v'yd.: Wiege.

Heurige
    Means both new wine and the tavern where it is drunk.

Kahlenberg Vienna w. ★★ D.Y.A.
    Village and v'yd. hill n. of VIENNA, famous for HEURIGEN.

Kamp Langenlois (r.) w. dr. or sw. ★→★★

Tributary of the Danube (Donau) giving its name to wines from its valley, n. and e. of the WACHAU, incl. pleasant Veltliner (see Grüner Veltliner) and RIESLING.

Klöch Steiermark (r.) p. w. ★→★★

The chief wine town of Styria, the s.e. province. No famous wines, but agreeable ones, esp. Traminer.

Klosterneuberg

Famous monastery, now a wine college and research station with magnificent cellars, just n. of VIENNA.

Krems Danube. w. ★→★★★

Town and district just e. of the WACHAU with good GRÜNER VELTLINER and Rheinriesling (see Riesling).

Langenlois Langenlois r. w. ★→★★★

Chief town of the KAMP valley with many modest and some good wines, esp. peppery GRÜNER VELTLINER and Rheinriesling (see Riesling). Reds less interesting.

Lenz Moser

Austria's best known and most progressive grower, invented a high vine system and makes good to excellent wine at Röhrendorf near KREMS, APETLON, MAILBERG and elsewhere.

Mailberg Weinviertel r. w. ★★

Town of the WEINVIERTEL known for lively light wine, esp. LENZ MOSER's Malteser.

Morandell, Alois

Big-scale Viennese wine-merchant.

Mörbisch Burgenland r. w. dr. or sw. ★→★★★

Leading wine-village of BURGENLAND. Good sweet wines. Reds and dry whites not inspiring.

Müller-Thurgau

9% of all Austria's white grapes are Müller-Thurgau.

Muskat-Ottonel

The strain of muscat grape grown in e. Europe, incl. Austria.

Niederösterreich

Lower Austria: i.e. all the n.e. corner of the country.

Neuberger

Popular white grape: pleasant wine in KREMS/LANGENLOIS but soft and coarse in BURGENLAND.

Neusiedlersee

Shallow lake in sandy country on the Hungarian border, creating autumn mists and giving character to the sweet wines of BURGENLAND.

Nussdorf Vienna w. ★★

Suburb of VIENNA with well-known HEURIGEN.

Oggau Burgenland (r.) w. sw. ★★→★★★

One of the wine-centres of BURGENLAND, famous for Beerenausleses (see Germany) and AUSBRUCH.

Portugieser

With BLAUFRÄNKISCH, one of the two main red-wine grapes of Austria, giving dark but rather characterless wine.

Retz Weinviertel (r.) w. ★

Leading wine-centre of the WEINVIERTEL, known for pleasant GRÜNER VELTLINER, etc.

Ried

Vineyard: when named it is usually a good one.

Riesling

German Riesling is always called Rheinriesling. "Riesling" is Wälschriesling.

Rotgipfler

Good and high-flavoured grape peculiar to BADEN and GUMPOLDSKIRCHEN. Used with ZIERFÄNDLER to make lively whites. Very heavy/sweet on its own.

Ruländer

The PINOT GRIS grape.

Rust Burgenland (r.) w. dr. or sw. ★→★★★

Most famous wine centre of BURGENLAND, long and justly famous for its AUSBRUCH, often made of mixed grape varieties.

St. Laurent

Traditional Austrian red grape, faintly muscat-flavoured.

Schilcher

Pleasant sharp rosé, speciality of STYRIA.

Schloss Grafenegg

Famous property of the Metternich family neat KREMS. Good standard white and excellent Ausleses.

Schluck

Name for the common white wine of the WACHAU, good when drunk very young.

Seewinkel

"Sea corner": the sandy district around the NEUSIEDLERSEE.

Sievering Vienna w. ★★

Suburb of VIENNA with notable HEURIGEN.

Spätrot

Another name for ZIERFÄNDLER.

Spitzenwein

Top wines—as opposed to TISCHWEIN: ordinary "dish wines".

Steiermark

Province in the s.e., not remarkable for wine but well-supplied with it.

Stift

The word for a monastery. Monasteries have been, and still are, very important in Austria's wine-making, combining tradition and high standards with modern resources.

Styria

English name for STEIERMARK.

Thallern Vienna (r.) w. dr. or sw. ★★ →★★★

Village near GUMPOLDSKIRCHEN and trade-name of wines from Stift HEILIGENKREUZ.

Tischwein

Everyday wine, as opposed to SPITZENWEIN.

Traiskirchen Vienna (r.) w. ★★

Village near GUMPOLDSKIRCHEN with similar wine.

Veltliner

See Grüner Veltliner

Vienna

See Wien

Vöslau Baden r. (w.) ★

Spa town s. of BADEN (and VIENNA) known for its reds made of PORTUGIESER and BLAUFRÄNKISCH: sound and refreshing but no more.

Wachau

District on the n. bank of the Danube round DÜRNSTEIN with cliff-like slopes giving some of Austria's best whites, esp. Rheinriesling (see Riesling) and GRÜNER VELTLINER.

Weinviertel

"The wine quarter": name given to the huge and productive district between VIENNA and the Czech border. Mainly light white wines.

Wien (Vienna)

The capital city, with 1,800 acres of v'yds. in its suburbs to supply its cafés and HEURIGEN.

Zierfänder

White grape of high flavour peculiar to the BADEN area. Used with ROTGIPFLER.

Hungary

Aszu

Word meaning "syrupy" applied to very sweet wines, esp. Tokay (TOKAJI), where the "aszu" is late-picked and "nobly rotten" as in Sauternes. (See p. 52.)

Badacsony Balaton w. dr. sw. **→★★★**

1,400 ft. hill on the n. shore of La. BALATON whose basalt soil gives rich high-flavoured wines, among Hungary's best.

Balatonfüred Balaton (r.) w. dr. sw. ★★

Town on the n. shore of La. BALATON e. of BADACSONI. Good but softer, less fiery wines.

Balaton Balaton r. w. dr. sw. ★ **→★★★**

Hungary's inland sea and Europe's largest lake. Many wines take its name and most are good. The ending "i" (e.g. Balatoni, Egri) is the equivalent of -er in German names, or in Londoner.

Bársonyos-Császár

Wine-district of n. Hungary. MÓR is its best-known centre.

Bikavér

"Bull's Blood"—or words to that effect. The historic name of the best-selling red wine of EGER: full-bodied and well-balanced, improving considerably with age.

Csopak

Village next to BALATONFÜRED, with similar wines.

Debrő Mátraalya w. sw. ★★★

Important centre of the MÁTRAALYA famous for its pale, aromatic and sweet HÁRSLEVELÜ.

Eger Mátraalya r. w. dr. sw. ★→ ★★

Best-known MÁTRAALYA wine-centre: fine baroque city of cellars full of BIKAVÉR. Also delicate white LEANYKA and dark sweetish MERLOT, known as MÉDOC NOIR.

Eszencia

The fabulous quintessence of Tokay (TOKAJI): intensely sweet grape-juice of very low, if any, alcoholic strength, reputed to have miraculous properties. Now almost unobtainable.

Ezerjó

The grape grown at MÓR to make one of Hungary's best dry white wines: distinguished, fragrant and fine.

Furmint

The classic grape of Tokay (TOKAJI), with great flavour and fire, also grown for table wine on La. BALATON with excellent results.

Hajós Mecsek r. ★

Town in s. Hungary becoming known as a centre for good CABERNET SAUVIGNON reds.

Hárslevelü

The "lime-leaved" grape used at DEBRŐ to make good gently sweet wine.

Kadarka

The commonest red grape of Hungary, grown in vast quantities for everyday wine on the plains in the s.; also used at EGER; capable of ample flavour and interesting maturity.

Kékfrankos

Hungarian for GAMAY, literally "blue French". Makes good light red at SOPRON on the Austrian border.

Kéknelyü

High-flavoured white grape making the best and "stiffest" wine of Mt. BADACSONY: fiery and spicy stuff.

Leanyka

East-European white grape better known in Romania but making admirable pale soft wine at EGER.

Mátraalya

Wine-district in the foothills of the Matra range in n. Hungary, incl. DEBRÖ and EGER.

Mecsek

District in s. Hungary known for the good reds of VILÁNY and whites of PÉCS.

Médoc Noir

Hungarian name for MERLOT, used to make sweet red at EGER.

Monimpex

The Hungarian state export monopoly, with great cellars at Budafok, near Budapest.

Mór North Hungary w. dr. ★★★

Town in n. Hungary famous for its fresh dry EZERJÓ.

Muskotály

Hungarian muscat, used to add aroma to Tokay (TOKAJI) and occasionally alone at EGER, where its wine is long-lived and worth tasting.

Nágyburgundi

Literally "black burgundy"—the PINOT NOIR makes admirable wine in s. Hungary, esp. round VILÁNY.

Olasz Riesling

The Hungarian name for the Italian, or Wälsch riesling.

Pécs Mecsek (r.) w. dr. ★★

Town in the Mecsek hills known in the West for its agreeable well-balanced (if rather sweet) Riesling.

Puttonyos

The measure of sweetness in Tokay (TOKAJI). A 7-gal. container from which ASZU is added to SZAMORODNI. One "putt" makes it sweetish; 5 (the maximum) very sweet indeed.

Siller

Pale red or rosé. Usually made from KADARKA grapes.

Somló North Hungary w. dr. ★★★

Isolated small v'yd. district n. of BALATON making intense white wines of high repute from FURMINT and RIESLING.

Sopron Burgenland r. ★★

Little Hungarian enclave in Burgenland s. of the Neusiedlersee (see Austria) specializing in KÉKFRANKOS (Gamay) red.

Szamorodni

Word meaning "as it comes": i.e. fully fermented (therefore dry) wine from all the grapes not specially selected. Used to describe the unsweetened form of Tokay (TOKAJI).

Szürkebarát

Literally means "grey friar": Hungarian for PINOT GRIS, which makes rich heavy wine in the BALATON v'yds.

Szekszárdi Vörös Mecsek r. ★★

The red (KADARKA) wine of Szekszárd in south-central Hungary. Dark strong wine which needs age.

Tokaji (Tokay) Tokaji w. dr. sw. ★★ →★★★★

Hungary's famous strong sweet wine, comparable to an oxidized Sauternes, from hills on the Russian border in the n.e. See Aszu, Eszencia, Furmint, Puttonyos, Szamorodni.

Tramini

The TRAMINER grape; little grown in Hungary.

Vilány Mecsek r. p. (w.) ★★

Southernmost city of Hungary and well-known centre of red wine production. Vilányi Burgundi is largely PINOT NOIR—and very good.

Wälschriesling

Austrian name sometimes used for Olasz (Italian) Riesling.

Zöldszilváni

"Green Sylvaner"—i.e. Sylvaner. Grown round La. BALATON.

Romania

Alba Iulia

Town in the TIRNAVE area in Transylvania, known for off-dry whites blended from Italian Riesling, FETEASCA and MUSKAT-OTTONEL.

Aligoté

The junior white burgundy grape makes pleasantly fresh white wine in Romania.

Babeaşca

Traditional red grape of the FOCSANI area: agreeably sharp wine tasting slightly of cloves.

Banat

The plain on the border with Serbia. Workaday Riesling and light red CADARCA.

Cabernet

Increasingly grown in Romania, particularly at DEALUL MARE, to make dark intense wines often too sweet for French-trained palates.

Cadarca

Romanian spelling of the Hungarian Kadarka.

Chardonnay

The great white burgundy grape is used at MURFATLAR to make honey-sweet dessert wine.

Cotesti

Part of the FOCSANI area making reds of PINOT NOIR, MERLOT, etc., and dry whites said to resemble Alsace wines.

Cotnari

Romania's most famous historical wine: light dessert wine from MOLDAVIA. Like very delicate Tokay.

Dealul Mare

Important up-to-date v'yd. area in the s.e. Carpathian foothills. Red wines from CABERNET, MERLOT, PINOT NOIR, etc.

Dobruja

Black Sea region round the port of Constanta. MURFATLAR is the main v'yd. area.

Dragaşani

Region on the R. Olt s. of the Carpathians, growing both traditional and "modern" grapes. Good MUSKAT-OTTONEL.

Feteasca

Romanian white grape of mild character, the same as Hungary's Leanyka (and some say Switzerland's Chasselas).

Focsani

Important eastern wine region including those of COTESTI, ODOBESTI and NICORESTI.

Grasa

A form of the Hungarian Furmint grape grown in Romania and used in, among other wines, COTNARI.

Moldavia

The n.e. province, now largely within the USSR.

Murfatlar

Big modern v'yds. near the Black Sea specializing in sweet wines, incl. very sweet CHARDONNAY.

Muskat-Ottonel

The e. European muscat, at its best in Romania.

Nicoresti

Eastern area of FOCSANI best known for its red BABEAŞCA.

Odobesti

The central part of FOCSANI; mainly white wines of FETEASCA, RIESLING, etc.

Perla

The speciality of TIRNAVE: a pleasant blended semi-sweet white of RIESLING, FETEASCA and MUSKAT-OTTONEL.

Pitesti
>Principal town of the Arges region s. of the Carpathians. Traditionally whites from FETEASCA, TAMIIOASA, RIESLING.

Riesling
>That is Italian Riesling. Very widely planted. No exceptional wines.

Sadova
>Town in the SEGARCEA area exporting an unexciting sweetish rosé.

Segarcea
>Southern wine area near the Danube. Exports rather sweet CABERNET.

Tamiioasa
>A traditional white-wine grape variety of no very distinct character.

Tirnave
>Important Transylvanian wine region, known for its PERLA and MUSKAT-OTTONEL.

Valea Calugareasca
>"The Valley of the Monks", part of the DEALUL MARE v'yd. with a well-known research station. CABERNET, MERLOT and PINOT NOIR are made into heavy sweet wines.

Jugoslavia

Amselfelder
>German marketing name for the Red Burgundac (Spätburgunder or PINOT NOIR) wine of KOSOVO.

Banat
>North-eastern area, partly in Romania, with up-to-date wineries making adequate RIESLING.

Beli Pinot
>The PINOT BLANC, a popular grape in SLOVENIA.

Bijelo
>White.

Blatina
>The red grape and wine of MOSTAR. Not in the same class as the white ZILAVKA.

Bogdanusa
>Local white grape of the Dalmatian islands, esp. Hvar and Brac. Pleasant fresh faintly fragrant wine.

Burgundac Bijeli
>The CHARDONNAY, grown a little in SLAVONIA and VOJVODINA.

Cabernet
>See grapes for red wine. Now introduced in many places, so far with pleasant, not outstanding, results.

Crno
>Black—i.e. red wine.

Čviček
>Traditional pale red or dark rosé of SLOVENIA.

Dalmaciajavino
>Important co-operative based at Split and selling a full range of coastal and island wines.

Dalmatia
>The middle coast of Jugoslavia from Rijeka to Dubrovnik. Has a remarkable variety of wines of character.

Dingac
>Heavy sweetish red from the local PLAVAC grape, speciality of the mid-Dalmatian coast.

Fruska Gora

Hills in VOJVODINA, on the Danube n.w. of Belgrade, with a growing modern v'yd. and a wide range of wines, incl. good Traminer and Sauvignon Blanc.

Graşevina

Slovenian for Italian Riesling (also called Walschriesling, LASKI RIZLING, etc.). The normal Riesling of Jugoslavia.

Grk

Strong almost sherry-like white from the Grk grape. Speciality of the island of Korcula.

Istria

Peninsula in the n. Adriatic, Porec its centre, with a variety of pleasant wines, the MERLOT as good as any.

Jerusalem

Jugoslavia's most famous v'yd., at LJUTOMER.

Kadarka

The major red grape of Hungary, widely grown in SERBIA.

Kosovo

Region in the s., between SERBIA and Macedonia, with modern v'yds. The source of AMSELFELDER.

Laski Rizling

Yet another name for Italian Riesling.

Ljutomer (or Lutomer)-Ormoz

Jugoslavia's best known and probably best wine district, in n.e. SLOVENIA, famous for its RIESLING: full-flavoured, full-strength and at its best rich and satisfying wine.

Malvasia

White grape giving luscious heavy wine, used in w. SLOVENIA.

Marastina

Strong dry white of the Dalmatian islands.

Maribor

Important wine-centre of n. SLOVENIA. White wines incl. SIPON, Ruländer, etc., as well as RIESLING and Austrian BOUVIER (see Austria).

Merlot

The Bordeaux red grape, grown in SLOVENIA and ISTRIA with reasonable results.

Mostar

Islamic-looking little city inland from DALMATIA, making admirable dry white from the ZILAVKA grape. Also BLATINA.

Muskat-Ottonel

The East European muscat, grown in VOJVODINA.

Navip

The big growers' co-operative of SERBIA, with its headquarters at Belgrade.

Opol

Pleasantly light pale red made of PLAVAĆ grapes round Split and Sibenik in DALMATIA.

Plavać Mali

Native red grape of SLOVENIA and DALMATIA: makes DINGAC, POSTUP, OPOL, etc.

Plavina

Light red of the DALMATIAN coast round Zadar.

Plovdina

Native red grape of Macedonia in the s., giving mild wine. Grown and generally blended with PROKUPAC.

Portugizac

Austria's Portugieser: plain red wine.

Posip

Pleasant, not-too-heavy white wine of the Dalmatian islands, notably Korcula.

Postup

Sweet and heavy DALMATIAN red from the Peljesac peninsula near Korcula. Highly esteemed locally.

Prokupac

Principal native red grape of s. SERBIA and Macedonia: 85% of the production. Makes good dark rosé (RUZICA) and full-bodied red of character. Some of the best comes from ZUPA. PLOVDINA is often added for smoothness.

Prosek

The dessert wine of DALMATIA, of stupefying natural strength and variable quality. The best is excellent, but hard to find.

Radgonska Ranina

Ranina is Austria's BOUVIER grape (see Austria). Radgona is near MARIBOR. The wine is sweet and carries the trade name TIGROVO MLJEKO (Tiger's Milk).

Rajnski Rizling

The Rhine Riesling, rare in Jugoslavia but grown a little in LJUTOMER-ORMOZ.

Refosco

Italian grape grown in e. SLOVENIA and ISTRIA under the name TERAN.

Renski Rizling

Alternative spelling for Rhine Riesling.

Riesling

Without qualification means Italian Riesling.

Ruzica

Rosé, usually from PROKUPAC. Darker than most; and better.

Serbia

The e. state of Jugoslavia, with nearly half the country's v'yds., stretching from VOJVODINA to Macedonia.

Sipon

Jugoslav name for the FURMINT grape of Hungary, also grown in SLOVENIA.

Slavonia

Northern Croatia, on the Hungarian border between SLOVENIA and SERBIA. A big producer of standard wines, mainly white.

Slovenia

The n.w. state, incl. Jugoslavia's most European-style v'yds. and wines: LJUTOMER, etc. Slovenija-vino, the sales organization, is Jugoslavia's biggest.

Teran

Stout dark red of ISTRIA. See REFOSCO.

Tigrovo Mljeko

See Radgonska Ranina

Tocai

The PINOT GRIS, making rather heavy white wine in SLOVENIA.

Traminac

The TRAMINER. Grown in SLOVENIA and VOJVODINA. Particularly successful in the latter.

Vojvodina

An autonomous province of n. SERBIA with substantial, growing and improving v'yds. Wide range of grapes, both European and Balkan.

Zilavka

The white wine of MOSTAR in Hercegovina. One of Jugoslavia's best: dry, pungent and memorably fruity, with a faint flavour of apricots.

Zupa

Central SERBIAN district giving its name to above-average red and rosé (or dark and light red) of PROKUPAC and PLOVDINA: respectively Zupsko Crno and Zupsko Ruzica.

Bulgaria

Cabernet
The Bordeaux grape is highly successful in n. Bulgaria. Excellent dark, vigorous, fruity and well-balanced wine.

Chardonnay
The white burgundy grape is scarcely less successful . Very dry but full and deep-flavoured wine.

Dimiat
The common native white grape, grown in the e. towards the coast. Agreeable dry white without memorable character.

Euxinograd
Brand of blended white wine produced for export.

Fetiaska
The same grape as Romania's Feteasca and Hungary's Leanyka. Rather neutral but pleasant pale wine, best a trifle sweet, sold as Donau Perle.

Gamza
The common red grape, Hungary's Kadarka: gives fairly light but "stiff" and worthwhile wine.

Hemus
A pale medium to sweet muscat from KARLOVO.

Iskra
The national brand of sparkling wine, normally sweet but of fair quality.

Karlovo
Town in central Bulgaria famous for the "Valley of Roses" and its very pleasant white MISKET.

Mavrud
Darkly plummy red from s. Bulgaria. Improves with age.

Melnik
City of the extreme s.e. Such concentrated MAVRUD that the locals say it can be carried in a handkerchief.

Misket
Bulgaria's muscat: locally popular flavour in sweet whites.

Pamid
The light, quite soft, everyday red of s. and central Bulgaria.

Rcatzitelli
One of Russia's favourite white grapes for strong sweet wine. Grown in n.e. Bulgaria.

Riesling
Normally refers to Italian Riesling, though some Rhine Riesling is grown. In the brand known as Rosenthaler Riesling (for export to Germany) the two are blended.

Saperavi
Russian red grape, presumably used for export to Russia: the biggest export market.

Sonnenküste
Brand of medium-sweet white sold in Germany.

Sungurlare
Eastern town giving its name to a sweet MISKET, similar to that of KARLOVO.

Sylvaner
Some pleasant dry SYLVANER is exported as "Klosterkeller".

Tamianka
Sweet white; sweeter than HEMUS.

Tirnovo
Strong sweet red wine.

Tgakia
Dry or medium-dry white.

Vinimpex
The "State Commercial Enterprise for Export and Import of Wines and Spirits".

Greece

Achaia-Clauss

    The best-known Greek wine-merchant, with cellars at Patras, n. PELOPONNESE.

Attica

    Region round Athens, the chief source of RETSINA.

Cambas, Andrew

    Important Athenian wine-growers and merchants.

Castel Danielis

    One of the best brands of dry red wine, from ACHAIA-CLAUSS.

Corfu

    Adriatic island with wines scarcely worthy of it. Ropa is the traditional red.

Crete

    Island with the name for some of Greece's better wine, esp. MAVRO ROMEIKO.

Demestica

    A reliable standard brand of dry red and white from ACHAIA-CLAUSS.

Hymettus

    Standard brand of red and dry white without resin.

Kokkineli

    The rosé version of RETSINA: like the white. Drink very cold.

Lindos

    Name for the higher quality of RHODES wine, whether from Lindos itself or not. Acceptable; no more.

Malvasia

    The famous grape is said to originate from Monemvasia in the s. PELOPONNESE.

Mavro

    "Black"—the word for dark red wine.

Mavrodaphne

    Literally "black laurel": dark sweet concentrated red; a speciality of the Patras region, n. PELOPONNESE.

Mavro Romeiko

    The best red wine of Crete, reputedly among the best of Greece: dry and full-bodied.

Mavroudi

    The red wine of Delphi and the n. shore of the Gulf of Corinth: dark and plummy.

Naoussa

    Above-average strong dry red from Macedonia in the n.

Nemea

    Town in the e. PELOPONNESE famous for its lion (a victim of Hercules) and its fittingly forceful MAVRO.

Peloponnese

    The s. landmass of mainland Greece, with a third of the whole country's v'yds.

Pendeli

    Reliable brand of dry red from ATTICA, grown and bottled by Andrew CAMBAS.

Retsina

    White wine with pine resin added, tasting of turpentine and oddly appropriate with Greek food. The speciality of ATTICA. Drink it very cold.

Rhodes

    Easternmost Greek island. Its sweet MALVASIAS are its best wines. LINDOS is the brand name for tolerable table wines.

Rombola

    The dry white of Cephalonia; island off the Gulf of Corinth.

Ropa

    See Corfu

Samos

Island off the Turkish coast with a reputation for its sweet pale-golden muscat. The normal commercial quality is nothing much.

Santorin

Island north of Crete, making sweet Vinsanto from sun-dried grapes, and dry white Thira.

Verdea

The dry white of Zakinthos, the island just w. of the PELOPONNESE.

Cyprus

Afames

Village at the foot of Mt. Olympus, giving its name to one of the better red (MAVRON) wines.

Aphrodite

Full-bodied medium-dry white, named after the Greek goddess of love.

Arsinöe

Dry white wine, named after an unfortunate female whom Aphrodite turned to stone.

Bellapais

Rather fizzy medium-sweet white named after the famous abbey near Kyrenia.

Christoforou

Family-directed wine firm at LIMASSOL.

Commandaria

Good-quality brown dessert wine made since ancient times and named after a crusading order of knights. The best is superb, of incredible sweetness. Normal qualities are much used as Communion wine.

Haggipavlu

Well-known wine-merchant at LIMASSOL.

Keo

One of the biggest firms in the wine trade at LIMASSOL.

Kokkineli

Rosé: the name is related to "cochineal".

Limassol

"The Bordeaux of Cyprus". The wine-port in the s.

Mavron

The black grape of Cyprus (and Greece) and its dark wine.

Mosaic

The brand-name of KEO's Cyprus sherries.

Othello

Perhaps the best dry red: solid, satisfying wine.

Pitsilia

Region s. of Mt. Olympus producing the best white and COMMANDARIA wines.

Rosella

Brand of strong medium-sweet rosé.

St Panteleimon

Brand of strong sweet white.

Sherry

Cyprus makes a full range of sherry-style wines, the best (particularly the dry) of very good quality.

SODAP

Major wine firm at LIMASSOL.

Xynisteri

The native white grape of Cyprus.

California

California has been making wine for 150 years, but her modern wine industry has grown from scratch in scarcely more than 25. Today it leads the world in good-quality cheap wines and startles it with a handful of luxury wines of brilliant quality. In the last six years the industry has expanded and altered at a frenzied pace, which is reflected in the entries that follow: nearly 40 of them start "new winery...". Quality ratings must therefore be tentative.

Grape-varieties (combined with brand-names) are the key to California wine. Since grapes in California play many new roles they are separately listed on the next two pages. For recent vintages see p. 127.

The areas referred to in the winery entries (and shown on the map) are listed below.

Vineyard areas

Amador
> County in the Sierra foothills e. of Sacramento. Grows fine Zinfandel.

Central Coast
> A long sweep of coast with scattered wine activity, from San Francisco Bay s. to Santa Barbara.

Central Coast/Santa Barbara
> Some of the newest planting in the state is round the Santa Maria river n. of Santa Barbara, where coastal fog gives particularly cool conditions.

Central Coast/Santa Cruz Mts.
> Wineries are scattered round the Santa Cruz Mts. s. of San Francisco Bay, from Paul Masson at Saratoga down to the HECKER PASS.

Central Coast/Hecker Pass
> Pass through the Santa Cruz Mts. s. of San Francisco Bay with a cluster of small old-style wineries.

Central Coast/Salinas Valley
> The main concentration of new planting in the Central Coast: the Salinas Valley runs inland s.e. from Monterey.

Livermore
> Valley e. of San Francisco Bay long famous for white wines but now largely built over.

Lodi

    Town and district at the n. end of the San Joaquin Valley, its hot climate modified by a westerly air-stream.

Mendocino

    Northernmost coastal wine country; a varied climate, much of it hotter than Sonoma and Napa farther s.

Napa

    The Napa Valley, n. of San Francisco Bay, well established as the top-quality wine area.

San Joaquin Valley

    The great central valley of California, fertile and hot, the source of most of the jug wines and dessert wines in the State.

Sonoma and Sonoma/Russian River (R-R.)

    County n. of San Francisco Bay, between Napa and the sea. Most v'yds. are in the n. round the Russian River. A few, historically important, are in the Valley of the Moon in the s.

Sonoma/Alexander Valley

    New quality area in Sonoma county, along the Russian River n. of the Napa Valley.

Temecula (Rancho California)

    Very new small area in s. California, 25 miles inland halfway between San Diego and Riverside.

California: grape varieties

Barbera

Darkly plummy variety from Piemonte (see Italy). Gives full-blooded and astringent wine in cool areas, good but softer wine in hot ones.

Cabernet Sauvignon

The best red-wine grape in California with a wide range of styles from delicately woody to overpoweringly fruity. The classic Napa grape.

Carignane

Common bulk-producing red grape rarely used as a "varietal", but occasionally with some success.

Charbono

Rare red grape of Italian origin and no distinction, like eviscerated Barbera.

Chardonnay

The best white-wine grape—indeed the best wine-grape—in California. Styles of making vary from merely clean and grapy to rich, concentrated and complex like the best white burgundies.

Chenin Blanc

A work-horse white grape with a surprising turn of speed when made dry and in limited, concentrated quantities. But usually made soft and sweet.

Emerald Riesling

A Californian original in the German manner. Clean, flowery/fruity and a touch tart.

Flora

Another California-bred white grape. Mildly flowery; best made sweet.

Folle Blanche

Acidic white with good performance but little used.

French Colombard

Another high-acid white coming into favour for clean semi-dry wines made more German-style than French.

Fumé Blanc

See Sauvignon Blanc.

Gamay (or Napa Gamay)

The red grape of Beaujolais. Agreeable but never remarkable in California.

Gamay Beaujolais

Not the red grape of Beaujolais, but a selection of Pinot Noir good for light summer wines.

Gewürztraminer

Generally softer and less aromatically thrilling in California than in France, but at best one of the real successes.

Green Hungarian

A minority interest: rather tasteless white. Can be lively.

Grenache

The most successful grape for rosé in California; generally, alas, made sweet.

Grey Riesling

Not a Riesling but a minor French grape used for full-bodied but scarcely notable white.

Grignolino

Highly seasoned grape good for young reds and rosés.

Johannisberg Riesling

Real Rhine Riesling (also known as White Riesling). Often rather strong and bland in California, but at its best (esp. in Auslese-style wines) gloriously complex and satisfying.

Merlot

The St-Emilion grape has a growing acreage in California. Very good heavy reds have been made.

Muscat
> Light sweet pale gold muscat is one of California's treats.

Petite Syrah or Syrah
> The name of the Rhône's and Australia's great red grape has been wrongly applied to a poor one. Generally used in Burgundy blends. But the real one is present in small quantities, and has great promise.

Pinot Blanc
> Much in the shade of the better Chardonnay.

Pinot Noir
> Has yet to reach consummation in California. Most wine with the name is disappointing; a minute proportion thrilling.

Pinot St George
> Only used by one winery—The Christian Brothers—to make a thoroughly agreeable sturdy red.

Riesling
> See Johannisberg Riesling. Also Sylvaner.

Ruby Cabernet
> A California-bred cross between Carignan and Cabernet Sauvignon with enough of the character of the latter to be interesting. Good in hot conditions.

Sauvignon Blanc
> Excellent white grape used either Sancerre style (fresh, aromatic, effervescent) or Graves style (fat, chewable). The former usually called Fumé Blanc.

Semillon
> High-flavoured whites from the cooler areas; bland ones from hotter places. The most memorable are sweet.

Sylvaner
> Is often labelled Riesling, but has none of its finesse or balance. Often decent semi-dry wine.

Zinfandel
> California's own red grape, open to many interpretations from light-weight fruity to galumphing. Capable of ageing to great quality.

Recent vintages

The Californian climate is far from being as consistent as its reputation. Although on the whole the grapes ripen regularly, they are subject to severe spring frosts in many areas, sometimes a wet harvest-time, and such occasional calamities as the two-year drought of 1975–7.

Wines from the San Joaquin Valley tend to be most consistent year by year. The vintage date on these, where there is one, is more important for telling the age of the wine than its character.

Vineyards in the Central Coast are mainly so new that no pattern of vintage qualities has yet emerged.

The Napa Valley is the one area where comment can be made on the last ten vintages of the top varietal wines: Cabernet Sauvignon and Chardonnay.

	Chardonnay	Cabernet Sauvignon
1978	Promising.	Promising.
1977	Generally excellent.	Scarcely ripe. Few good.
1976	Difficult: variable.	Small crop but splendid.
1975	Good.	Good.
1974	Good.	Difficult: but many superb.
1973	Very good.	Big and good.
1972	The best wines of a cool year.	Uneven: rain: many poor wines.
1971	Good balance: long lived.	Average.
1970	Good all round: not great: mature.	Best ever.
1969	Weak.	Good, not great.
1968	Well-balanced: now ageing.	Fine, well balanced, now ready.
1967	Weak.	Weak.

California wineries

Alexander Valley Vineyards Alexander Valley. Table **→****

New small winery. CHARDONNAY, CABERNET esp. good.

Almaden Central Coast. Full range *→ **

Big winery famous for pioneer varietal labelling and pioneer planting in the Central Coast. Now owned by National Distillers. Best regular wines incl. SAUV BL., CABERNET. New Charles le Franc label for top vintage wines.

Ambassador

Brand name of PERELLI-MINETTI.

Assumption Abbey

Brand name of BROOKSIDE.

Barengo Lodi. Table and dessert *→**

Small firm making wines of character, especially ZINFANDEL and RUBY CABERNET.

Beaulieu Napa. Table and sp. **→****

Rightly famous medium-size growers and makers of esp. CABERNET and CHARDONNAY. Top wine: De Latour Private Reserve Cabernet. Now owned by Heublein Corp.

Beringer Napa. Table and dessert ** →***

Century-old winery recently modernized by Nestlé Co. Increasingly interesting wines incl. Auslese types.

Boeger Amador. Table **

Small winery in Sierra foothills. Good ZIN and SAUV BLANC.

Brookside S. California. Table and dessert *→**

Traditional dessert wine firm also making table varietals from TEMECULA under the Assumption Abbey label.

Bruce, David Central Coast. Table ****

Small luxury winery with heavy-weight old-style wines.

Buena Vista Sonoma. Table **

Historic pioneer winery with inproving recent record esp. in whites (RIESLING, FUMÉ BLANC). Reds include old-style ZINFANDEL from its reputed original v'yd.

Burgess Cellars Napa. Table ***

Small hillside winery, originally called Souverain, making good CHARDONNAY, late harvest RIESLING, CABERNET.

B.V.

Abbreviation of BEAULIEU VINEYARDS used on their labels.

Cakebread Napa. Table **

Started 1974. Increasing reputation, esp. for SAUVIGNON BLANC; also CHARDONNAY, CABERNET, ZIN.

Calera Monterey-San Benito. Table **

New winery with good ZIN and ambitious with PINOT NOIR.

California Growers San Joaquin. Table and dessert *

Known for sherry and brandy, now also varietal table wines, some labelled Setrakian (now the owner).

Callaway S. California. Table **

Small new winery in new territory at TEMECULA. Early reds are strong, dark, conservative.

Château St Jean Sonoma. Table and sp. ***

New small winery specializing in richly flavoured whites from individual v'yds., incl. CHARDONNAY, PINOT BLANC and esp. late harvest RIESLING.

Christian Brothers Napa and San Joaquin. Full range **→****

The biggest Napa winery, run by a religious order, specializing in consistent undated blends, incl. excellent CABERNET, useful PINOT ST GEORGE, sweet white Ch. La Salle and very good brandy. Vintage-dated special lots replace the former Brother Timothy Selection.

Clos du Val Napa. Table ***

New small French-owned winery making strong rustic ZINFANDEL and fine delicate CABERNET.

Concannon Livermore. Table ★★
>Substantial family winery famous for SAUVIGNON BLANC and SEMILLON, but with reds of similar quality.

Congress Springs Santa Clara/Santa Cruz. Table ★★
>Tiny new winery above Saratoga. Well-made whites, esp. SAUVIGNON BLANC, SEMILLON.

Conn Creek Napa. Table ★★→★★★
>Still formative. New winery building on Silverado Trail. 1974 CABERNET was a critical success.

Cresta Blanca Mendocino and San Joaquin. Table and dessert ★★
>Old name from Livermore revived on the n. coast by new owners, GUILD co-op. Husky ZINFANDEL and PETITE SYRAH. Mild whites.

Cuvaison Napa. Table ★★
>Small winery with expert new direction. Shows promise.

Davis Bynum Sonoma. Table ★→★★
>Established maker of standard varieties, w. of Healdsburg.

Diamond Creek Napa. Table ★★
>Small winery since the 60s with CABERNET from hills w. of Calistoga. Growing in reputation.

Domaine Chandon Napa. sp. ★★★
>Californian outpost of Moët & Chandon Champagne. Launched 1976. Early promise is being fulfilled.

Dry Creek Sonoma. Table ★★★
>New small winery with high ideals, making old-fashioned dry wines, esp. whites, incl. CHARDONNAY, CHENIN BLANC and FUMÉ BLANC.

East-Side San Joaquin. Table and dessert ★
>Progressive growers' co-operative best known for its Royal Host label. Good RUBY CABERNET, EMERALD RIESLING, ZIN.

Edmeades Mendocino. Table ★★
>Tiny winery in Anderson Valley near Pacific. Known for CABERNET and a French Colombard Ice Wine.

Eleven Cellars
>Brand name of PERELLI-MINETTI.

Estrella River San Luis Obispo/Santa Barbara. Table ★★
>Impressive new winery with 600 acres. CHARDONNAY, RIESLING, MUSCAT, SYRAH are promising.

Felton-Empire Vineyards Cent. Coast/Santa Cruz Mts. Table ★★.
>The old Hallcrest property recently revived by new owners. Excellent first RIESLING. A label to watch.

Fetzer Mendocino. Table ★★
>Ten-year-old small winery with interesting but inconsistent wines, incl. CABERNET, SAUVIGNON BLANC, ZIN, SEMILLON.

Ficklin San Joaquin. Dessert (and table) ★★★
>Family firm making California's best "port" and minute quantities of table wine.

Field Stone Sonoma (Alexander Valley). Table ★★
>Newcomer owned by mechanical harvester manufacturer, pressing grapes in the v'yd. for whites and CABERNET rosé.

Firestone Central Coast/Santa Barbara. Table ★★
>Ambitious new (1975) winery in a new area n. of Santa Barbara. Cool conditions are producing interesting wines, incl. PINOT NOIR and RIESLING.

Foppiano Sonoma. Table ★★
>Old winery at Healdsburg refurbished with vintage varieties incl. CHENIN BLANC, FUMÉ BLANC, CAB, ZIN, PETITE SYRAH.

Franciscan Vineyard Napa. Table ★★→★★★
>Small-to-medium winery run by an ex-Christian Brother. Good ZINFANDEL, and Silver Oak CABERNET, RIESLING.

Franzia San Joaquin. Full range *

Large old family winery now owned by Coca Cola. Various labels, but all say "made and bottled in Ripon". Noteworthy Burgundy and ZINFANDEL.

Freemark Abbey Napa. Table ***

Small connoisseur's winery with high reputation for CABERNET, CHARDONNAY, PINOT NOIR and RIESLING.

Gallo, E. & J. San Joaquin. Full range *→ **

The world's biggest winery, pioneer in both quantity and quality. Family owned. Hearty Burgundy and Chablis Blanc set national standards. Varietals incl. good SAUVIGNON BLANC, FRENCH COLOMBARD, RUBY CABERNET, BARBERA.

Gemello Santa Clara/Santa Cruz. Full range **

Old winery with reputation for reds, esp. PETITE SYRAH, ZIN, sometimes CABERNET.

Geyser Peak Sonoma. Table **

Old winery recently revived and expanded by Schlitz Brewery. More steady than inspired.

Giumarra San Joaquin. Table *

Recent installation making sound RUBY CABERNET and PETITE SYRAH from family v'yds. in hottest part of valley.

Grand Cru Sonoma. Table **→***

New small winery making good GEWÜRZ, light ZIN and increasingly CABERNET and SAUVIGNON BLANC.

Grgich-Hills Cellars Napa. Table ***

New winery. Grgich (formerly of CH. MONTELENA) is winemaker, Hills grows the grapes—esp. CHARDONNAY and RIESLING.

Guild San Joaquin. Table and dessert *

Big growers' co-operative famous for Vino da Tavola semisweet red and B. Cribari label. New line of varietals with Winemasters label incl. good ZINFANDEL.

Gundlach-Bundschu Sonoma. Table ***

Very old small family winery revived by the new generation. Excellent CABERNET, MERLOT, ZIN and good whites: CHARDONNAY, GEWÜRZ, RIESLING.

Hacienda Sonoma. Table ** ***

New small winery specializing in high-quality CHARDONNAY.

Hanzell Sonoma. Table ***

Small winery which revolutionized Californian CHARDONNAYS in the '50s under its founder, now in new hands. PINOT NOIR now also good.

Harbor Winery San Joaquin. Table ***

Tiny winery using AMADOR and NAPA grapes to make first-rate ZINFANDEL and CHARDONNAY.

Heitz Napa. Table (and dessert) ****

In many eyes the first name in California. An inspired individual wine-maker who has set standards for the whole industry. His CABERNETS (esp. "Martha's Vineyard") are dark, deep and emphatic, his best CHARDONNAYS peers of Montrachet.

Hoffmann Mtn. Ranch Cen. Coast San Luis Obispo. Table ***

New small winery in new area near Paso Robles. CHARDONNAY and PINOT NOIR are promising.

Inglenook Napa and San Joaquin. Table and dessert * →***

One of the great old Napa wineries recently much changed by new owners: Heublein Corp. Special Cask CABERNET SAUVIGNON remains best wine. Other varieties sound. Inglenook Vintage is a second label, Inglenook Navalle a third and the best value: good cheap RUBY, ZINFANDEL and FRENCH COLOMBARD.

Italian Swiss Colony   San Joaquin and Sonoma. Full range ★→★★
Honourable old name from Sonoma transferred to San Joaquin by new owners: Heublein Corp. Adequate standards. Lejon is a second label.

Johnsons of Alexander Valley   Sonoma. Table (Probable★★)
New small winery with good v'yd. land. Style not yet established.

Jordan   Sonoma. Table N.Y.A.
Extravagant winery specializing in CABERNET. First vintage, '75, to be released in 1980.

Kenwood Vineyards   Sonoma. Table ★★→★★★
Steady small producer of increasingly stylish reds, esp. CABERNET and ZIN. Also good CHARDONNAY and CHENIN BLANC.

Korbel   Sonoma. Sp. and table ★★★
Long-established sparkling wine specialists. "Natural" and "Brut" are among California's best standard "champagnes".

Kornell   Napa. Sp. ★★★
Fine sparkling wine house making excellent full-flavoured dry wines: Brut and Sehr Trocken.

Krug, Charles   Napa. Table and dessert ★★→★★★
Important old winery with reliable range, incl. good CABERNET SAUVIGNON, CHARDONNAY, sweet CHENIN BLANC and very sweet Moscato di Canelli. C.K. is the jug-wine brand.

Lambert Bridge   Sonoma. Table ★★
New small winery nr. Healdsburg has made promising CHARDONNAY; also CABERNET.

Lamont, M.   San Joaquin. Table and desert ★
New name for old Bear Mountain coop, now owned by Labatt brewery. Well-made varietals, inc. FRENCH COLOMBARD.

Landmark   Sonoma. Table ★★
New winery nr. Windsor with sound CHARDONNAY and CABERNET tending to improve.

Lejon
Brand name of ITALIAN SWISS COLONY.

Los Hermanos
Second label of BERINGER.

Mark West   Sonoma Table ★★
New winery in cool sub-region starting well with whites: GEWÜRZ, RIESLING.

Markham   Napa. Table N.Y.A.
New winery with 200 acres. Samples show promise.

Martini, Louis   Napa. Table and dessert ★★→ ★★★
Large but individual winery with very high standards, from jug wines (called "Mountain") up. CABERNET SAUVIGNON one of California's best. BARBERA, PINOT NOIR, ZINFANDEL, GEWÜRZ, FOLLE BLANCHE and Moscato Amabile are all fine.

Martini & Prati   Sonoma. Table ★★
Important winery selling mainly in bulk to others, but using the name Fountaingrove for a small quantity of good CABERNET SAUVIGNON.

Masson, Paul   Central Coast. Full range ★→ ★★
Big, lively and reliable middle-quality winery with good-value varietals, incl. Emerald Dry (EM. RIES.) Rubion (RUBY), CHARDONNAY, ZINFANDEL, good cheap sparkling and very good Souzão port-type.

Mayacamas   Napa. Table ★★★
First-rate very small v'yd. and winery offering CABERNET SAUVIGNON, CHARDONNAY, ZINFANDEL (sometimes).

Mill Creek   Sonoma. Table ★★
New winery near Healdsburg with ex-Simi winemaker Mary Ann Graf. First wines are CHARDONNAY, MERLOT, CABERNET.

Mirassou Central Coast. Full range ★★→★★★
Dynamic mid-sized growers and makers, the fifth generation of the family. Pioneers in SALINAS v'yds. Notable ZINFANDEL, GAMAY BEAUJOLAIS, PETITE SYRAH, GEWÜRZ and sparkling.

Mondavi, Robert Napa. Table ★★★
Ten-year-old winery with a brilliant record of innovation in styles, equipment and technique. Wines of grace and character incl. CABERNET SAUVIGNON, SAUVIGNON BLANC (sold as Fumé Blanc), CHARDONNAY, PINOT NOIR.

Monterey Peninsula Central Coast/Salinas. Table ★★★
Very small new winery near Carmel making chunky chewable ZINFANDEL and CABERNET from SALINAS grapes.

Monterey Vineyard Central Coast/Salinas. Table ★★★
The first big modern winery of SALINAS, opened 1974. Superb direction has already produced first-class ZINFANDEL, GEWÜRZ and SYLVANER and fruity feather-weight GAMAY BEAUJOLAIS.

Monteviña Amador. Table ★★
Pioneer small winery in new area: the Shenandoah Valley, Amador County, in the Sierra foothills. ZINFANDEL, BARBERA and SAUVIGNON BLANC.

J. W. Morris Port Works North Coast (Oakland). Dessert ★★★
Small specialist in high-quality port-types, both vintage and wood-aged. Mainly SONOMA grapes.

Mount Eden Central Coast. Table ★★
New company owning a major share of what were MARTIN RAY Vineyards. Excellent (and expensive) first wines.

Mount Veeder Napa. Table ★★
Ambitious little new winery. High prices but early signs of quality.

Nichelini Napa. Table ★★
Small old-style family winery selling sound varietals at the cellar door.

Novitiate of Los Gatos Central Coast. Dessert and Table ★★
Jesuit-run altar-wine-orientated unrevolutionary winery with some adequate varietals, inadequately distributed.

Papagni, Angelo San Joaquin. Table and sp. ★★→★★★ ★
Grower of an old family with a technically outstanding modern winery at Madera. Dry coastal-style varietals include excellent ZINFANDEL, good Alicante Bouschet, light "Moscato d'Angelo".

Parducci Mendocino. Table ★★
Well-established mid-sized winery with v'yds. in several locations. Good sturdy reds: CABERNET SAUVIGNON, PETITE SYRAH, ZINFANDEL, Burgundy. Also pleasant FRENCH COLOMBARD.

Pedroncelli Sonoma R-R. Table ★★
Second-generation family business with recent reputation for well-above-average ZINFANDEL, PINOT NOIR and CHARDONNAY in a ripe rural style.

Perelli-Minetti San Joaquin. Table and dessert ★
Big firm with chequered history as California Wine Association, now in family hands. Two principal labels: Ambassador and Eleven Cellars.

Phelps, Joseph Napa. Table ★★★→★★★★
New very de luxe small winery and v'yd. Late harvest RIESLING exceptional. Very good CHARDONNAY, CABERNET and ZIN.

Preston Sonoma. Table (Possible ★★★)
Tiny new winery with very high standards in Dry Creek Valley, Healdsburg. So far SAUVIGNON BLANC and CABERNET.

Rafanelli, J. Sonoma. Table ★★
Tiny local cellar specializing in outstanding ZIN; also GAMAY BEAUJOLAIS.

Ray, Martin Central Coast S. Cruz Mts. Table ★★★★
Eccentric small winery famous for high prices and unpredictable wines, occasionally very good.

Raymond Vineyards Napa. Table ★★★
New small winery with experienced owners. Early ZIN, CHARDONNAY, CHENIN BLANC and CABERNET all excellent.

Ridge Central Coast S. CRUZ. Table ★★★★
Small winery of high repute among connoisseurs for powerful concentrated reds needing long maturing in bottle. Notable CABERNET and very strong ZINFANDEL.

Robert Keenan Napa. Table (Possible ★★★)
Newcomer with very good first CHARDONNAY and CABERNET. V'yds. on Spring Mountain; wine-maker ex-CHAPPELLET.

Robert Pecota Napa. Table (Probable ★★)
New small cellar of ex-Veringer man with high standards. Wines are FLORA, PETITE SIRAH, SAUVIGNON BLANC.

Rondon-Smith Santa Clara/Santa Cruz ★★
New small winery with well-received CHARDONNAY and CABERNET.

Royal Host
Brand name for EAST-SIDE winery.

Rutherford Hill Napa. Table ★★
Recent larger stable-mate of FREEMARK ABBEY. Good early GEWÜRZ, MERLOT, ZIN. Promising CHARDONNAY and CABERNET.

Rutherford Vintners Napa. Table ★★★
New small winery started in 1977 by Bernard Skoda, former LOUIS MARTINI manager. CABERNET and RIESLING will be specialities; also PINOT NOIR, MERLOT, CHARDONNAY.

St. Clement Napa. Table ★★★
New owner has made very good CHARDONNAY. CABERNET is expected.

Sandford and Benedict San Luis Obispo/Santa Barbara Table
New winery whose first CHARDONNAY and PINOT NOIR (1976) caused a stir.

San Martin Central Coast. Table and dessert ★★→ ★★★
Newly restructured old company using SALINAS and SAN LUIS OBISPO grapes to make clean, correct varietals of increasing quality. ZIN from AMADOR COUNTY.

San Pasqual S. California. Table ★→★★
New winery near San Diego with pleasant whites, esp. CHENIN BLANC, SAUVIGNON BLANC.

Santa Ynez San Luis Obispo/Santa Barbara. Table ★★
Promising whites, esp. SAUVIGNON BLANC, from new winery.

Schramsberg Napa. Sp. ★★★★
A dedicated specialist using historic old cellars to make California's best "champagne".

Sebastiani Sonoma. Table ★★
Substantial and distinguished old family firm with robust appetizing wines, esp. BARBERA, GAMAY BEAUJOLAIS, PINOT NOIR.

Setrakian
See California Growers.

Simi Alexander Valley. Table ★★★
Restored old winery with expert direction. Several notable wines, incl. racy GEWÜRZ, gentle ZINFANDEL, delicate CABERNET.

Smith-Madrone Napa. Table ★★
New v'yd. high on Spring Mountain made good RIESLING in '77. CHARDONNAY and CABERNET are expected.

Smothers Santa Clara/Santa Cruz. Table ?
Tiny winery owned by T.V. comic made remarkable first wines. The world waits.

Sonoma Vineyards Sonoma R-R. Table and sp. **★★** → **★★★**
> Quick-growing business, well-regarded for varietals, esp. RIESLING and CHARDONNAY. Range includes single-v'yd. wines, esp. Alexander's Crown CABERNET.

Souverain Alexander Valley. Table **★★**
> Luxurious new mid-sized winery with highly competent wines, both red and white, if no great ones.

Spring Mountain Napa. Table ★★★
> Recently renovated small 19th-century property with new winery already noted for good CHARDONNAY, SAUVIGNON BLANC and CABERNET.

Stag's Leap Wine Cellars Napa. Table ★★★→★★★★
> New small v'yd. and cellar with high standards. Excellent CABERNET, fresh GAMAY, soft RIESLING, fine CHARDONNAY.

Sterling Napa. Table **★★★**
> Spectacular new mid-sized winery, now owned by Coca-Cola, with already startling achievements. Rich heavy SAUVIGNON BLANC and CHARDONNAY; fruity CABERNET and MERLOT.

Stonegate Napa. Table ★★→★★★
> Small privately owned winery and v'yd. making CHENIN BLANC, SAUVIGNON BLANC, CHARDONNAY, PINOT NOIR.

Stony Hill Napa. Table ★★★★
> Many of California's very best whites have come from this minute winery over 25 years. Alas owner Fred McCrea died in 1977, but his wife Eleanor carries on. Stony Hill CHARDONNAY, GEWÜRZ and RIESLING are all delicate and fine.

Story Vineyard Amador City. Table **★★**
> Old vineyard producing very good ZIN.

Sutter Home Napa. Table **★★**
> Small winery revived, specializing in ZINFANDEL from Amador County grapes: excellent heavy-weight.

Swan, J. Sonoma. Table ★★
> New one-man winery with a name for rich ZINFANDEL.

Trefethen Napa. Table ★★★
> Small family-owned winery in Napa's finest old wooden building. Good RIESLING, CHARDONNAY and CABERNET.

Trentadue Sonoma R-R. Table ★★
> Small v'yd. and smaller winery making sound big-flavoured wines, incl. some from unorthodox varieties.

Turgeon & Lohr Central Coast. Table ★★
> Small winery in San Jose with its own v'yds. in SALINAS. Reliable PINOT BLANC and CABERNET.

Veedercrest Napa. Table ★★
> Still nascent small winery with promise of talent.

Villa Armando Livermore/San Joaquin. Table ★
> Specialist in the American-Italian market for coarse sweet table wines.

Villa Mount Eden Napa. ★★★
> Small Oakville estate with excellent dry CHENIN BLANC, good CHARDONNAY, and CABERNET outstanding.

Weibel Central Coast. Table and sp. ★
> Veteran mid-sized winery without high ambitions.

Wente Livermore and Central Coast. Table ★★→★★★
> Important and historic specialists in Bordeaux-style whites. Fourth-generation Wentes are as dynamic as ever. CHARDONNAY, SAUVIGNON BLANC and RIESLING are all standards. PINOT NOIR is also good.

Winemasters
> Brand name of GUILD.

Z-D Wines Napa. Table ★★★
> Very small winery (moved from Sonoma to Rutherford) with a name for powerful PINOT NOIR and CHARDONNAY.

New York

New York State and its neighbours Ohio and Ontario make their own style of wine from grapes of native American ancestry, rather than the European vines of California. American grapes have a flavour known as "foxy"; a taste acquired by many easterners. Fashion is slowly moving in favour of hybrids between these and European grapes with less, or no, foxiness. The entries below include both wineries and grape varieties.

Aurora

One of the best white French-American hybrid grapes, the most widely planted in New York. Formerly known as Seibel 5279. Good for sparkling wine.

Baco Noir

One of the better red French-American hybrid grapes. High acidity but good clean dark wine.

Benmarl

Highly regarded and expanding v'yd. and winery at Marlboro on the Hudson River. Wines are mainly from French-American hybrids, but European vines also make good wine.

Boordy Vineyards

The winery which pioneered French-American hybrid grapes in the USA. Started by Philip Wagner in Maryland in the '50s, now also in the FINGER LAKES.

Brights

Canada's biggest winery, in Ontario, now tending towards French-American hybrids and experiments with European vines. Their CHELOIS and BACO NOIR are pleasant reds, respectively lighter and more full-bodied.

Bully Hill

New (since 1970) FINGER LAKES winery using both American and hybrid grapes to make varietal wines.

Château Gai

Canadian (Ontario) winery making European and hybrid wines, incl. successful GAMAY and PINOT NOIR.

Catawba

One of the first American wine-grapes, still the second most widely grown. Pale red and foxy flavoured.

Chautauqua

The biggest grape-growing district in the e., along the s. shore of La. Erie from New York to Ohio.

Chelois

Popular red French-American hybrid grape, formerly called Seibel 10878. Makes dry red wine with some richness, slightly foxy.

Concord

The archetypal American grape, dark red, strongly foxy, making good grape jelly but dreadful wine. By far the most widely planted in New York (23,000 acres).

Delaware

Old American white-wine grape making pleasant, slightly foxy dry wines. Used in "Champagne" and for still wine.

De Chaunac

A good red French-American hybrid grape, popular in Canada as well as New York. Full-bodied dark wine.

Finger Lakes

Century-old wine district in upper New York State, best-known for its "Champagne". The centre is Hammondsport.

Fournier, Charles

The top quality of "Champagne" made by the GOLD SEAL company, named for a former distinguished wine-maker.

Frank, Dr. Konstantin
> A controversial figure in the FINGER LAKES: the protagonist of European vinifera vines. See Vinifera Wines.

Gold Seal
> One of New York's biggest wineries, makers of Charles FOURNIER "Champagne" and the HENRI MARCHANT range. Known for high quality and readiness to experiment.

Great Western
> The brand name of the PLEASANT VALLEY WINE CO's "Champagne", one of New York's best wines.

Henri Marchant
> Brand name of GOLD SEAL's standard range of mainly traditional American-grape wines.

High Tor
> Well-known small winery on the Hudson River only 28 miles from Manhattan. Vines are French-American hybrids.

Inniskillin
> Small new Canadian winery at Niagara making European and hybrid wines, incl. good MARÉCHAL FOCH.

Isabella
> Old CONCORD-style red grape making strongly foxy wine.

Phylloxera is an insect that lives on the roots of the vine. Its arrival in Europe from North America in the 1860s was an international catastrophe. It destroyed almost every vineyard on the continent before it was discovered that the native American vine is immune to its attacks. The remedy was (and still is) to graft European vines on to American rootstocks. Virtually all Europe's vineyards are so grafted today. Whether their produce is just as good as the wine of pre-phylloxera days is a favourite debate among old-school wine-lovers

---

Maréchal Foch
> Promising red French hybrid between PINOT NOIR and GAMAY. Makes good burgundy-style wine in Ontario.

Niagara
> Old American white grape used for sweet wine. Very foxy.

Pleasant Valley Wine Co.
> Winery at Hammondsport, FINGER LAKES, owned by TAYLOR'S, producing GREAT WESTERN wines.

Seibel
> One of the most famous French grape hybridists, responsible for many successful French-American crosses originally known by numbers, since christened with such names as AURORA, DE CHAUNAC, CHELOIS.

Seyve-Villard
> Another well-known French hybridist. His best-known cross, no. 5276, is known as Seyval Blanc.

Taylor's
> The biggest wine-company of the Eastern States, based at Hammondsport in the FINGER LAKES. Brands incl. GREAT WESTERN and LAKE COUNTRY. Most vines are American.

Vinifera Wines
> Small but influential winery of Dr Frank, pioneer in growing European vines, incl. RIESLING, CHARDONNAY and PINOT NOIR, in the FINGER LAKES area. Some excellent wines.

Widmers
> Major FINGER LAKES winery selling native American varietal wines: DELAWARE, NIAGARA, etc.

South America

The flourishing vineyards of Argentina (the world's fifth largest) and Chile are known to the world chiefly as a source of cheap wine of sometimes remarkable quality. Most of it is drunk within South America.

ARGENTINA

The quality vineyards are concentrated in Mendoza province in the Andean foothills at about 2,000 feet. They are all irrigated. San Raphael, 140 miles s. of Mendoza city, is centre of a slightly cooler area. San Juan, to the north, is hotter and specializes in sherry and brandy.

Bianchi, Bodegas

Well-known premium wine producer at San Raphael. "Don Valentin" is a best-seller. "1887" and "particular" are top Cabernets.

Cooperation San Raphael

Enormous cooperative for bulk wines and concentrated grape juice.

Crillon, Bodegas

Brand-new (1972) winery owned by Seagram's, principally for tank-method sparkling wines.

Furlotti, Angel

Big bodega at Maipu, Mendoza. 2,500 acres making its best red wine from a blend of CABERNET, MERLOT and Lambrusco, white from PINOT BLANC and RIESLING.

Giol

The State winery of Maipu province. Mainly bulk wines. Premium range is called "Canciller".

Gonzales Videla, Bodegas

Old-established family firm re-equipped for modern methods. Brands include "Tromel" and "Panquehua".

Goyenechea, Bodegas

Basque family firm making old-style wines.

Greco Hermanos

1,750 acre v'yds at St. Martin, Mendoza, with Malbec, Lambrusco, BARBERA, SEMILLON, PALOMINO, etc. Range incl. El Greco "selection" and Oro del Rhin (PINOT BLANC).

La Rural, Bodegas

Family-run winery at Coquimbito specializing in Riesling and Traminer whites.

Lopez, Bodegas

Family firm best known for their 10-year-old "Chateau Montchenot" Cabernet/Malbec red.

Norton, Bodegas

Old firm, originally English, at Perdriol. "Perdriel" is brand-name of 10-year-old premium Cabernet in flask-bottle.

Orfila, José

Long-established bodega at St. Martin, Mendoza. Top export wines are CABERNET and white Extra Dry (PINOT BLANC).

Penaflor

Four bodegas and 3,000 acres in San Juan and Mendoza. Specialities: sherry and desert wine, also red in cans. Tio Quinto is their popular medium sherry.

Proviar, Bodega

Producers of "champana" (sparkling wine) under contract with MOET ET CHANDON! Premium brand is "Baron B".

Santa Ana, Bodegas

Old-established family firm at Guaymallen. Wide range of wines.

Suter, Bodegas

Swiss-founded firm best-known for "Etiquetta Marron" white and "Juan Suter" reds.

Toso, Pascual
Old Mendoza winery at San José, making one of Argentina's best reds, Cabernet Toso. Also RIESLING and sparkling wines.

CHILE
The principal bodegas exporting wine from Chile are:

Canepa, José
A modern establishment at Valparaiso handling wine from several areas. Very good French-style CABERNET from Lontüé, Talca, 100 miles south; dry SEMILLON, sweet Moscatel. Exports to Switzerland, Mexico, U.K., etc.

Concha y Toro
The biggest wine firm, with several bodegas and 2,500 acres in the Maipo valley. Remarkable dark and deep CABERNET, MERLOT, Verdot. Good SAUVIGNON BLANC. Wines go to Venezuela, Brazil, etc., Canada and Germany.

Cousiño Macul
Distinguished estate near Santiago. Very dry "green" SEMILLON and CHARDONNAY. Don Luis light red, Don Matias dark and tannic, tastes of oak and cheese. Colombia is a big market, also Benelux.

Santa Carolina
A bodega with pleasant widely available dry wines.

San Pedro
Brand name for Wagner Stein & Co., long-established at Lontüé, Talca. Range of good wines sold all over S. America, esp. Bordeaux-like CABERNET.

Santa Rita
Bodega in the Maipo valley s. of Santiago. Pleasant soft wines including the "120" brand.

Tocornal, José
Considerable exporter to Venezuela and Canada.

Undurraga
Famous family business; one of the first to export to the U.S.A. Wines in both old and modern styles: good clean SAUVIGNON BLANC and oaky yellow "Viejo Roble". "Gran Vino Tinto" is one of the best buys in Chile.

England

The English wine industry started again in earnest in the late 1960s after a pause of some 400 years. More than a million bottles a year are now being made; almost all white and generally Germanic in style, many from new German and French grape varieties designed to ripen well in cool weather. In such a young industry results of prize competitions are studied with interest. The annual Gore-Brown Trophy is awarded for the best English wine.

Adgestone nr. Sandown, Isle of Wight. K. C. Barlow
Prize-winning 9-acre v'yd on chalky hill site. Vines are Müller-Thurgau, Reichensteiner, Seyval Blanc. First vintage was 1970. Light, fragrant, dryish wines.

Beaulieu Abbey nr. Lymington, Hampshire. The Hon. Ralph Douglas Scott-Montagu
6-acre v'yd, principally of Müller-Thurgau, established in 1960 by the Gore-Brown family on an old monastic site.

Biddenden nr. Tenterden, Kent. R. A. Barnes
16-acre mixed v'yd since 1973 making crisp med-dry white of Huxelrebe and Müller-Thurgau; also a rosé with Pinot Noir. First vintage 1973.

Brede nr. Rye, Sussex. R. D. Thorley
The first winner of the Gore-Brown Trophy, in 1974. Planted 1965. Medium dry Müller-Thurgau and medium-sweet Seyval Blanc from 1¼ acres.

Cavendish Manor nr. Sudbury, Suffolk. B. T. Ambrose
10-acre v'yd of Müller-Thurgau planted on a farm. Fruity dry wine has won several awards since 1974.

Chilford Hundred Linton, nr. Cambridge. S. Alper
18 acres of Müller-Thurgau, Schonburger, Huxelrebe and Siegerrebe making fairly dry wines since 1974.

Chilsdown nr. Chichester, Sussex. I. R. Paget
10½ acres of Müller-Thurgau, Reichensteiner and Seyval Blanc making full dry French-style white since 1974.

Elmham Park nr. East Dereham, Norfolk. R. Don
7½-acre v'yd of a wine-merchant/fruit farmer, planted with Müller-Thurgau, Madeleine-Angevine, etc. "Mosel-style" light dry flowery wines. First vintage 1974.

Felstar Felsted, nr. Dunmow, Essex J. G. Barrett
Well-established 10½-acre v'yd of many varieties, selling Madeleine Sylvaner, Müller-Thurgau, Seyval Blanc/ Chardonnay, Muscat, a rosé and an occasional Auslese. A sparkling wine won a medal in 1978.

Hambledon nr. Petersfield, Hampshire. Maj. Gen. Sir Guy Salisbury Jones
The first modern English v'yd, planted in 1954 on a chalk slope with advice and grapes from Champagne; principally Chardonnay. Now 5¼ acres. Fairly dry wines.

Hascombe Godalming, Surrey. Lt. Cdr. T. P. Baillie-Grohman
5¾-acre v'yd, principally Müller-Thurgau, making dry delicate wines since 1971.

Kelsale nr. Saxmundham, Suffolk. S. T. Edgerley
2¼-acre v'yd owned by a retired barrister, making stylish wines. Winner of 1977 Gore-Brown Trophy with a Madeleine Angevine.

Lamberhurst Priory nr. Tunbridge Wells, Kent. K. McAlpine
England's biggest v'yd with 35 acres, planted 1972. Largely Müller-Thurgau, Seyval Blanc, etc., but some also more experimental reds (sold in Germany). Produces half a million bottles a year including wine-making for other small v'ds.

Merrydown Wine Co. Heathfield, E. Sussex. J. L. Ward
A major influence on English wine-making, having started in 1946 with cider and since 1969 acted as a co-operative for the young wine industry. Now making an estate Müller-Thurgau, "Horam Manor" (2 acres).

New Hall nr. Maldon, Essex. S. W. Greenwood
21 acres of a mixed farm making award-winning whites, chiefly of the fragrant Huxelrebe. Experimental reds.

Pilton Manor nr. Shepton Mallet, Somerset. N. de m. Godden
4½-acre hillside v'yd, chiefly of Müller-Thurgau and Seyval Blanc, planted 1966. Twice winner of Gore-Brown Trophy. Also a méthode champenoise sparkling wine.

Pulham nr. Norwich, Norfolk. P. W. Cook
New 16-acre v'yd (since 1976); principally Müller-Thurgau.

Rock Lodge nr. Haywards Heath, Sussex. N. C. Cowderoy
2¼-acre v'yd of Müller-Thurgau and Reichensteiner making very dry white since 1970.

St. Etheldreda nr. Ely, Cambridge. N. Sneesby
2¼-acre mixed v'yd making a Müller-Thurgau and a Chardonnay since 1974.

Wootton nr. Wells, Somerset. Major C. L. B. Gillespie
6-acre v'yd of Schönburger, Müller-Thurgau, etc., making award-winning fresh and fruity wines since 1973.

Australia

It is only 20 years since modern wine technology revolutionized Australia's 150-year-old wine industry, ending the dominance of fortified wines and making table wines of top quality possible. Already the results are as impressive as California's. The Australians know it: little is left for export.

Traditional-style Australian wines were thick-set and burly Shiraz reds or Semillon or Riesling whites. The modern taste is for lighter wines, especially Rhine Rieslings, and for Cabernet reds, but the best still have great character and the ability to age splendidly.

Australia's wine labels are among the world's most communicative. Since Australians started to take their own wine seriously they have become longer and longer winded, with information about grapes, soil, sunshine, fermenting periods and temperatures, wine-makers' biographies and serving hints. Little of this is pure salesmanship. It is intended to be, and really is, helpful. Bin-numbers mean something. They need to be noted and remembered. Prizes in shows (which are highly competitive) mean a great deal. In a country without any sort of established grades of quality the buyer needs all the help he can get.

Wine areas

The vintages mentioned here are those rated as good or excellent for the reds of the areas in question in an authoritative chart published by the Rothbury Estate Society.

Adelaide 66 67 70 71 72 73 75 76 77 79
The capital of South Australia had the state's first v'yds. A few are still making wine.

Barossa 66 68 72 73 75 76 77 79
Australia's biggest quality area, of German origin, specializing in white (esp. Riesling; best from the Eden Valley at 1,500 feet), good-quality reds and good dessert wines.

Clare-Watervale 66 68 70 71 72 75 76 77 78 79
Small cool-climate area 90 miles n. of Adelaide best known for Riesling; also planted with Shiraz and Cabernet.

Central Victoria 66 68 71 73 74 76 79
Scattered v'yds. remaining from vast pre-phylloxera plantings include GT. WESTERN, CH. TAHBILK, AVOCA and BENDEGO.

Coonawarra   66 68 70 71 72 73 74 75 76 77 79

Southernmost v'yd. of South Australia, long famous for well-balanced reds, recently successful with Riesling.

Hunter Valley   66 67 70 72 73 74 75 76 77 79

The great name in N.S.W. Broad deep Shiraz reds and Semillon whites with a style of their own. Now also Cabernet and Chardonnay. Recent expansion at Wybong, etc., to the w.

Keppock/Padthaway

Large new area in southern S. Australia being developed by big companies as an overspill of Coonawarra. Cool climate and good potential for commercial reds and whites.

Langhorne Creek

See Southern Vales.

Lilydale/Yarra Valley

Historic wine area near Melbourne destroyed by phylloxera, now being redeveloped by enthusiasts with small wineries. A bewildering range of varieties and styles.

N.E. Victoria   66 70 71 72 73 75 76

Historic area incl. Rutherglen, Corowa, Wangaratta. Heavy reds and magnificent sweet dessert wines.

Margaret River/Busselton

New area of great promise for fine wines, s. of Perth in W. Australia.

McLaren Vale and S. Adelaide

See Southern Vales

Mudgee

Small traditional wine area in a N.S.W. fruit-growing district. Big reds of great colour and flavour and full coarse whites.

Murray Valley   N.V.

Important scattered v'yds. irrigated from the Murray river, incl. Swan Hill, Mildura, Renmark, Berri, Loxton, Waikerie. Largely sherry, brandy, "jug" and dessert wines.

Riverina   N.V.

Fruit- and vine-growing district irrigated from the Murrumbidgee river. Mainly jug wines, but good light "varietals".

Southern Vales   66 67 70 71 72 73 75 76 77 79

General name for several small pockets of wine-growing s. of Adelaide of which McLaren Vale is the most important. Big full-blooded reds and rather coarse whites.

Swan Valley

The main v'yd. of Western Australia, on the n. outskirts of Perth. Hot climate makes strong low-acid wines.

Upper Hunter

New region 60 miles N.W. of Hunter Valley, N.S.W. with more extreme climate, specializing in white wines, lighter and quicker-developing than Hunter whites.

Wineries

All Saints   N.E. Vic. Full range *→**

Big old family-run winery in dessert-wine country. Sturdy reds. Sweet brown MUSCAT is sometimes exceptional.

Angle Vale   S. Aus. Table wine *→**

Big new winery s. of Barossa with good SEMILLON white and pleasant soft reds.

Angove's   S.A. Table and dessert *→**

Family business in Adelaide and Renmark in the Murray Valley. Sound traditional wines.

Arrowfield   N.S.W. Table *

The largest Upper Hunter vineyard, on irrigated land. Some pleasant dry whites, including RH. RIESLING.

Bailey's N.E. Vic. Table and dessert `**`
　　Small family concern making rich old-fashioned reds of great character, and admirable dessert MUSCAT.

Balgownie Vic. Table `***`
　　Specialist in fine reds, particularly straight CABERNET.

Berri Coop. S. Aus. Full range `*→**`
　　Aus's largest winery, selling mostly to other companies. Lately developing their own name with success; particularly robust oaky reds.

Best's Central Vic. Full range `*→**`
　　Conservative old family winery at Great Western with good strong old-style claret, hock, etc.

Bilyara N. Barossa. S. Aus. Table and Sp. `**→***`
　　Wolf Blass is the ebullient German wine-maker with dazzling products and propaganda. His oak wines are not for keeping.

Bleasdale Langhorne Creek, S.A. Full range `*→**`
　　Small family business making above-average reds of CABERNET and SHIRAZ.

Brand Coonawarra, S.A. Table `***`
　　Small privately owned winery. Outstandingly fine and stylish CABERNET and SHIRAZ under the Laira label.

Brokenwood N.S.W. Dry red. `**`
　　New small winery owned by lawyers. Exciting quality of CABERNET SAUVIGNON since 1973.

Brown Brothers Milawa, N.E. Victoria. Full range `*→***`
　　Old family firm with new ideas, wide range of rather delicate wines, not the blood-and-guts style of the area.

Buring, Leo Barossa, S.A. Full range `*→***`
　　"Château Leonay", old white-wine specialists, now owned by LINDEMAN. Very good "Reserve Bin" RHINE RIESLING.

Château Tahbilk Central Vic. Table `*→***`
　　Family-owned wine-estate making CABERNET, SHIRAZ, RHINE RIESLING and Marsanne. "Special Bins" are outstanding.

Château Yaldara Barossa, S.A. Full range `*`
　　A showpiece of Barossa, popular with tourists. Sparkling wines are a speciality.

Craigmoor N.S.W. Table and Port `*→**`
　　The oldest Mudgee winery. Robust reds and whites, and port matured in rum barrels.

d'Arenberg McLaren Vale, S.A. Table and dessert `*→**`
　　Small-scale old-style family outfit s. of Adelaide. Strapping rustic reds; CABERNET, SHIRAZ and Burgundy.

Drayton Hunter Valley, N.S.W. Table `**`
　　Traditional Hunter wines, Hermitage red and SEMILLON white, from the old Bellevue estate.

Elliott Hunter Valley, N.S.W. Table `**`
　　Long-established grower. "Tallawanta" reds and "Belford" whites are in the bosomy, deep-flavoured Hunter style.

Emu S.A. Table and dessert `*`
　　Bulk shippers of high-strength wine to Britain and Canada.

Gramp Barossa, S.A. Full range `*→***`
　　Great pioneering family company, now owned by Reckitt & Colman. Range includes sweet fizzy "Barossa Pearl", good standard CABERNET, etc., and some of Australia's best RHINE RIESLING: Steingarten. Typed labels on special wines.

Hamilton's S. Adelaide and Barossa, S.A. Full range `*`
　　Big family business making popular rather light and "modern" wines, e.g. Ewell Moselle and Springton Riesling.

Hardy's Southern Vales, S.A., Barossa, etc. Full range `*→**`
　　Famous wide-spread family-run company using and blending wines from several areas, incl. a CABERNET, reliable light St. Thomas Burgundy and good Old Castle Riesling.

Henschke Barossa, S.A. Table *
    Family business known for white wines, esp. RHINE RIESLING.

Houghton Swan Valley, W.A. Table and dessert *→**
    The one famous winery of W. Australia. Now belongs to EMU. Soft, ripe "White Burgundy" is the top wine.

Hungerford Hill Hunter Valley, N.S.W. Table *→**
    Big new winery with over 1,000 acres and modern ideas.

Huntingdon Estate N.S.W. Table *→**
    New small winery; the best in Mudgee. Fine award-winning reds and clean SEMILLON and CHARDONNAY.

Kaiser Stuhl Barossa, S.A. Full range *→***
    The Barossa growers' co-operative. A fine modern winery with high standards. "Individual v'yd." Rieslings are excellent. So is "Special Reserve" CABERNET.

Lake's Folly Hunter Valley, N.S.W. Table ***
    The work of an inspired surgeon from Sydney. A new style for the Hunter Valley: CABERNET and new barrels to make rich complex California-style reds. Also excellent CHARDONNAY.

Lindeman Orig. Hunter, now everywhere. Full range *→***
    One of the oldest firms, now a giant owned by Phillip Morris Corp. Its Ben Ean "Moselle" is Australia's best-selling wine. Owns BURINGS in Barossa and Rouge Homme in Coonawarra. Dessert-wine v'yds. at Corowa, N. Victoria. Many inter-state blends. Pioneers in modernizing wine styles.

McWilliams Hunter Valley and Riverina, N.S.W. Full range *→***
    Famous and first-rate Hunter wine-makers at Mount Pleasant and Lovedale (HERMITAGE and SEMILLON). Pioneers in RIVERINA with lighter wines, incl. sweet white "Lexia" and fine varieties.

Mildara Murray Valley, S.A. Full range *→***
    Sherry and brandy specialists at Mildura on the Murray river also making fine CABERNET and RIESLING at COONAWARRA.

Morris N.E. Vic. Table and dessert **→****
    Old winery at Rutherglen making Australia's best brown "liqueur" muscat. Now owned by Reckitt & Colman.

Orlando See GRAMPS.

Penfold's Orig. Adelaide, now everywhere. Full range *→****
    Ubiquitous and excellent company: in BAROSSA, HUNTER VALLEY, RIVERINA, COONAWARRA, etc. Grange Hermitage is ****, St. Henri Claret not far behind. Bin-numbered wines are usually outstanding. "Grandfather Port" is remarkable.

Petaluma S.A. ***
    Very promising newcomer, a recent rocket-like success with CHARDONNAY and RIESLING, now centred around new winery in ADELAIDE HILLS.

Quelltaler Clare-Watervale, S.A. Full range *→**
    Old winery n. of Adelaide known for good "Granfiesta" sherry and full dry "hock". Recently good Rhine Riesling.

Redman Coonawarra, S.A. Table ***
    Small new winery making only COONAWARRA claret of SHIRAZ and CABERNET of top quality.

Reynella Southern Vales, S.A. Full range *→***
    Red-wine specialists s. of ADELAIDE. Highly esteemed rich CABERNET and "Vintage Reserve" claret.

Rosemount N.S.W. Table *→**
    Bustling newcomer in Upper HUNTER. Agreeable RH. RIESLING and Traminer/Riesling blend.

Rothbury Estate Hunter Valley, N.S.W. Table ***
    Important new syndicate-owned wine estate concentrating on traditional HUNTER wines: "Hermitage" and "Riesling" also new plantings of CABERNET, CHARDONNAY, PINOT NOIR.

Rycroft McLaren Vale, S.A. Table ★→★★
> Specialists in typical sturdy CABERNET and SHIRAZ.

Saltram Barossa, S.A. Full range ★→★★★
> One of the smaller wineries making a notable CABERNET, "Mamre Brook" and good "Selected Vintage" claret and RHINE RIESLING.

Sandleford W. Aus. Table ★→★★
> New small winery with contrasting styles of red and white varietals from Swan and Margaret River.

Saxonvale N.S.W. Table ★★
> Large newcomer at Fordwich, N.W. of Hunter. After early difficulties now making very good SEMILLON and CHARDONNAY.

Seaview Southern Vales, S.A. Table and dessert ★★
> Old-established winery now owned by Toohey's Brewery. Well-known CABERNET, SAUVIGNON and RHINE RIESLING.

Seppelt Barossa, S.A. Central Vic. and elsewhere. Full range ★→★★
> Far-flung producers of Australia's best "champagne" (Gt. Western Brut), good dessert wines (from Rutherglen, the Murray Valley, Barossa), the reliable Moyston claret and some good private bin wines from Gt. Western in Victoria.

Smith's Yalumba Barossa, S.A. Full range ★→★★★
> Big old family firm. Best wines incl. Rhine Riesling from Pewsey Vale above Barossa, good "Galway Vintage" claret, "Galway Pipe" port and Chiquita sherry.

Southern Vales Wine Co. S. Aus. Full range ★→★★
> Co-op in McLaren Vale developing fine table wines, esp. dry white varietals.

Stanley Clare, S. Aus. Full range ★→★★
> Important medium size quality winery owned by Heinz. Among Aus's best RH. RIESLING and CABERNET SAUVIGNON and complex Cabernet-Shiraz-Malbec blends under Leasingham label.

Stonyfell Adelaide, S.A. Full range ★→★★
> Long-established company best known for "Metala" CABERNET SHIRAZ from Langhorne Creek.

Tollana Barossa, S.A. Full range ★→★★
> Old company famous for brandy, has latterly made some remarkable CABERNET and RHINE RIESLING.

Tulloch Hunter Valley, N.S.W. Table ★★
> An old name at Pokolbin, with good dry reds and "Riesling".

Tyrrell Hunter Valley, N.S.W. Table ★★→★★★
> Up-to-date old family business at "Ashman's". Some of the best traditional Hunter wines, Hermitage and RIESLING, are distinguished by Vat Numbers. Also big rich CHARDONNAY.

Valencia W. Aus. Full range ★→★★
> W. Aus's largest company owned by Thos. Hardy, located in Swan Valley. Interesting white varietals of CHENIN BLANC from Gin Gin w. of Perth.

Woodleys Adel, S. Aus. Table ★★
> Melbourne-owned; well-known for Queen Adelaide label claret and Riesling.

Wyndham Estate Branxton, N.S.W. Full range ★→★★
> Frantic marketers of full range, but some fine Hunter varietals occasionally emerge. Geo. Wyndham's original estate is now a tourist attraction.

Wynns S. Aus. and N.S.W. Table ★→★★★
> Large inter-state company, originators of flagon wines, with winery in RIVERINA and vineyards at Coonawarra, making good CABERNET. Owned by Toohey's Brewery.

South Africa

South Africa has made excellent sherry and port for many years, but has taken table wine seriously only in the last decade. Since 1972 a new system of Wines of Origin and registered "estates" has started a new era of competitive modern wine-making. The following list includes areas of origin, wineries, grape varieties and other label terms. Star-ratings have been omitted for the present until more information is available.

Allesverloren
Estate in MALMESBURY with over 325 acres of v'yds., formerly well known for "port", now specializing in red wines made with modern technology. Distributed by BERGKELDER.

Alphen
Estate originally at Constantia, owned by the famous Cloete family (see GROOT CONSTANTIA), now at Somerset West with a new winery. Expert direction should make good wines.

Alto
STELLENBOSCH estate of about 200 acres best known for massive-bodied CABERNET and a good blend: Alto Rouge. Distributed by BERGKELDER.

Backsberg
Name formerly associated with commercial blends, now a prize-winning 400-acre estate at PAARL with notably good varietal reds.

Bergkelder
Big wine concern at STELLENBOSCH, member of the OUDÈ MEESTER group, making and distributing many brands and estate wines, incl. FLEUR DU CAP, ALTO, HAZENDAL, etc.

Bertrams
Major wine company owned by Gilbeys with a wide range of well-made varietals.

Blaauwklippen
Estate s. of STELLENBOSCH.

Boberg
Controlled area of origin consisting of the regions of PAARL and TULBAGH, applying only to their fortified or dessert wines.

Boschendal
Estate in PAARL area being developed on old fruit farm. Anglo-American owned.

Bukettraube
New German white-wine grapes with acidity and aroma, popular in S. Africa for blending.

Cabernet
The great Bordeaux grape particularly successful in the STELLENBOSCH area. Sturdy, long-ageing wines.

Cavendish Cape
Range of remarkably good sherries from the K.W.V..

Château Libertas
Also Oude Libertas. Two standard good-quality blended reds from the STELLENBOSCH FARMERS' WINERY.

Cinsaut
Bulk-producing French red grape formerly known as Hermitage in S. Africa. Chiefly blended with CABERNET, but can make good wine on its own.

Colombard
The "FRENCH COLOMBARD" of California. Prized in S. Africa for its high acidity and fruity flavour.

Constantia

Once the world's most famous muscat wine, from the Cape. Now the southernmost area of origin ("Constantia and Durbanville"). See also GROOT CONSTANTIA.

Delheim

Winery at Driesprong in the best and highest area of STELLENBOSCH, known for delicate STEEN whites and also light reds, PINOTAGE, SHIRAZ and CABERNET.

Drostdy

Well-known growers' co-operative in TULBAGH.

Estate wine

A strictly controlled term applying only to some 40 registered estates making wines made of grapes grown on the same property.

Fleur du Cap

Popular and well-made range of wines from the BERGKELDER, Stellenbosch. Particularly good SHIRAZ.

Gewürztraminer

The famous spicy grape of Alsace, successfully grown in the TULBAGH area.

La Gratitude

Well-known brand of dry white from the STELLENBOSCH FARMERS' WINERY.

Groot Constantia

Historic estate, now government-owned, near Cape Town. Source of superlative muscat wine in the early 19th century. Now making CABERNET, PINOT NOIR, PINOTAGE and SHIRAZ reds, the Shiraz apparently being best. Also a blend Heerenrood.

Grünberger

A good brand of dry STEEN white from the BERGKELDER, though flagrantly dressed up as a German Franconian "Steinwein".

Hazendal

Family estate in w. STELLENBOSCH making STEEN, CINSAUT and PINOTAGE, all marketed by the BERGKELDER.

Kanonkop

Estate in n. STELLENBOSCH, specializing in high-quality and particularly full-bodied CABERNET and PINOTAGE.

Klein Karoo

The easternmost S. African wine region, warm and dry, specializing in dessert and distilling wine.

K.W.V.

The Kooperatieve Wijnbouwers Vereniging, S. Africa's national wine co-operative, originally organized by the State to absorb embarrassing surpluses, now at vast and splendidly equipped premises in PAARL making a range of good wines, particularly sherries.

Landgoed

South African for Estate; a word which appears on all estate-wine labels and official seals.

Landskroon

Family estate owned by Paul and Hugo de Villiers. Mainly port-type wines for K.W.V. but recently some exc. dry reds – PINOTAGE and Tintas das Baroccas.

Malmesbury

Wine region on the w. coast n. of Cape Town, specializing in dry whites and distilling wine.

Meerendal

Estate near Durbanville producing robust reds marketed by the BERGKELDER.

Meerlust

    Estate s. of STELLENBOSCH making CABERNET marketed by the BERGKELDER.

Monis

    Well-known wine concern of PAARL now merged with the STELLENBOSCH FARMERS' WINERY.

Montagne

    Relatively new but successful estate of 300+ acres near STELLENBOSCH. Wines incl. CABERNET, STEEN (sold as "Chenin Blanc"), RIESLING, and a dry rosé now owned by Gilbeys.

Montpellier

    Famous pioneering TULBAGH estate with 350 acres of v'yds. specializing in white wine. Produced the first two whites to be officially designated SUPERIOR (RIESLING and GEWÜRZTRAMINER), also French CHENIN BLANC and a small quantity of excellent méthode champenoise sparkling wine.

Muratie

    Ancient estate in STELLENBOSCH, best known for its Pinot Noir. 160 acres of v'yds. also grow CABERNET, RIESLING, STEEN and CINSAUT.

Nederburg

    The most famous wine farm in modern S. Africa, now operated by the STELLENBOSCH FARMERS' WINERY. Pioneer in modern cellar practice, popularized both CABERNET and the idea of estate wines, although no longer technically an estate itself. Recent innovations have included an Auslese-type STEEN: Nederburg Edelkeur.

Olifantsrivier

    The northernmost demarcated wine region of the Cape with a warm dry climate. Mainly distilling wine.

"I only drink Champagne to wake me from the dead"—said Hilaire Belloc—"a thing I constantly need!" Why does Champagne have such an instantly stimulating effect? The latest theory is that the CO_2 in the bubbles not only helps the alcohol in the wine to pass through the stomach wall into the bloodstream; but that in passing into the bloodstream itself it speeds up the circulation—the system puts on a spurt to get rid of the CO_2 and replace it with oxygen—thus carrying the alcohol to where it can do most good with the least delay. Which is a justification for the infinite pains champagne-makers take to see that as much CO_2 as possible is dissolved in their wine. In real Champagne the CO_2 is produced by slow fermentation in the bottles: it can't escape: instead it goes into solution in the wine. No short-cut process can persuade the wine to dissolve so much of the luxury laughing gas.

Overgaauw

    Estate w. of STELLENBOSCH making good whites and reds.

Paarl

    South Africa's wine capital, 50 miles n.e. of Cape Town, and the surrounding demarcated region, among the best in the country, particularly for white wine and sherry. Most of its wine is made by co-operatives.

Paarlsack

    Well-known range of sherries made at PAARL by the K.W.V.

Pinotage

    South African red grape, a cross between PINOT NOIR and CINSAUT, useful for high yields, hardiness and good quality.

Piquetberg

    Small demarcated region on the w. coast round Porterville. A warm dry climate gives mainly dessert and distilling wine.

Riesling

South African Riesling makes some of the country's better white wines, but is not the same as Rhine Riesling, which has only recently been planted in any quantity in S. Africa.

Robertson

Small demarcated region e. of the Cape and inland. Mainly dessert wines (notably MUSCAT), but red and white table wines are on the increase.

Roodeberg

High-quality brand of blended red wine from the K.W.V. Has good colour, body and flavour and ages well in bottle.

Rustenberg

Effectively, if not officially, an estate red wine from just n.e. of STELLENBOSCH. Rustenberg and SCHOONGEZICHT are managed together and the name Rustenberg used for the red of CABERNET and CINSAUT, one of S. Africa's best.

Schoongezicht

Partner of RUSTENBERG, one of S. Africa's most beautiful old farms and producer of agreeable white wine from STEEN, RIESLING and Clairette Blanche.

Shiraz

The red Rhône grape, recently gaining in popularity in S. Africa for rich deep-coloured wine.

Simonsig

Estate owned by F.J. Malan, Chairman of the Cape Estate Wine Producers' Association. Produces a successful "Méthode Champenoise" wine among others.

Simonsvlei

One of S. Africa's best-known co-operative cellars, just outside PAARL. A prize-winner with both whites and reds.

Spier

Estate of five farms w. of STELLENBOSCH producing reds and whites.

Steen

South Africa's commonest white grape, said to be a clone of the CHENIN BLANC. It gives strong, tasty and lively wine, sweet or dry, normally better than S. African RIESLING.

Stein

Name used for any medium dry white wine.

Stellenbosch

Town and demarcated region 30 miles e. of Cape Town, extending to the Ocean at False Bay. Most of the best estates, esp. for red wine, are in the mountain foothills of the region.

Stellenbosch Farmers' Winery

South Africa's biggest winery (after the K.W.V.) with several ranges of wines, incl. NEDERBURG, ZONNEBLOEM, Lanzerac, Oude Libertas and the popular TASSENBERG. Also new low-alcohol white and rosé "Vinotas Light".

Superior

An official designation of quality for WINES OF ORIGIN. The wine must meet standards set by the Wine & Spirit Board.

Swellendam

Demarcated region of the s.e., with Bonnievale as its centre. Dessert, distilling and light table wines.

Taskelder

Range of good value wines from the STELLENBOSCH FARMERS' WINERY, including CH. LIBERTAS, Lanzerac Rosé, LA GRATITUDE and Tasheimer.

Tassenberg

Popular and good-value red table wine known to thousands as Tassie. "Oom Tas" is a low-price white.

Tawny

In Portugal means port-style wines aged in wood.

Theuniskraal

Well-known TULBAGH estate specializing in white wines, esp. RIESLING. Also STEEN, Semillon and GEWÜRZTRAMINER. Distributed by the BERGKELDER.

Tulbagh

Demarcated region n. of PAARL best known for the white wines of its three famous estates, MONTPELLIER, THEUNISKRAAL and TWEE JONGEGEZELLEN, and the dessert wines of its co-operative at Drostdy. See also BOBERG.

Twee Jongegezellen

Estate at TULBAGH. One of the great pioneers which revolutionized S. African wine in the 1950s, still in the family of its 18th-century founder. Mainly white wine, incl. RIESLING, STEEN and SEMILLON. Best wine: "T.J.39". The name means "two young friends". Now also producing a CABERNET grown by a large dam (reservoir) to get the "Médoc" effect.

Uiterwyk

Estate w. of STELLENBOSCH making a very good CABERNET SAUVIGNON.

Uitkyk

Old estate at STELLENBOSCH formerly famous for Cabernet red and Carlsheim white, recently recovering from a bad patch with good CABERNET, STEEN, etc. Now over 350 acres. Distribution by BERGKELDER.

Union Wine

Company with HQ in Wellington, Boberg area. Brand names Culemborg, Bellingham and Val du Charron.

Van Riebeck

Co-operative at Riebeck Kasteel, MALMESBURY, known for pioneering work in white wine technology.

Verdun

Estate w of STELLENBOSCH, best known for its Gamay red, but also producing an excellent SAUVIGNON BLANC.

Vergenoegd

Old family estate in s. STELLENBOSCH supplying high-quality sherry to the K.W.V. but recently offering prize-winning reds under an estate label.

Wine of Origin

The S. African equivalent of Appellation Controlée. The demarcated regions involved are all described on these pages.

Worcester

Demarcated wine region round the Breede and Hex river valleys, e. of PAARL. Many co-operative cellars make mainly dessert wines, brandy and dry whites.

Zandvliet

Estate in the Robertson area marketing a SHIRAZ red through the BERGKELDER. Later will add a Cabernet-Merlot blend.

Zonnebloem

Popular brand of CABERNET, RIESLING, PINOTAGE, SHIRAZ and STEEN from the STELLENBOSCH FARMERS' WINERY. The Cabernet is vintage-dated and ages well in bottle.

Sherry, Port & Madeira

The original, classical sherries of Spain, ports of Portugal and madeiras of Madeira are listed in the A–Z below. Their many imitators in South Africa, California, Australia, Cyprus, Argentina are not. References to them will be found under their respective countries.

The map on page 99 locates the port and sherry districts. Madeira is an island 400 miles out in the Atlantic from the coast of Morocco, a port of call for west-bound ships: hence its traditional market in North America.

In this section most of the entries are shippers' names followed by a brief account of their wines. The names of wine-types are included in the alphabetical listing.

Amontillado
>In general use means medium sherry; technically means a wine which has been aged to become more powerful and pungent. A FINO can be amontillado.

Amoroso
>A style of sweet sherry, not noticeably different from a sweet OLOROSO.

Barbeito
>Shippers of good-quality Madeira, including the driest and best apéritif Madeira, "Island Dry".

Bertola
>Sherry shippers, owned by the giant Rumasa group, best known for their Bertola Cream Sherry.

Blandy
>Old family firm of Madeira shippers at Funchal. Duke of Clarence Malmsey is their most famous wine.

Blazquez
>Sherry bodega at JEREZ with outstanding FINO, "Carta Blanca", and "Carta Oro" amontillado "al natural" (unsweetened).

Brown sherry
>British term for a style of dark sweet sherry, not normally of the best quality.

Bual
>One of the grapes of Madeira, making a soft smoky sweet wine, not as sweet as Malmsey.

Caballero
>Sherry shippers best known for Gran Señor Choice Old Cream. Their best FINO is Don Guisa.

Cockburn
>British-owned port shippers with a range of good wines. Fine vintage port from very high v'yds. can look light when young, but has great lasting power. Vintages: **55 60** 63 67 70 75.

Cossart Gordon
>Leading firm of Madeira shippers founded 1745, best known for their "Good Company" range of wines.

Cream sherry
>A style of fairly pale sweet sherry made by sweetening a blend of well-aged OLOROSOS.

Crofts

The second-oldest firm shipping vintage port: 300 years old in 1978. Bought early this century by Gilbey's. "Particular" is an excellent old tawny. Well-balanced vintage wines last as long as any. Vintages: **55 60 63 66 70 75**, and lighter vintage wines under the name of their Quinta da Roeda in several other years. Also now in the sherry business with Croft Original (pale cream), Croft Fino and Gilbey's sherries.

Crusted

Term for a vintage-style port, but blended from several vintages not one, bottled young and aged in bottle, so forming a "crust" in the bottle. Needs decanting.

Cuvillo

Sherry bodega at Puerto de Santa Maria best known for their Cream, dry Oloroso Sangre y Trabajadero and Fino "C" and a fine Palo Cortado.

Delaforce

Port shippers particularly well known in Germany. "His Eminence" is an excellent tawny. "Vintage character" is also good. Vintage wines are very fine, among the lighter kind: **55 58 60 63 66 70 75**.

Domecq

Giant family-owned sherry bodega at JEREZ. Double Century Oloroso is their biggest brand, La Ina their excellent FINO. Other famous wines: Celebration Cream and Rio Viejo (dry oloroso). Now also in Rioja (p. 104).

Dow

Old name used on the British market by the port shippers Silva & Cosens, well known for their relatively early maturing vintage wines, said to have a faint "cedarwood" character. Vintages: **55 57 58 60** 63 66 70 75 77.

Duff Gordon

Sherry shippers best known for their El Cid AMONTILLADO. Owned by the big Spanish firm Bodegas Osborne.

Findlater's

Old established London wine merchant shipping his own very successful brand of medium sherry: Dry Fly.

Fino

Term for the lightest and finest of sherries, completely dry, very pale and with great delicacy. Fino should always be drunk cool and fresh: it deteriorates rapidly once opened. TIO PEPE is the classic example.

Flor

The characteristic natural yeast which gives FINO sherry its unique flavour.

Fonseca

British-owned port shipper of high reputation. Vintage character "Bin 27" makes robust, deeply coloured vintage wine, sometimes said to have a slight "burnt" flavour. Vintages: **55 60 63 66** 70 75.

Garvey's

Famous old sherry shippers at JEREZ. Their finest wines are Fino San Patricio, Tio Guillermo Dry Amontillado and Ochavico Dry Oloroso. San Angelo Medium Amontillado is their most popular.

Gonzalez Byass

Enormous concern shipping the world's most famous and one of the best sherries: Tio Pepe. Other brands incl. La Concha Medium Amontillado, Elegante Dry Fino, San Domingo Pale Cream, Romano Cream.

Graham

> Port shippers famous for one of the richest and sweetest of vintage ports, largely from their own Quinta Malvedos, also excellent brands, incl. Ruby and Tawny and 'Late Bottled Vintage'. Vintages: **55 58 60 63** 66 70 75 77.

Harvey's

> World-famous Bristol shippers of Bristol Milk and Bristol Cream sweet sherries, Club Amontillado and Bristol Dry, which are medium. Luncheon Dry and Bristol Fino, which are dry.

Henriques & Henriques

> Well-known Madeira shippers of Funchal. Their range includes a good dry apéritif wine: Ribeiro Seco.

Jerez de la Frontera

> Centre of the sherry industry, between Cadiz and Seville in s. Spain. The word sherry is a corruption of the name, pronounced in Spanish "Hereth". In French, Xérés.

Late-bottled vintage

> Port of a single good vintage kept in wood for twice as long as vintage port (about 5 years). Therefore lighter when bottled and ageing quicker.

Leacock

> One of the oldest firms of Madeira shippers. Most famous wine is "Penny Black" Malmsey.

Lustau

> The largest independent family-owned sherry bodega in JEREZ, making many wines for other shippers, but with a very good "Dry Lustau" range and "Emilio" Palo Cortado.

Macharnudo

> One of the best parts of the sherry v'yds., n. of Jerez, famous for wines of the highest quality, both FINO and OLOROSO.

Malmsey

> The sweetest form of Madeira; dark amber, rich and honeyed yet with Madeira's unique sharp tang.

Manzanilla

> Sherry, normally FINO, which has acquired a peculiar bracing salty character from being kept in bodegas at Sanlucar de Barrameda, on the Guadalquivir estuary near JEREZ.

Offley Forester

> Port shippers and owners of the famous Quinta Boa Vista. Their vintage wines tend to be round, "fat" and sweet, good for relatively early drinking. Vintages: **55 60 62 63** 66 67 70 72 75.

Oloroso

> Style of sherry, heavier and less brilliant than FINO when young, but maturing to greater richness and roundness. Naturally dry, but generally sweetened for sale, as CREAM.

Palo Cortado

> A style of sherry close to OLOROSO but with some of the character of a FINO. Dry but rich and soft. Not often seen.

Palomino & Vergara

> Sherry shippers of JEREZ, best known for Palomino Cream, Medium and Dry. Best FINO: Tio Mateo. Rumasa group.

Puerto de Santa Maria

> The port and second city of the sherry area with a number of important bodegas.

P.X.

> Short for Pedro Ximenez, the grape used in JEREZ for sweetening blends. P.X. wine alone is almost like treacle.

Quinta   Portuguese for "estate".

Quinta do Noval

Great Portuguese port house making splendidly dark, rich and full-bodied vintage port; a few pre-phylloxera vines still at the Quinta make a small quantity of "Nacional"—very dark, full and slow-maturing wine. Vintages: **55 58 60 63 66 67 70 75**.

Rainwater

A fairly light, not very sweet blend of Madeira—in fact of VERDELHO wine—popular in the USA and Canada.

Real Tesoro, Marques de

Sherry shippers of SANLUCAR, specializing in MANZANILLA.

Rebello Valente

Name used for the vintage port of ROBERTSON. Their vintage wines are light but elegant and well-balanced, maturing rather early. Vintages: **55 60 63 66 67** 70 75.

La Riva

Distinguished firm of sherry shippers making one of the best FINOS, Tres Palmas, among many good wines.

Rivero

Considerable sherry concern best known for their CZ range of wines.

Robertson

Subsidiary of SANDEMAN'S, shipping REBELLO VALENTE vintage port and Gamebird Tawny and Ruby.

Ruby

The youngest (and cheapest) style of port: very sweet and red. The best are vigorous and full of flavour. Others can be merely strong and rather thin.

Ruiz Mateos

The sherry bodega which gave its name to the mammoth Rumasa group of bodegas, banks, etc. Its Don Zoilo sherries are some of the most expensive and best. Ruiz Hermanos is a cheaper range.

Rutherford & Miles

Madeira shippers with one of the best known of all Bual wines: Old Trinity House.

Saccone & Speed

British sherry shippers owned by Courage's the Brewers, make the popular Troubador and Lysonder ranges and a good Fino.

Sandeman

Giant of the port trade and a major figure in the sherry one. Still family controlled. "Partners" is their best-known tawny port; their vintage wines are robust—some of the old vintages were superlative [**55 58 60** 63 66 67 70 75]. Of the sherries, Medium Dry Amontillado is the best-seller, their Fino "Apitiv" is particularly good and Armada Cream and Dry Don Amontillado are both well known.

Sanlucar

Seaside sherry-town (see Manzanilla) 15 miles from JEREZ.

Sercial

Grape (reputedly a RIESLING) grown in Madeira to make the driest of the island's wines—a good apéritif.

Solera

System used in making both sherry and Madeira, also some port. It consists of topping up progressively more mature barrels with slightly younger wine of the same sort: the object to attain continuity in the final wine. Most commercial sherries are blends of several solera wines.

Tarquinio Lomelino

Madeira shippers famous for their collection of antique wines. Their standard range is called Dom Henriques.

Tawny

A style of port aged for many years in wood (in contrast to vintage port, which is aged in bottle) until it becomes tawny in colour.

Taylor

One of the best port shippers, particularly for their full, rich, long-lived vintage wine and tawnies of stated age (40-year-old, 30-year-old, etc.). Their Quinta de Vargellas is said to give Taylor's its distinctive scent of violets. Vintages: 55 60 63 66 70 75. Some lesser vintages are shipped with the Quinta name.

De Terry, Carlos y Javier

Family-owned bodega at PUERTO DE SANTA MARIA with a good range of sherries known as "501".

Tio Pepe

The most famous of FINO sherries (see Gonzalez Byass).

Valdespino

Famous bodega at JEREZ, owner of the Inocente v'yd., making the excellent FINO of the same name. Tio Diego is their splendid dry AMONTILLADO, Matador the name of their popular range.

Varela

Sherry shippers, members of the Rumasa group, best-known for their Varela Medium and Cream.

Verdelho

Madeira grape making fairly dry wine without the distinction of SERCIAL. A pleasant apéritif.

Vintage Port

The best port of exceptional vintages is bottled after only 2 years in wood and matures very slowly, for up to 20 years or even more, in its bottle. It always leaves a heavy deposit and therefore needs decanting.

Vintage port is almost as much a ritual as a drink. It always needs to be decanted with great care (since the method of making it leaves a heavy deposit in the bottle). The simplest and surest way of doing this is by filtering it through clean muslin or a coffee filter-paper into either a decanter or a well-rinsed bottle. All except very old ports can safely be decanted the day before drinking. At table the decanter is traditionally passed from guest to guest clockwise.

Vintage port can be immensely long-lived. Particularly good vintages older than those mentioned in the text include 1950, 48, 45, 35, 34, 27, 20, 11, 08, 04.

Vintage Character

Somewhat misleading term used for a good-quality full and meaty port like a first-class RUBY made by the solera system. Lacks the splendid "nose" of vintage port.

Warre

Probably the oldest of all port shippers. Makes fine long-maturing vintage wines, a good TAWNY, Nimrod and Vintage Character Warrior. Vintages: 55 60 63 66 70 75.

White Port

Port made of white grapes and therefore golden in colour. Formerly made sweet, now more often dry: a good apéritif but a heavy one.

Williams & Humbert

Famous and first-class sherry bodega now owned by the giant Rumasa group. Dry Sack (medium AMONTILLADO) is their best-selling wine. Pando is an excellent FINO. Canasta Cream and Walnut Brown are good in their class.

Wine newspeak

The last ten years has seen a revolution in wine technology. They have also heard a matching revolution in wine-talk. Attempts to express the characters of wines used to get little further than terms as vague as "fruity" and "full-bodied". Your modern wine-lover is made of sterner stuff. He is satisfied with nothing less than the jargon of laboratory analysis. Rather than expound the old imagery (which should after all be self-explanatory) I therefore give below a summary of the new hard-edge wine-talk.

The most frequent references are to the ripeness of grapes at picking; the resultant alcohol and sugar content of the wine; various measures of its acidity; the amount of sulphur dioxide used as a preservative, and the amount of "dry extract"—the sum of all the things that give wine its characteristic flavours.

The **sugar** in wine is mainly glucose and fructose, with traces of arabinose, xylose and other sugars that are not fermentable by yeast, but can be attacked by bacteria. Each country has its own system for measuring the sugar content or ripeness of grapes, known as the **"must-weight"**. The chart below relates the three principal ones (German, French and American) to each other, to specific gravity, and to the potential alcohol of the resulting wine if all the sugar is fermented out.

Specific Gravity	°O °Oechsle	Baumé	Brix	% Potential Alcohol v/v
1.065	65	8.8	15.8	8.1
1.070	70	9.4	17.0	8.8
1.075	75	10.1	18.1	9.4
1.080	80	10.7	19.3	10.0
1.085	85	11.3	20.4	10.6
1.090	90	11.9	21.5	11.3
1.095	95	12.5	22.5	11.9
1.100	100	13.1	23.7	12.5
1.105	105	13.7	24.8	13.1
1.110	110	14.3	25.8	13.8
1.115	115	14.9	26.9	14.4
1.120	120	15.5	28.0	15.0

Residual sugar is the sugar left after fermentation has finished or been artificially stopped, measured in grammes per litre.

Alcohol content (mainly ethyl alcohol) is expressed as a percentage by volume of the total liquid.

Acidity is both fixed and volatile. **Fixed acidity** consists principally of tartaric, malic and citric acids which are all found in the grape, and lactic and succinic acids, which are produced during fermentation. **Volatile acidity** consists mainly of acetic acid, which is rapidly formed by bacteria in the presence of oxygen. A small amount of volatile acidity is inevitable and attractive. With a larger amount the wine becomes "pricked"—i.e. starts to turn to vinegar.

Total acidity is fixed and volatile acidity combined. As a rule of thumb for a well-balanced wine it should be in the region of 1 gramme/thousand for each 10°Oechsle (see above).

pH is a measure of the strength of the acidity, rather than its volume. A pH above 7 is alkaline; below is acid; the lower the figure the more acid. Wine normally ranges in pH from 2.8 to 3.8. Cold northerly climates with less ripe grapes tend to lower pHs; wine-makers in hot climates can have problems getting the pH low enough. Lower pH gives better colour, helps prevent bacterial spoilage, allows more of the SO_2 to be free and active as a preservative.

Sulphur dioxide (SO_2) is added to prevent oxidation and other accidents in wine-making. Some of it combines with sugars, etc., and is known as "bound". Only the **free SO_2** that remains in the wine is effective as a preservative. **Total SO_2** is controlled by law according to the level of residual sugar: the more sugar the more SO_2 is needed.

QUICK REFERENCE VINTAGE CHARTS FOR FRANCE AND GERMANY

These charts give a rough and generalized picture of the range of qualities made in the principal areas (since every year has its relative successes and failures) and a guide as to whether the wine is ready to drink or should be kept.

0 no good   **10** the best

ı drink now   **—** needs keeping

✓ can be drunk with pleasure now, but the better wines will continue to improve

Combinations of these symbols mean that there are wines in more than one of the categories.

FRANCE

	Red Bordeaux		White Bordeaux	
	Médoc/Graves	Pom/St-Em.	Sauternes & sw.	Graves & dr.
78	6–9 —	6–8 —	4–6 ✓	7–9 ✓
77	3–6 —	2–5 —	2–4 ✓	6–9 ✓
76	6–8 —	7–8 —	7–8 ✓	4–8 ✓
75	9–10 —	8–10 —	9–10 —	8–10
74	4–7 ✓	3–5 ✓	0	6–7
73	5–6 ✓	5–7 ✓	0–4 ✓	7–8
72	2–5 ı	2–4 ı	2–4 ı	4–7 ı
71	5–8 ✓	6–8 ı	8–9 ı	8–10 ✓
70	9–10 ı	9–10 ı	9–10 ı	9–10 ı
69	1–4 ı	0–3 ı	6–7 ı	8–9 ı
68	0–2	0	0	0
67	5–7 ✓	6–8 ı	7–10 ı	8–10 ı
66	7–9 ✓	8–9 ✓	4–7 ı	7–8
65	0–2	0		
64	2–7 ı	5–9 ı		
63	0	0		
62	4–8 ı	3–6 ı		
61	10 ✓	10 ı		

	Red Burgundy	White Burgundy		
	Côte d'Or	Côte d'Or	Chablis	Alsace
78	8–10 —	7–8 —	7–9 ✓	6–8 ✓
77	2–4 —	4–7 ✓	5–7 ✓	6–7 ✓
76	7–9 —	7–9 ✓	8–9 —	10 ✓
75	0–5 ✓	4–8 ✓	8–10 ı	9
74	2–5 ı	7–9 ı	6–8 ı	6–7 ı
73	4–7 ı	8	7–8 ı	7–8 ı
72	4–9 ✓	6–10 ✓	1–4 ı	3 ı
71	8–10 ✓	8–10 ✓	7–9 ı	10 ✓
70	6–8 ı	7–8 ı	6–8 ı	7–8 ı
69	9–10 ı	8–10 ı	7–9 ı	

Beaujolais: 78 and 76 are the vintages to buy. Mâcon-Villages (white): 78, 76 and 75 are good now.
Loire: Sweet wines of Anjou and Touraine. Best recent vintages: 78, 76, 75, 73, 71, 70, 69, 64.
Upper Loire: Sancerre and Pouilly-Fumé 78, 76, 75 are all good now.
Muscadet: Drink the new vintage.

GERMANY

	Rhône	Rhine	Moselle
78	7–9 ✓	5–7 ✓	4–6 ✓
77	5–7	5–7	4–6
76	8–10 ✓	9–10 ✓	9–10 ✓
75	0–5 ı	10 ✓	10 ı
74	4–7 ı	3–6 ı	2–4 ı
73	5–8 ı	6–7 ı	6–8 ı
72	6–9 ✓	2–5 ı	1–4 ı
71	7–9 ✓	9–10 ✓	10 ✓

N.B. Fully detailed charts will be found on pages 20, 21 (France), 65 (Germany).